DATE DUE	
MAY 07 1993		
OCT 0 1 1993		
NOV 23 1996		
FEB 11 1997		
APR 1 0 1997		
MAR 2 6 1998		
Scott Pbl.b		
due 13 oct 09		

Springer Series on Behavior Therapy and Behavioral Medicine

MICHAEL ROSENBAUM, Ph.D., (University of Illinois) is an Associate Professor of Psychology and head of the clinical psychology training program in the Department of Psychology at Tel Aviv University. He is the cofounder and past president of the Israeli Association for Behavior Therapy. He is the past director of the psychology departments at Geha Psychiatric Hospital and at Lowenstein Rehabilitation Center. He is on the editorial board of the *Journal of Cognitive Psychotherapy* and on the international advisory board of the journal *Child and Family Behavior Therapy*. He has widely published in the areas of self-control, learned resourcefulness, and behavioral medicine.

Learned Resourcefulness

On Coping Skills, Self-Control, and Adaptive Behavior

Michael Rosenbaum

Editor

SPRINGER PUBLISHING COMPANY
New York

Springer Publishing Company, Inc.
536 Broadway
New York, NY 10012

90 91 92 93 94 / 5 4 3 2 1

Library of Congress Cataloging-in-Publication Data

Learned resourcefulness : on coping skills, self-control, and adaptive
    behavior / edited by Michael Rosenbaum.
        p.   cm. — (Springer series on behavior therapy and behavioral
    medicine ; v. 24)
    Includes bibliographical references.
    ISBN (invalid) 0-8261-4860-3
    1. Cognitive therapy.   2. Adjustment (Psychology)
I. Rosenbaum, Michael.   II. Series.
    [DNLM: 1. Adaptation, Psychological.   2. Behavior Therapy.
3. Cognitive Therapy.   4. Internal-External Control.   5. Stress,
Psychological.   W1 SP685NB v. 24 / WM 425 L4375]
RC489.C63L43   1990
616.89'142—dc20
DNLM/DLC
for Library of Congress   90-9637
                                                               CIP

Printed in the United States of America

To my daughters, Yael and Nurit, who I hope have
acquired enough resourcefulness to go through life
with a smile.

Contents

RESOURCEFULNESS IN SPECIFIC AREAS

Foreword

The story of stress and coping is the tale of resilience and courage. The research and clinical literatures are replete with accounts of individuals who have endured and, in some cases, have even become strengthened by the most unimaginable stressful life events. Whether these stressors are environmental or human, people have shown remarkable fortitude and courage when confronting stressful events such as the holocaust, the Hiroshima bombing, personal loss, injury, illness, and the like (Rachman, 1978).

Researchers have struggled to understand what distinguishes those who "cope" more effectively from those who do not. A number of concepts have been offered to explain such differential coping abilities. Illustrative of these concepts are an individual or group's dispositional optimism (Scheier & Carver, 1985), sense of coherence (Antonovsky, 1979), hardiness (Kobasa, 1982), coping resources (Roskies & Lazarus, 1978), and sense of self-efficacy (Bandura, 1977). Now to be added to this list of constructs is that of learned resourcefulness.

Like other psychological concepts, learned resourcefulness has its own unique history. In the 1970s, my graduate students (Roy Cameron, Dennis Turk, and Myles Genest) and I conducted research on the role that cognitive and affective factors play in behavior therapy. We addressed the question of why such therapeutic procedures were not more effective in fostering treatment generalization and maintenance. This series of studies contributed to the emergence of a cognitive–behavioral treatment approach and to the development of a number of innovative integrative treatment techniques, including Stress Inoculation Training (SIT). The SIT intervention was designed to help both clients and high-risk populations develop, both on a treatment and preventive basis, a flexible coping repertoire to be practiced on graded levels of stressors. This treatment approach is similar to what Gray (1982) subsequently characterized as a "toughening-up process." A major byproduct of the SIT intervention was that individuals developed a greater sense of confidence and stronger feelings of resource-fulness so that they could handle future stressors. Clients often enter therapy with an internal dialogue characterized by feelings of helplessness and hopelessness, and expressions of demoralization and victimization, due to their symptoms and situations. Cognitive–behavioral interventions are designed to translate these feelings of "learned helplessness" (Seligman, 1975) into what we called "learned resourcefulness" (Meichenbaum, 1977) or what Bandura (1977) has called "self-efficacy." The treatment outcome literature attests to the promise of SIT and related cognitive–behavioral interventions in fostering coping resources and learned resourcefulness (Meichenbaum, 1985; Meichenbaum & Jaremko, 1983). In this volume, Frederick (Chapter 9) provides further clinical evidence for a similar notion, that of "psychological immunization," when discussing the experience of hostages and their families. Whether it is by means of experience or as the result of treatment, it appears that learned resourcefulness can be both acquired and trained.

But what exactly is learned resourcefulness and how does it relate to the other psychological concepts offered to explain an individual's ability to cope? An important contribution toward the answer to this question was offered in 1980 by Rosenbaum who developed a 36-item self-report scale to measure learned resourcefulness (Self-Control Schedule). Rosenbaum (1983) defined learned resourcefulness as an acquired repertoire of behavioral and cognitive skills with which the person is able to regulate internal events such as emotions and cognitions that might otherwise interfere with the smooth execution of a target behavior. The 36 test items were designed to assess a variety of diverse skills including (a) cognitive strategies for dealing with unpleasant emotional and physiological responses, (b) problem solving strategies, (c) ability to delay gratification, and (d) a general belief in one's ability to self-regulate internal events or self-efficacy expectations.

In order to obtain a feel for the construct of learned resourcefulness, I strongly encourage the reader to pause, turn to Appendix A, and take the learned resourcefulness test. This personal assessment will give you a feel for the potential usefulness of the learned resourcefulness construct. This effort is warranted since the self-report scale has been found to be both reliable and valid (having both concurrent and predictive validity). Research has indicated that learned resourcefulness relates to an individual's ability to (a) tolerate clinical and laboratory-induced pain, (b) cope with seasickness, (c) succeed in weight reduction programs, (d) control nail biting, (e) handle helplessness manipulations, (f) cope with the emotional sequelae of epilepsy, and (g) comply with demanding medical treatment regimens such as dialysis and diabetes regulation.

In this volume, we also learn what role the learned resourcefulness construct plays in the onset of depression (Lewinsohn & Alexander, Chapter 8), in the responses of agoraphobics to cognitive–behavioral treatment (Biran, Chapter 7), in the promotion of health-engendering behaviors (Rosenbaum, Chapter 1), and in the courageous acts of bomb disposal experts and parachutists (Rachman, Chapter 6). Moreover, the authors thoughtfully explore how learned resourcefulness relates to constructs such as sense of coherence (with its components of comprehensibility, manageability, and meaningfulness) (Antonovsky, Chapter 2), hardiness (with its components of commitment, control, and challenge) (Orr & Westman, Chapter 3), to preferred coping styles (monitoring-blunting) (Miller, Chapter 4), and to help-seeking behaviors (Nadler, Chapter 5). In each analysis, theoretical, assessment, and practical clinical questions are considered. The contributors address such questions as whether learned resourcefulness should be conceptualized as a dispositional trait or state variable, as a set of specifiable coping behaviors, or as a general problem-solving ability. For instance, consider Rachman's proposal that "resourcefulness is the ability to use one's personal and social resources for successfully dealing with problems, especially those with elements of novelty." Although Rachman's definition of resourcefulness is broader than Rosenbaum's initial definition, both authors highlight the influence of resourcefulness when automatic means of coping break down. How individuals learn to anticipate, notice, interrupt, self-regulate (self-monitor, plan, alter coping strategies accordingly), and cope with failure influence the nature and degree of resourcefulness. Conversely, learned resourcefulness can exert its influence by affecting an individual's (a) initial evaluation of the stressful event and his or her ability to handle it [what Lazarus (1981) has called "primary and secondary appraisal processes"]; (b) ability to reduce interfering effects of one's reaction to stressor; (c) ability to engage in self-corrective functions and initiate self-change (stress buffering effects); and (d) ability to seek, mobilize, and use social as well as personal resources.

The possibility that such processes may indeed be affected by learned resourcefulness, is highlighted by Biran (Chapter 7), who reported that it is the presence and frequency of negative or maladaptive cognitions, rather than paucity of positive coping cognitions, that is most important in contributing to behavioral problems. Learned resourcefulness may exert more of its influence in controlling negative interfering ideation and affect than in fostering positive coping alternatives.

Frederick (Chapter 9) reminds us that another hallmark of competent copers is flexibility in their adapting a varied coping repertoire to the demands of the situation. For instance, he enumerates the diverse coping responses employed by hostages. These responses included (a) belief in the innate strength of oneself, (b) reflections and thoughts of loved ones and friends, (c) faith in some superordinate power, (d) hope that captivity will end favorably, (e) use of calculating powers to favorably interact and plan for possible escape, (f) physical exercise, (g) expression of anger via appropriate self-assertion, and (h) ability to focus attention and become task-oriented.

It is not only flexibility, but an individual's ability to tailor coping repertoire to the specific needs of the situation that is critical. Miller (Chapter 4) highlights the transactional and developmental origins of learned resourcefulness. In her thoughtful discussion of different preferred modes of coping (monitoring-vigilance versus blunting-avoidance), she raises questions about the conditions under which each coping style might be most adaptive. She reminds us that we need to take into consideration not only the level of the individual's learned resourcefulness, but also we need to consider the demands of the situation.

In order to personalize such concerns, it is useful to reflect on your performance on the learned resourcefulness test (see Appendix A). How did you score on the learned resourcefulness self-report scale? What exactly does your level of resourcefulness reflect? Besides using a self-report measure, how else can we assess resourcefulness? How does such resourcefulness develop, and what accounts for individual differences in learned resourcefulness? Can learned resourcefulness be trained, and, if so, what exactly changes? The chapters in this welcomed volume address these questions.

DONALD MEICHENBAUM, PH.D.

References

Antonovsky, A. (1979). *Health, stress and coping : New perspectives on mental and physical well-being.* San Francisco: Jossey-Bass.

Bandura, A. (1977). Self-efficacy: Toward a unifying theory of behavioral change. *Psychological Review, 84,* 191–215.

Gray, J. (1982). *The neuropsychology of anxiety.* Oxford: Oxford University Press.

Kobasa, S. C. (1982). The hardy personality: Toward a social psychology of stress and health. In J. Suls and G. Sanders (Eds.), *Social psychology of health and illness.* Hillsdale, NJ: Erlbaum.

Lazarus, R. (1981). The stress and coping paradigm. In Eisdorfer (Ed.), *Models of clinical psychology*. Englewood Cliffs, NJ: Prentice-Hall.

Meichenbaum, D. (1977). *Cognitive-behavior modification: An integrative approach*. New York: Plenum

Meichenbaum, D. (1985). *Stress inoculation training*. New York: Pergamon Press.

Meichenbaum, D., & Jaremko, M. (1983). *Stress reduction and Prevention*. New York: Plenum.

Rachman, S. (1978). *Fear and courage*. San Francisco: Freeman.

Rosenbaum, M. (1980). A schedule for assessing self-control behaviors: Preliminary findings. *Behavior Therapy, 11,* 109–121.

Rosenbaum, M. (1983). Learned resourcefulness as a behavioral repertoire for the self-regulation of internal events: Issues and speculations. In M. Rosenbaum, C. M. Franks, & Y. Jaffe (Eds.), *Perspectives on behavior therapy in the eighties* (pp. 54–73). New York: Springer Publishing Co.

Roskies, E., & Lazarus, R. (1978). Coping theory and the teaching of coping skills. In P. Davidson and S. Davidson (Eds.), *Behavioral Medicine*. New York: Brunner Mazel.

Scheier, M. F., & Carver, C. S. (1985). Optimism, coping and health: Assessment and implications of generalized outcome expectancies. *Health Psychology, 4,* 219–247.

Seligman, M. E. P. (1975). *Helplessness: On depression, development and death*. San Francisco: Freeman.

Preface

Being born and raised in Israel, I admired the resiliency and resourcefulness of my people and was at the same time puzzled by it. As a young child I witnessed the immigration of over a million people to the newly established State of Israel. At that time the population of Israel numbered only about 600,000 people and Israel was at war with armies that by far outnumbered its own small and ill-equipped army. The majority of the new immigrants were either survivers of the Nazi death camps or escapees of antiSemitic persecutions in countries in North Africa and the Middle East. Many of the new immigrants were literally taken from the boats in which they had just arrived to the battle fields. But even those who did not join the fighting had to go through extreme economical hardship and cultural shocks in order to adjust to their new country.

Common sense and most of the psychological theories on stress and coping would have predicted that such stressful experiences would have had devastating effects on the psychological well-being of the new immigrants. Yet, in what appeared to be a miracle, these people were able to rehabilitate their own lives and to devote their energies to the development of a new and a modern society. What are the unique human qualities that make people resourceful and creative even under the most dire circumstances?

Surprisingly this question has received relatively little attention in the psychological literature. The science of human behavior preferred to focus on the factors that account for psychopathology rather than for mental health. Psychological theories and research have mainly focused on the study of the minority of human beings who succumbed to stressful life events and developed depression, anxiety reactions, and other psychopathologies. Human resourcefulness and resiliency that become manifested when individuals are faced with extreme and challenging life experiences are of interest to only a small minority of behavioral scientists. Yet, by unravelling the mystery of human resourcefulness and resiliency we may be able to enhance the well-being of humankind.

I hope that this book will provide the impetus for advancing research and theory on human resourcefulness. For those who are in clinical practice, this book is intended to encourage them to uncover the "strong" rather than the "weak" qualities of their clients. This book should also be of value for those who are interested in the process of coping with stress.

Many individuals have influenced my thinking and my work on learned resourcefulness and self-control. I would like, however, to single out three individuals whose work had the greatest impact on my thinking: Frederick Kanfer, Donald Meichenbaum, and Richard Lazarus. Kanfer provided me with invaluable insights into the process of self-control and self-regulation. Meichenbaum's work contributed to my idea that individuals acquire throughout their lives a cognitive–behavioral repertoire that helps them to cope effectively with stressful life events. And finally, Lazarus' seminal work on coping resources and his transactional concept of stress provided the foundations of much of my thinking on human resourcefulness.

I am indebted to the authors who have been very cooperative and patient throughout the long gestation period of this book. I gratefully acknowledge the encouragement and help received from Cyril M. Franks, Senior Editor of the Springer Series on Behavior Therapy and Behavioral Medicine. I am also grateful with the support and encouragement received from Ursula Springer, Barbara Watkins, Pamela Lankas, and other members of Springer Publishing Company throughout the preparation of this book.

Thanks are also due to my friend and colleague, Noach Milgram who introduced me to Calvin Frederick, one of the contributors to this book. I owe a great debt to Attorney Frederick L. Simmons, the First Trustee of the Schwartz Memorial Fund, Los Angeles, for the provision of continuous financial support for my research and for this book. I would also like to thank Sharona Goldberg and Shmuel Michelson for their secretarial help in typing and proofreading the manuscripts.

MICHAEL ROSENBAUM

Contributors

CAROLYN ALEXANDER, Ph.D., (University of Oregon) is a school psychologist in the Children Clinical Services Division of Multnomah County, Portland, Oregon. Prior to her current position, she coordinated the Coping with Depression Program, and assisted in the development of that program for Adolescents at the University of Oregon. She worked in depression research with Peter Lewinsohn for six years, and has also practiced clinically in the fields of rehabilitation and neuropsychology.

AARON ANTONOVSKY, Ph.D., (Yale University) is a Kunin-Lunenfeld Professor of Medical Sociology and chair of the Department of the Sociology of Health in the Faculty of Health sciences, Ben-Gurion University of the Negev, Beer Sheba, Israel. His doctorate in sociology led to a strong crosscultural perspective and work in ethnic and race relations and social stratification. Since his migration to Israel in 1960, he has worked largely in what used to be called "medical sociology" but thanks to his work, is now widely referred to as "the sociology of health." In 1973 he moved to Beer Sheba to take an active part in setting up a community-oriented medical school.

MIA W. BIRAN, Ph.D., (Rutgers University), is an Associate Professor of Psychology at Miami University, Oxford, Ohio. Her research activity has focused on the area of anxiety disorders. She has conducted several treatment-based projects on agoraphobia and social phobias, published her work in reputable journals, and has given numerous presentations in national and international conferences. Her current interest is in social phobias(e.g., public-speaking anxiety) with an emphasis on etiological factors and personality patterns among social-anxious patients. She also combines a social-learning approach with a psychodynamic conceptualization in an integrative way.

CALVIN J. FREDERICK, Ph.D., (University of California at Los Angeles) is a professor in the Department of Psychiatry and Biobehavioral Sciences at the University of California at Los Angeles and Chief of Psychological Services at the Veterans Affairs Medical Center in West Los Angeles. He was formerly on the faculties of the George Washington University School of Medicine in Washington, DC and The Johns Hopkins University School of Medicine in Baltimore, Maryland. From 1972–1974, he served as Chief of Training and Research Fellowships in the Center for Studies of Crime and Delinquency at the National Institute of Mental Health. From 1974–1981 he directed the NIMH programs in Emergency Mental Health and Disaster Assistance. During 1973–1974, he served as Advisor to the Pan American Health Organization on the mental health aspects of violent deaths in Central and South America. His work which has been widely published, has encompassed more than 2000 cases covering such major stressors as hostage-taking, catastrophic disasters, former prisoners of war, victims of physical assault and victims of sexual abuse. He has served on numerous government committees dealing with emergency mental health, including his most recent appointment as the Chair of the Committee on Emergency Mental Health by the World Federation for Mental Health.

PETER M. LEWINSOHN, Ph.D., (The Johns Hopkins University) is an Emeritus Professor at the University of Oregon, Research Scientist at Oregon Research Institute, and Adjunct Professor of Psychiatry at Oregon Health Sciences University. He has been on the faculties of the Temple University Medical School, Indiana University Medical School, and Southern Illinois University and for four years served as Chief Psychologist at the Larue D. Carter Memorial Hospital in Indianapolis. During the years 1965–1987 he was Professor of Psychology and Director of the Neuropsychology Laboratory at the University of Oregon. For five years he also served as the Director of Training in Clinical Psychology at the University of Oregon. He is the author of many scientific articles on depression and has co-authored books on geropsychology as well as depression. He is a diplomate in Clinical Psychology, American Board of Examiners in Professional Psychology, and in 1978 was the recipient of the Professional Award of the Mental Health Association of Oregon.

DONALD MEICHENBAUM, Ph.D., (University of Illinois) is a Professor of Psychology at the University of Waterloo, Ontario, Canada. Among his many distinctions, he is a fellow of the Royal Society of Canada. He is one of the founders of Cognitive Behavior Modification, and his 1977 book, *Cognitive behavior modification: An integrative approach* is considered a classic in the field. He is the author of numerous other books and is on the editorial boards of over a dozen journals.

SUZANNE M. MILLER, Ph.D, (University of London Institute of Psychiatry) is an Associate Professor of Psychology and Medicine at Temple University in Philadelphia, Pennsylvania. She has been on the faculties of the University of Western Ontario and the Department of Psychiatry at the University of Pennsylvania. She was also a visiting scholar at Stanford University in California. She is the author of numerous articles and book chapters on stress, health, and the coping process. Her current research interests include also the study of developmental psychopathology.

ARIE NADLER, Ph.D., (Purdue University) is a Professor of Psychology and a past chairperson of the Department of Psychology at Tel Aviv University. He is affiliated with a number of Israeli, European, and American professional associations and is an elected Fellow of the American Psychological Association. His research interests concern the social psychology of helping relations. Within this area he has been studying the processes and determinants of help-seeking and receiving behaviors. Some of his other interests include research on holocaust survivors and their families, and processes of personal change. He has published numerous articles and book chapters in these areas.

EMDA ORR, Ph.D., (Hebrew University in Jerusalem) is an Assistant Professor in the departments of Education and Behavioral Sciences at Ben Gurion University of the Negev, Beer Sheba, Israel. During the academic year 1986–1987 she participated in the post-doctoral training program of the City University of New York doing research on "hardiness" with Suzanne Kobasa. Her current research activities are in the areas of coping with cancer and "hardiness."

STANLEY RACHMAN, Ph.D., (University of London) is a Professor of Psychology in the Department of Psychology at the University of British Columbia. From 1961 to 1982 he was on the faculty of the University of London. He is a fellow of the Royal Society of Canada, and his awards and distinctions include the 1984 Distinguished Scientific Contribution Award, presented by Division 12 of the American Psychological Association, and the Killam Research Prize for 1988. He is the editor of *Advances in Behavior Research and Therapy* and is a member of the editorial boards of a number of psychological journals. He has carried long-term research on fearlessness and courage in military and clinical situations, and on the nature and treatment of neurotic disorders. He has published many books and articles on various psychological topics.

MINA WESTMAN, Ph.D., (Tel Aviv University) is an Assistant Professor of Organizational Behavior in the Leon Recanati Graduate School of Business Administration at Tel Aviv University. She did joint research projects on "hardiness" with Suzanne Kobasa at the City University of New York. Her current research interests include studies of the impact of hardiness on the relationship between stress and performance, coping strategies, and issues in social support.

Introduction: From Helplessness to Resourcefulness

Michael Rosenbaum

Seligman and Maier coined the phrase "learned helplessness" in 1967 to describe the debilitated escape-avoidance responding shown by dogs exposed to uncontrollable shocks in a laboratory. Research on learned helplessness proliferated, and has been applied to both animal and human behavior; in 1975, Seligman published the classic *Helplessness: On depression, development, and death.* According to the learned helplessness hypothesis, "When an animal or a person is faced with an outcome that is independent of his responses, he [or she] learns that the outcome is independent of his [or her] responses" (Seligman, 1975, p. 46). Frequent exposure to uncontrollable events (either good or bad) can produce the motivational, cognitive, and emotional deficits that characterize depressed people.

The learned helplessness hypothesis fitted in well with the early stages of behavioral therapy. It used learning theory and experimental research with animals and humans to provide a parsimonious explanation of a psychopathological syndrome. Although it had a cognitive component, it was based mainly on the principles of operant and classical conditioning.

In many respects, however, Seligman's book marked the end of an era in behavior therapy dominated by the principles derived from conditioning theory. Two years after its publication, Meichenbaum published *Cognitive-behavior modification: An integrative approach* (1977). In this well-cited book, Meichenbaum laid the foundation of cognitive–behavior therapy—the intermarriage of behavioral and cognitive approaches to psychological treatment. It postulates that behavior is changed through a sequence of mediating processes involving the interaction of inner speech, cognitive structures, and behavior and their resultant outcomes.

Meichenbaum's book represents the increased domination of cognitive factors in behavior therapy and a conceptual shift as well. In the past, environmental factors were held to be almost solely responsible for human behavior; now, intrapersonal factors have become the focus of change. It is not only the exposure to uncontrollable events that causes people to become helpless, but the way in which they cope with these events. Training in specific coping skills can help them deal effectively with external stressors. By controlling cognitive processes, people can achieve control over their reactions to problematic and stressful life events; "helplessness" can be replaced by "resourcefulness" (Meichenbaum, 1977).

The increasing emphasis on cognitive processes that characterizes psychology in general and not just behavior therapy led to changes in Seligman's learned helplessness theory. In a special issue of the *Journal of Abnormal Psychology* published in February 1978, Abramson, Seligman, and Teasdale presented a reformulation of the theory. According to this reformulation, depression will result when individuals expect bad events will occur, expect that they can do nothing to prevent them, and attribute this state of affairs to internal, stable, and global factors.

Later, Abramson, Garber, and Seligman (1980) proposed a personality variable that accounts for the kind of attributions people make when confronted with failure or success. "So, those people who typically tend to attribute failure to global, stable, and internal factors should be most prone to general and chronic helplessness depressions with low self-esteem. Moreover, such a style may predispose these individuals to depression" (p. 32). The characteristic way in which people make attributions has been labeled "attributional" or "explanatory" style. Individual differences in attributional style are hypothesized to predict vulnerability to helplessness and depression.

Thus, over a period of five years, the helplessness theory has shifted its emphasis from environmental factors to factors within the person himself. Although environmental factors are not ignored, personality variables play a more significant role in current theorizing of learned helplessness (Peterson & Seligman, 1984). However, Silver and Wortman (1980) criticized the reformulated helplessness model as being too narrow, focusing solely on the reactions of helplessness and depression. They faulted it for not incorporating other emotional reactions and for devoting relatively little attention to the process by which people cope with uncontrollable life events.

Silver and Wortman, as well as the other contributors to Garber and Seligman's (1980) second book on learned helplessness, were apparently unaware of Meichenbaum's cognitive theory of behavior change. Meichenbaum's (1977) model provides a viable alternative to the reformulated model of learned helplessness, since it incorporates a wide range of emotional reactions and focuses on the process of coping with these reactions. Meichenbaum (1985) developed a Stress Inoculation Training (SIT) program that "is designed to nurture and develop coping skills, not only to resolve specific immediate problems but also to apply to future difficulties. It provides individuals and groups with a proactive defense or a set of coping skills to deal with future stressful situations" (p. 21). Those who completed the SIT program were expected to develop a sense of "learned resourcefulness" by experiencing success in coping with manageable levels of stress. They developed "psychological antibodies" or coping skills that helped them stay healthy.

Meichenbaum's stress inoculation program and Seligman's learned helplessness model have their roots in two diametrically different theoretical orientations. Whereas Seligman and colleagues seek to explain why people get sick, Meichenbaum seeks to explain why people stay healthy despite their exposure to various risk factors. In the terminology proposed by Antonovsky (1979, 1987, Chapter 2, this volume), the concept of learned helplessness is based on the pathogenic model, whereas the concept of stress inoculation is based on the salutogenic model.

The search for the pathogenic factors responsible for mental illness dominates the fields of clinical psychology and psychiatry regardless of specific theoretical orientations. Those who ascribe to psychoanalysis believe that mental disorders are a function of aberrations in psychosexual development. Behaviorally oriented psychologists assume that maladaptive behaviors are produced and maintained by environmental contingencies. Cognitively oriented psychologists believe that mental disorders originate from irrational beliefs and "cognitive distortions." However divergent these schools of thought may be, they share a common ground: the pathogenic model. They search for deviant and abnormal personality and situational variables that produce mental illness.

Antonovsky (1979, 1987, Chapter 2, this volume) has cogently argued for abandonment of the pathogenic model in favor of the salutogenic model. Those who adopt the solutogenic model study the cultural, social, and personal resources that contribute to the health xxviii Introduction

and the psychological well-being of human beings. Antonovsky rejects the traditional medical model, which assumes that germs, lesions, and other foreign insults are the sole cause for physical illness. Similarly, he rejects the utility of the pathogenic model for understanding mental disorders; it fails to explain why most people remain healthy despite their exposure to various risk factors. For example, Marks (1983) pointed out that many people acquire trivial fears and rituals at some point in their lives but are able to overcome them without developing full-blown phobias or obsessive-compulsive syndromes. Similarly, although most individuals suffer occasionally from depressive moods, very few develop a full-blown depressive episode.

In a similar vein, Rodin and Salovey (1989), in a recent review of the health psychology literature, argued that the search for specific pathogenic fators leads "to narrow definitions and assumptions about the desirability of encouraging health-promoting behaviors that may not in fact be healthy when one takes the whole person into account" (p. 563). For example, elite athletes are considered to be models of health, yet they suffer from a high incidence of anorexia nervosa and bulimia. Eysenck (1988) argued that specific risk factors such as smoking may eventually be found to be less predictive of cancer and cardiac diseases than are personality variables. Hence, in studying what keeps people in good health, the focus should be on the whole person rather than on specific risk-producing behaviors.

Instead of focusing on what makes people sick, this volume focuses on what keeps people healthy in an inevitably stressor-rich environment. Instead of seeking specific risk factors, the contributors suggest various personality variables that could explain why most people do not succumb to an illness-producing environment.

What makes people resourceful rather than helpless? In Chapter 1, I present my answer to this question. The ability to control their behavior frees people, to a great extent, from environmental control. Once people become independent of situational pulls, they acquire the personal resources that keep them healthy.

My concept of learned resourcefulness is rooted in the self-control models developed by cognitive behavior therapists such as Bandura (1977), Kanfer (1977), and Meichenbaum (1977), which emphasize the role of cognitive factors. My model describes not only the cogntive processes by which individuals control their behavior, but also the role of specific personality repertoires in promoting self-control.

When I first developed the concept of "learned resourcefulness" (Rosenbaum, 1983), I was unaware of Antonovsky's concept of "sense of coherence" described in *Health, stress, and coping* (1979). Antonovsky is a medical sociologist who usually publishes in nonpsychological journals and was rarely cited by psychologists. Even now, I am not sure that many psychologists are aware of his work.

This lack of awareness is reinforced by the fact that very few studies have tested Antonovsky's ideas. Antonovsky (1987) considers himself a theoretician and would rather leave the testing of hypotheses to experimentalists. I believe that the concept of sense of coherence can be very useful in understanding the reasons why people stay healthy.

Learned resourcefulness refers to what people do when stressful circumstances call for self-direction: The sense of coherence refers to a set of personal beliefs that guide people's coping with stress. A sense of coherence expresses the belief that life is comprehensible, manageable, and meaningful: In Chapter 2, Antonovsky provides sound theoretical arguments that such a personal philosophy may promote health and facilitate coping with stress.

Similar to the sense of coherence, the concept of hardiness refers to a set of beliefs that provide the basis for healthful adaptation to a stressful environment. Kobasa (1979) developed this personality-based concept and sees it as a composite of three inextricably intertwined components: commitment, control, and challenge. In Chapter 3, Orr and Westman provide an up-to-date review of the hardiness literature; they conclude that there is strong support for the hypothesis that hardy persons are healthier, less depressed, and perform better than do nonhardy people.

On a specific-to-global scale, I would rank learned resourceful as being more specific than hardiness or the sense of coherence. Miller's concept of blunting-monitoring, which describes a very specific coping style, would be even closer to the specific pole. It refers to the way people attend to threatening information. Monitors seek information about a threatening event, whereas blunters prefer to cognitively avoid or transform threat-relevant information (see Miller, Chapter 4).

At first glance, Miller's concept is reminiscent of the well-known concept of repression-sensitization personality styles (Byrne, 1961); here, Miller spells out the differences between the two concepts. Repression has been considered to be a less effective coping style than sensitization (Byrne, 1961); more recently, it has been associated with poor health (Rodin & Salovey, 1989). However, Miller claims that blunting is not necessarily more pathological than monitoring; it all depends on the specific characteristics of the stressful event. When a person faces uncontrollable events, blunting may be more effective than monitoring; under controllable conditions, monitoring is the preferred coping style. Whereas previous research on repression focused on its pathogenic aspects, Miller points to the beneficial and solutogenic effects of avoiding threatening information.

Miller focuses mainly on the fit between coping styles and situational characteristics; she did not study the interaction between blunting-monitoring and other personality repertoires. In a study described in my chapter (Piamenta, 1987), it was found that monitors who have a rich repertoire of self-control skills (i.e., are highly resourceful persons) cope better with stressful events than do monitors who have low resourcefulness, and low-resourceful blunters are better copers with stress than are low-resourceful monitors. In other words, under the particular conditions of this study, monitoring was the more effective coping strategy for highly resourceful individuals, whereas for low resourceful persons blunting was more effective.

This book presents three major personality variables that describe positive adaptation to stressful events: learned resourcefulness, sense of coherence, and hardiness. A specific scale was developed for assessing each of these variables. On the face of it, these scales appear to measure the same construct from different vantage points. Until now there are no published studies that compare these scales. However, unpublished data collected at Tel Aviv University reveal only low-to-moderate correlations among the three measures that assess learned resourcefulness, hardiness, and sense of coherence. Apparently, these scales share a certain amount of variance, but they do not assess exactly the same thing.

In a recent article (Rosenbaum, 1988) I suggested that learned resourcefulness, hardiness, and the sense of coherence mitigate the effects of stressful events at different phases of the self-control process. Hardiness and the sense of coherence are postulated as influencing a person's initial evaluation of a stressful event; learned resourcefulness is postulated as influencing his or her actions toward reducing the interfering effects of his or her reactions to the stressor. The self-control model that I present in Chapter 1 could be the basis for generating hypotheses on the roles played by the different personality variables in the process of adaptation to stress.

In Chapter 3, Orr and Westman also provide a conceptual comparison among hardiness, resourcefulness, and the sense of coherence. In addition, they compare hardiness to dispositional optimism, a concept developed by Scheier and Carver (1985). In relation to the other three personality variables, the concept of optimism is the most parsimonious. It assumes that when people have general expectancies for positive outcomes, their coping patterns will involve continued positive striving and they will make the best of whatever situations they confront. Whether people are optimistic or pessimistic probably depends on whether they are resourceful, hardy, or have a strong sense of coherence; this needs to be substantiated by research.

When confronted with a stressor, people not only turn to their own resources; they also enlist the help of others. In Chapter 5, Nadler focuses on help-seeking behavior, which he suggests is a way of positive coping with stress, as any other coping strategy. The process by which a person decides to seek the help of others is explained in terms of the self-control process described in Chapter 1. His theoretical conceptualization of help-seeking behavior provides the theoretical links between the self-control literature and the social psychology of help-seeking.

Nadler's exposition of help-seeking relates well to Rachman's (Chapter 6) broader definition of resourcefulness as "the ability to use one's personal and social resources for successful dealing with problems, especially those that are novel." Rachman also provides an important link between resourcefulness and Bandura's concept of self-efficacy (1977). According to this view, highly competent people are most likely to develop high expectancies of self-efficacy. However, there might be cases in which someone has the necessary competencies, but still has low expectations of self-efficacy. Learned resourcefulness was found to be positively correlated with self-efficacy expectancies mostly when the subjects had a previous experience with the stressful task (e.g., Rosenbaum & Ben-Ari Smira, 1986), but not when they had no experience with the stressful task (e.g., Weisenberg et al., 1988). Nevertheless, the relationship between resourcefulness and belief in self-efficacy is far from settled; more research is needed in this area.

Rachman's article is in the section of the book headed "Resourcefulness in Specfic Areas," whereas the other chapters mentioned so far come under the heading of "Major Conceptual Approaches." Although Rachman provides a critical review of the concept of learned resourcefulness, the major thrust of the chapter is on applying this concept to the training of soldiers to carry out hazardous tasks. The research indicates that it is indeed possible to train people to carry out hazardous tasks such as bomb-disposal and parachuting even without significantly reducing their basic fears of these tasks. The soldiers are taught to control their fears in a way that enables them to perform the required tasks in a smooth fashion; namely, they are taught to be resourceful.

Rachman noted that some of the soldiers were particularly capable of benefiting from such training and were especially able to carry out hazardous tasks. He speculated that these soldiers would likely score high on the Self-Control Schedule (SCS), which I developed as a measure of learned resourcefulness (Chapter 1).

Biran (Chapter 7) provides research data that supports Rachman's speculation, and is in line with the research reported in Chapter 1 on the relationship between clients' resourcefulness and their success in psychological treatment.

Biran studied the effectiveness of cognitive-behavioral treatments on agoraphobia. Subjects who scored high on the SCS (i.e., were highly resourceful) prior to therapy were more likely to benefit from therapy than were their low-resourceful counterparts. Furthermore, the highly resourceful patients were more ready to comply with the requirements of treatment; "they invested greater efforts in practicing approach behaviors on their own between sessions, and they tended to attend more therapy sessions." Biran discusses at some length her notions of why individual differences in learned resourcefulness may be related to the outcome of cognitive–behavioral treatment.

A major assumption underlying the concept of learned resourcefulness is that people who have a rich repertoire of self-control skills adjust better to life even when confronted by risk factors. Testing this assumption requires following large samples of the population for an extended period. Such a study is quite expensive in time and money, and is beyond the capabilities of the average researcher.

Fortunately, Lewinsohn included the SCS in a large prospective study as one of the many psychological measures used to predict unipolar depression. Because this study yielded numerous findings, they were reported in several published articles; the most detailed information on the methodology and some of the major findings can be found in Lewinsohn, Hoberman and Rosenbaum (1988). In this volume, Lewinsohn and Alexander (Chapter 8) summarize the findings concerning the relationship between resourcefulness and depression.

People who were low on learned resourcefulness were more likely to become depressed than were highly resourceful people. Stressful life events also increased the probabiity of becoming depressed. Unexpectedly, however, resourcefulness did not moderate the relationship between stress and the onset of depression. Resourcefulness and stress acted in an additive manner but not multiplicative or interactive.

Lewinsohn and Alexander noted that resourcefulness was related to various measure of effective coping with depression, but not with the rate of occurrence of stressful life events. Overall, their findings suggest that resourcefulness has a direct impact on mental health. It should be noted that also hardiness was found to have a direct impact on health (Chapter 3). These findings are in line with my reformulation of the concept of learned resourcefulness (Chapter 1; Rosenbaum, 1989). According to this reformulation, resourcefulness has not just a corrective function (i.e., stress-buffering effects); it also prompts people to initiate self-change, even if this entails facing new stressors.

In a recent article, I wrote, "The literature on stress and coping has focused mainly on the redressive function of self-control: the striving for homeostasis by eliminating any interfering factors. However, peopel are motivated not only to avoid stress and preserve homeostasis. The development of humankind has been characterized by a constant search for change and for new challenges, even if considerable stress and pain are involved. People often deliberately bring stressful interruptions into their lives to change their behavior, in anticipation of a more rewarding life in the future" (Rosenbaum, 1989, p. 251). I call this "reformative self-control" to contrast it with "redressive self-control." I believe that highly resourceful people, as well as people high on hardiness and with a strong sense of coherence, are physically and psychologically healthier—not only because they can better cope with stress, but also because they are more capable of adopting health-promoting behaviors and attitudes. A fuller discussion of this idea is presented in Chapter 1.

Lewinsohn and Alexander (Chapter 8) report that people who scored high on resourcefulness also scored high on measures reflecting self-confidence and self-perceived skill in social interaction. However, resourcefulness was not related to measures of perceived social support or emotional dependency on others. These findings support Rachman's (Chapter 6) contention that the definition of resourcefulness should be broadened to include the ability to use social resources, not just personal resources. In the final chapter of this book, Frederick brings the message that a time-limited severe trauma that occurs during adulthood can have positive sequelae for some people. He conducted a series of personal interviews with former hostages and members of their families. He lists various coping mechanisms they used to survive the severe stressors they were subjected to. More importantly, Frederick reports the salutogenic effects these traumatic events had on their lives. For example, one man noted that he changed for the better after being held for 444 days in an Iranian prison, he had a greater appreciation for life, and his marital relationship had improved. I would predict that this man would score high on measures that assess resourcefulnes, hardiness, and sense of coherence.

Rachman has correctly noted that learned resourcefulness is not simply a mirror image of learned helplessness. Whereas helplessness refers to a psychological state, resourcefulness refers to an enduring general attribute (as do hardiness and the sense of coherence). Furthermore, whereas helplessness originated from a pathogenic model, resourcefulness has its roots in a salutogenic orientation.

To summarize: this book focuses on the psychological factors that account for good mental and physical health. Obviously, no single concept or theory can provide a full explanation; different theories were advanced by the various contributors to the book. I hope that this book will provide an impetus for the study of health-promoting personality factors. If we ever get to the stage in which the mystery of health is unraveled, there will be little need to study pathology any longer.

References

Abramson, L. Y., Garber, J., & Seligman, M. E. P. (1980). Learned helplessness in humans: An attributional analysis. In J. Garber & M. E. P. Seligman (Eds.), *Human helplessness: Theory and applications* (pp. 3–34). New York: Academic Press.

Abramson, L. Y., Seligman, M. E. P., & Teasdale, J. (1978). Learned helplessness in humans: Critique and reformulation. *Journal of Abnormal Psychology, 87,* 49–74.

Antonovsky. A. (1979). *Health, stress, and coping.* San Francisco: Jossey-Bass.

Antonovsky, A. (1987). Unraveling the mystery of health: How people manage stress and stay well. San Francisco: Jossey-Bass.

Bandura, A. (1977). Self-efficacy: Toward a unifying theory of behavior change. *Psychological Review, 84,* 191–215.

Byrne, D. (1961). The repression-sensitization scale: Rationale, reliability and validity. *Journal of Personality, 29,* 334–349.

Eysenck, H. J. (1988). The respective importance of personality, cigarette smoking and interaction effects for the genesis of cancer and coronary heart disease. *Personality and Individual Differences, 9,* 453–464.

Garber, J., & Seligman, M. E. P. (Eds.) (1980). *Human helplessness: Theory and applications.* New York: Academic Press.

Kanfer, F. H. (1977). The many faces of self-control, or behavior modification changes its focus. In R. B. Stuart (Ed.), *Behavioral self-management: Strategies, techniques and outcomes.* New York: Brunner/Mazel.

Kobasa, S. C. (1979). Stressful life events, personality, health: Inquiry into hardiness. *Journal of Personality and Social Psychology, 37,* 1–11.

Lewinsohn, P. M., Hoberman, H. M., & Rosenbaum, M. (1988). A prospective study of risk factors for unipolar depression. *Journal of Abnormal Psychology, 97,* 251–264.

Marks, I. (1983). Behavioral concepts and treatment of neuroses. In M. Rosenbaum, C. M. Franks, & Y. Jaffe (Eds.), *Perspectives on behavior therapy in the eighties* (pp. 112–137). New York: Springer.

Meichenbaum, D. (1977). *Cognitive-behavior modification: An integrative approach.* New York: Plenum.

Meichenbaum, D. (1985). *Stress inoculation training.* New York: Pergamon Press.

Piamenta, R. (1987). The effect of learned resourcefulness and style of coping (blunter vs. monitor) on adjustment to surgery under local or general anesthesia. Unpublished master's thesis, Tel Aviv University, Tel Aviv.

Peterson, C., & Seligman, M. E. P. (1984). Causal explanations as a risk for depression: Theory and evidence. *Psychological Review, 91*, 347–374.

Rodin, J., & Salovey, P. (1989). Health psychology. *Annual Review of Psychology, 40*, 533–579.

Rosenbaum, M. (1983). Learned resourcefulness as a behavioral repertoire for the self-regulation of internal events: Issues and speculations. In M. Rosenbaum, C. M. Franks, & Y. Jaffe (Eds.), *Perspectives on behavior therapy in the eighties* (pp. 54–73). New York: Springer.

Rosenbaum, M. (1988). Learned resourcefulness, stress, and self-regulation. In S. Fisher & J. Reason (Eds.). *Handbook of life stress, cognition and health.* (pp. 483–496). Chichester, UK: John Wiley & Son.

Rosenbaum, M. (1989). Self-control under stress: The role of learned resourcefulness. *Advances in Behavior Research and Therapy, 11*, 249–258.

Rosenbaum, M., & Ben-Ari Smira, K. (1986). Cognitive and personality factors in the delay of immediate gratification of hemodialysis patients. *Journal of Personality and Social Psychology, 51*, 357–364.

Scheier, M. F., & Carver, C. S. (1985). Optimism, coping, and health: Assessment and implications of generalized outcome expectancies. *Health Psychology, 4*, 219–247.

Seligman, M. E. P. (1975). *Helplessness: On depression, development, and death.* San Francisco: Freeman.

Seligman, M. E. P., & Maier, S. F. (1967). Failure to escape traumatic shock. *Journal of Experimental Psychology, 74*, 1–9.

Silver, R. L., & Wortman, C. B. (1980). Coping with undesirable life events. In J. Garber & M. E. P. Seligman (Eds.), *Human helplessness: Theory and applications* (pp. 279–340). New York: Academic Press.

Weisenberg, M., Wolf, Y., Mittwoch, T., & Mikulincer, M. (1988). Learned resourcefulness and perceived control of pain. Unpublished manuscript, Bar-Ilan University, Ramat Gan, Israel.

Major Conceptual Approaches

1

The Role of Learned Resourcefulness in the Self-Control of Health Behavior

Michael Rosenbaum

Although modern medicine in its search for the causes of various illnesses made large strides in eliminating many infectious diseases, it failed to a large extent in promoting health-related behaviors. We know how to combat infectious diseases and how to remove by surgical means pathological factors within our body, but so far we have failed to prevent various diseases such as cardiovascular disorders and cancer that are at least partially determined by the kind of life-style that characterizes modern life. In fact, the conditions that have developed in most modern societies promote illness-related behaviors rather than health-related behaviors. Thus, for example, individuals learn to smoke, to overeat certain unhealthy food, and to engage in activities that do not require any physical exercises. Furthermore, because of the dynamical nature of modern society, most individuals are constantly faced with highly demanding and ever-changing situations that challenge their competencies and their well-established behavioral repertoires. These challenges produce intense physiological and emotional reactions that often have adverse effects on their physical and psychological well-being. Nevertheless, most people do not succumb completely to situational pulls of modern life and know how to self-manage behavior so it promotes health rather than illness. Without the ability to self-regulate and to self-manage their behaviors, often in opposition to environmental contingencies, people would be unable to engage in health-related behaviors. Thus, whereas illness-related behaviors are acquired and maintained by the general life-style of the individual in modern society, health-related behaviors are most frequently learned and maintained by self-control processes.

Hence, my basic premise is that a clear understanding of the process of self-control is paramount for developing methods and techniques that would promote health behavior and better coping with illness. The first part of this chapter is devoted to a theoretical discourse of our self-control model, and the second part focuses on research findings on learned resourcefulness. Learned resourcefulness refers to a set of well-learned behaviors and skills by which a person self-controls his or her behavior.

A Conceptual Model of Self-Control

Human actions can be characterized by the degree to which they require the activation of cognitive processes. On the one end of the continuum are those actions that require very little thinking and are performed almost automatically, and on the other end are actions that require considerable cognitive effort. Speaking one's mother tongue, driving a car, or brushing teeth are well-established behaviors that are performed in a "mindless" fashion with minimal cognitive effort. On the other hand, performance of a newly acquired skill or responding to an unfamiliar situation may require some "thinking" and cognitive effort. The former actions represent the "automatic" pole of the continuum, and the latter actions characterize the "controlled" pole of the continuum. When one is engaged in controlled actions one has to engage also in what has been labeled as "process-regulating cognitions" (PRC)(Rosenbaum, 1990). The PRC's function is to regulate the processes by which individuals determine their own behavior; they precede any self-control behavior. The PRC are similar to the cognitive functions of the self-system in Bandura's (1978) social learning theory. The "self-system" refers to "cognitive structures that provide reference mechanisms and to a set of subfunctions for the perception, evaluation, and regulation of behavior" (Bandura, 1978, p. 438). Whenever a person monitors his or her actions, assigns meanings to events, attributes causality to what has happened, and develops expectancies for the future, he or she engages his or her PRC.

Under the general rubric of "self-regulation," I distinguish between "automatic self-regulatory" processes and "self-control" processes. Whereas the former occur automatically often without the person's awareness, the latter are cognitively controlled by the person through his or her process regulating cognitions. Physiological reactions are effected by automatic self-regulatory processes (Schwartz, 1984). Self-control behaviors are controlled by deliberate cognitive processes that are under the voluntary control of the person.

There are four basic assumptions underlying our self-control model: (a) human behavior is goal directed; (b) self-control behavior is called for when individuals encounter obstacles in the smooth execution of goal directed behavior; (c) self-control behavior is always associated with certain process regulating cognitions (PRC); and (d) there are multiple and interactive factors that influence the PRC and the self-control behavior.

Cognitive Processes (PRC) that Foster Self-Control Behavior

On the basis of Kanfer's (1977) model of self-regulation and of theories of stress (Lazarus & Folkman, 1984; Mandler, 1982), I have proposed (Rosenbaum, 1988) that the processes that lead to the execution of the self-control behavior consists of a number of cognitive phases. First, there is the representational phase in which the individual experiences an emotional and/or a cognitive reaction to real or imagined changes within himself or herself, or within the environment. These reactions occur more or less automatically without any conscious effort. The disruption of ongoing behaviors, plans, and well-established expectations may trigger "automatic" thoughts about such things as one's self-worth and one's basic beliefs. These automatic thoughts are assumed to originate from deeply rooted cognitive self-schemata and should not be confused with conscious and deliberate attempts to appraise the situation at hand. The former fall under the rubric of "personality" in our model, whereas the latter are part of the PRC. Similarly, disruptions of the smooth flow of behavior and of habitual ways of thinking are often also associated with emotional reactions. In fact, emotional reactions are conceptualized as primitive and powerful knowing processes of changes that occur within the person or within the immediate environment (Mahoney & Gabriel, 1987).

An example would clarify what is meant by the representational phase. A highly successful executive was asked by his company to go through a routine physical check-up. The person felt healthy and physically capable, and thus he expected to be pronounced a healthy person. However, the examining physician told him that he is at high risk for coronary disease because of his high blood pressure, over-weightness, and excessive amount of cholesterol in his blood. Furthermore, the physician recommended that he change his eating habits, exercise regularly, and learn to relax. Each of these activities requires interruptions of well-established habits and the adoption of behaviors that in the short run have unfavorable consequences but in the long run are likely to prevent coronary disease. Yet none of these behaviors will be initiated if the person reacts indifferently to the information about the possible threat to his health. The results of the physical check-up must cause a disruption in the person's self-image as invulnerable to physical illness in order for the self-change program to take place.

Second, the initial automatic reaction to a disruption is followed by a shift in attention toward one's own behavior. The person then starts to gain information on his or her behavior by using self-monitoring. The PRC play a significant role in how this information is evaluated and what expectations develop. In the self-evaluation phase, individuals engage in what Lazarus and Folkman (1984) have labeled "primary and secondary appraisals." In primary appraisal, the person evaluates whether the disruption is desirable or undesirable. If the person concludes that there is nothing at stake for her in the disruption, she will ignore her reactions to it and no self-control behavior will ensue. However, if the person feels threatened by the disruption, she appraises whether there is anything she can do to minimize its adverse effects and to maximize potential benefits. The latter is referred to by Lazarus and Folkman (1984) as "secondary appraisal." In the example given above, after the executive's spontaneous reaction to the disturbing medical information, he is likely to evaluate the physician's report. He may ignore the implications of the medical information by saying to himself, "I know better than the doctor of what is going with me," or "I rather continue with my life as usual than being disturbed by what the doctor told me." Yet, if he concludes that "what the doctor told me, is extremely important for my well being," he will go ahead by appraising whether he could do something to improve his health status. If he concludes that there is something he can do to reduce his chances for a coronary disease, he will start to consider various courses of action that he could adopt in order to change his life-style. On the other hand, if he concludes that he can do nothing to reduce his chances of getting a coronary illness, no self-control behavior will be performed.

During the secondary appraisal stage of the self-evaluation phase, individuals develop expectations for the future. Bandura (1977, 1982) has proposed two basic expectancies that are important in guiding human behavior: outcome and self-efficacy expectancies. Outcome expectancies refer to the belief that the desired goal will be obtained if the person follows a specified course of action. Self-efficacy expectancies, on the other hand, refer to the person's evaluation that he or she is fully capable of performing the acts needed to attain the desired goal. Outcome expectation are based on the kind of explanations the person developed for the causes of his or her current situation. Individuals who believe that events are caused by their own actions and that these actions are modifiable (i.e., they do not reflect some global personal deficiency) are likely to pursue their attempts at self-control.

To summarize, before an individual engages in self-control behavior he or she must go through the following cognitive processes (PRCs): (a) notice a disruption in his or her habitual ways of thinking; (b) evaluate this disruption as important for his or her well-being; (c) believe that a specified course of action will lead to a desired outcome; and (d) expect that he or she will be capable of self-change (i.e., self-efficacy expectations) (Bandura, 1977).

Determinants of Process Regulating Cognitions (PRC)

How do people develop the kind of beliefs and expectations that we and others (e.g., Bandura, 1977; Kanfer and Hagerman, 1981) believe are crucial for self-control behavior? In Figure, 1.1, I present a schematic model of the variables that govern the PRC. The basic assumption of this model is that the PRC develop through a reciprocal interaction with personality, situational, and physiological variables.

In the context of the self-control literature, the most extensive studies were done on the development of self-efficacy expectations. Bandura (1977) has suggested that these expectations are derived from four principal sources of information: performance accomplishments, physiological states, vicarious experience, and verbal persuasion. It is interesting to note that two of the four sources reside in the social context of the person, and none are related to personality variables. In fact, this reflects the basic bias of many behaviorists and social learning theoreticians against the concept of personality [with a noted exception of Staats (1975)] in favor of social-situational variables. Bandura (1977) suggested that individuals appraise their abilities to self-control their own behavior according to the feedback they obtain on their own performance and/or on the performance of similar others under similar situations. When feedback is negative or noncontingent, individuals may either abandon any attempt to obtain their original goal or may search for new and potentially more rewarding goals.

Situational variables determine also how much pressure will be put

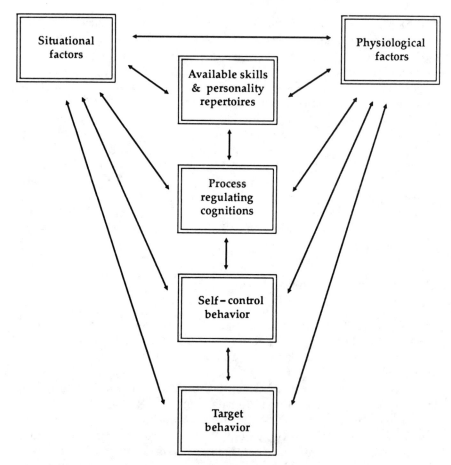

FIGURE 1.1. Schematic representation of interactions among factors which govern cognitions that foster self-control behavior.

on the person at a given time. If there are too many changes in the environment that call for the person's attention, the person could not adequately attend to these changes and self-evaluate her capabilities to cope with them. Thus, it is quite likely that excessive situational demands may lead to cognitions that are not conducive of self-control behavior.

Although physiological variables were introduced to various models of self-control (e.g., Bandura, 1977; Kanfer, 1977), their role in the process of self-control has received relatively little attention. Bandura (1977) suggested that physiological responses may provide the individual with another source of information about his or her ability to cope with fears. Schefft et al. (1985) suggested on the basis of Kanfer's model of self-regulation (Kanfer, 1977) that large discrepancies between the person's goals and the outcome of her behavior (presumably the trigger for self-control) may lead to increased brainstem-limbic activation (i.e., emotional arousal). This stage corresponds to the representational phase of the PRC in our model. Self-evaluation according to these authors is influenced by the function of the frontal lobes. "For example, in a situation perceived as threatening, increased brainstem-activation entrains the frontal lobes for evaluation and formulation of a response. The result may be calming self-statements that the threat is more perceived than real with subsequent reduction in brainstem-limbic activity through positive feedback (reflecting lack of goal-outcome discrepancies). However, if the threat is real, increased brainstem-limbic activation through negative feedback from the frontal lobes will entrain the appropriate fight-flight response" (Schefft et al., 1985, p. 210).

The focus of this chapter, however, is the role of personality repertoires in the execution of self-control behavior. Personality repertoires have been defined as "constellations of complex skills which are evoked by many situations but also have the quality of providing the basis for additional learning" (Staats, 1975, p. 63). A personality repertoire is not a personality trait, but rather a set of well-learned behaviors, cognitions, and affects that are in constant interaction with the social and physical environment of the person. It influences the way a particular individual will respond to her social and physical environment, and at the same time it is modified by the person's experiences, but not as easily as the PRC.

The individual's personality repertoire has a unique influence on the PRC and it partially accounts for the large individual differences in self-control behavior. It has an impact on how a person reacts to disruptive changes in one's life, how she evaluates their effect on her well-being, how she assesses her ability to cope with them, and how she plans to self-control her behavior in light of these changes (Rosenbaum, 1988). The focus of the present chapter is mainly on one such personality repertoire, namely, learned resourcefulness. However, in this section, I will mention just a few other personality variables that appear to influence various phases of the cognitive process that foster self-control behavior.

In the context of self-control theories, perhaps the largest attention was given to individual differences in attending to disruptive changes in oneself. Carver and Scheier (1982) and Schwartz (1984) bring evidence that individual differences in the disposition to be self-attentive determines whether or not an individual will start to self-regulate his or her behavior. For example, individuals who have a strong disposition to attend to the inner, unshared aspects of themselves (i.e., high on "private self-consciousness")(Buss, 1980) are more likely to react to changes in their bodily sensations and in their moods. Yet, individuals who are high on "public self-consciousness" (Buss, 1980) are more likely to react to changes in the response of others to them. Hypnotic ability is another personality repertoire that may account for persons' reactions to changes within themselves. People who are high on hypnotic ability have been found to be more responsive to psychological and physiological changes (Wickramasekera, 1986). Miller (Chapter 4) suggests that individuals can be divided into those who seek information on stressful events ("monitors") and those who avoid such information ("blunters"). In circumstances that call for self-control behavior, monitors are more likely to engage in self-control than blunters. Yet, as Miller has noted, this personality variable may also account for how persons cope with a specific stressful situation after they have recognized that there is a problem at hand.

Individual differences in other personality variables may account for how individuals appraise disruptive changes in their life (i.e., "primary appraisal"; Lazarus & Folkman, 1984). These include the "sense of coherence" (Antonovsky, 1979; Chapter 2, this volume) and "hardiness" (Kobasa, 1979; Orr & Westman, Chapter 3, this volume). Thus, by definition, individuals with a high sense of coherence are those who usually evaluate stressors in a positive way because they are generally confident that their "internal and external environments are predictable and that there is a high probability that things will work out as well as can be expected" (Antonovsky, 1979, p. 123). Similarly, it is expected that "hardy" individuals will emphasis the positive aspects of a stressor, in particular, because they view changes and disruptions in their life as challenging and desirable (Kobasa, 1979).

Personality variables were also hypothesized to influence the person's belief in his or her ability to control the outcome of his or her behavior (i.e., "secondary appraisal," Lazarus & Folkman, 1984). Peterson and Seligman (1984) reported that the habitual way people explain causes for bad or good events (explanatory style) predicts depression, achievement, and health. People who posses an "optimistic" explanatory style see the causes of bad events as unstable, specific, and external ("It just happened this time"; "It is a single and specific event"; "It is not because of anything I did"), and the causes of good events as stable, global, and internal (Seligman et al., 1988). The exact opposite explanatory style has been labeled as "pessimistic," and it was found to be related to helplessness, inaction, and depression (Seligman et al., 1988). Hence, it is quite likely that individuals who have an optimistic explanatory style are more likely to appraise noxious disruptions in their life in such a way as to promote actions and self-control behavior.

Under the rubric of secondary appraisal, we also include the person's self-efficacy beliefs in his or her ability to cope with a specific stressor (Bandura, 1977). Although Bandura (1977) did not include personality dispositions as a possible source for self-efficacy expectations, we have found, as will be indicated in the next sections, that these expectations are related to the person's learned resourcefulness (Rosenbaum & Ben-Ari Smira, 1986). On the other hand, Folkman, et al. (1986) found only a low correlation between the person's secondary appraisals and Pearlin and Schooler's (1978) Mastery Scale, which assesses a person's habitual belief in his ability to control his own behavior.

In sum, our self-control model suggests that the cognitive processes that foster self-control behavior (i.e., the PRC) are affected by situational, physiological, and personality variables. Bandura's (1977) work provides supporting evidence of how social situations influence the individual' self-efficacy expectations. Carver and Scheier (1982) and Schwartz (1984) provide research evidence on the role of personality variables in the person's initial attention to disruptive changes in his or her life. The primary and secondary appraisals of these disruptions are probably influenced by the following personality variables: sense of coherence, hardiness, and explanatory style. In a later section, I will expound on the role of learned resourcefulness as a personality variable in the development of the PRC. So far, the effect of physiological factors on the PRC has received little attention.

Redressive Versus Reformative Self-Control

Thus far we have discussed the cognitive processes that promote self-control behavior without discussing the functions of the self-control behavior itself. Most models of self-regulation focus on the corrective and return to homeostasis functions of the self-regulatory process (e.g., Kanfer & Hagerman, 1981; Schwartz, 1984). Namely, the self-regulatory process is initiated by an environmental disruption of an ongoing automatic behavior and the individual self-regulates his or her behavior in such a way as to minimize the interfering effects that this disruption has on the smooth execution of routinized actions. Kanfer and Schefft (1988) have labeled this kind of self-regulation as corrective self-regulation. For the purpose of the present discussion, I prefer to use the term "redressive self-control" (the term "self-regulation" is reserved for noncognitive, automatic self-regulation that has always a corrective function). Individuals who have to cope with physical pain or with the anxieties involved in threatening medical procedures usually engage in redressive self-control. However, many health-related behaviors, in particular those that are involved in changing of life-style in order to prevent future illness, are not initiated by external disruptions. In fact, these kinds of behavior require of the person to self-initiate a disruption in order to produce a change in illness-promoting habits. This kind of self-control is labeled "reformative self-control." Whereas in redressive self-control the person's efforts are directed at resuming normal functioning that was disrupted, in reformative self-control the person's efforts are directed at disrupting his or her customary way of functioning and adopting a new behavior. Furthermore, whereas in redressive self-control the person's behavior is guided and reinforced by immediate feedback from the environment, in reformative self-control the person's behavior is self-generated and is minimally influenced by proximal external feedback.

The distinction between redressive self-control and reformative self-control is not substantially different from the distinction of Nerentz and Leventhal (1983) between danger control and emotion control. "The danger-control system consists of representations of the health threat as objectively perceived and of plans and reactions for modifying the impact of the threat on the individual. The emotion- control system consists of the representation of the subjective feeling state and the cognitions specific to it and of plans and reactions for modifying the emotional state of the individual" (p. 15). In emotion control, the individual engages in redressive self-control: he or she attempts to reduce the interfering effects that internal responses such as anxiety, depression, and pain have on ongoing behavior. For example, a person that goes through an aversive medical procedure directs her efforts at self-controlling her anxiety and pain in order to improve her general feelings and to prevent any disturbances to the medical procedure. In danger control, a person has to modify his or her behavior in the face of information on a threat to health (i.e., "smoking is dangerous for your health"). In the latter situation the individual may engage in reformative self-control in order to reduce future threats to her health.

The two kinds of self-control behaviors can either compete with each other or complement each other (Rosenbaum, 1989). For example, patients who suffer from end-stage renal disease usually comply with the requirement to be on a dialysis machine three times a week, since noncompliance is lethal. However, dialysis patients often fail to follow the strict restrictions on fluid intake (De-Nour and Czaczkes, 1972). "The dialysis patients face a dilemma that is typical of situations that require self-control behavior. If they follow the required fluid diet they face a constant urge to drink, and they suffer from thirst. On the other hand, if they abuse the fluid diet, . . . their health deteriorates" (Rosenbaum & Ben-Ari Smira, 1986). The information that unrestricted fluid intake may eventually lead to additional physical illness may produce fear reactions in the dialysis patient, and she may prefer to ignore this information (as apparently some do) and reduce the fear reaction by telling herself, "Don't worry about the future; just enjoy your life as long as you can." In this case, she engages in some kind of redressive self-control. However, she may decide to adhere to the fluid intake restrictions despite the fact that it causes her stress and pain because she hopes to be rewarded with healthier life in the future. In this case, she engages in reformative self-control. Most likely, however, the relationship between these two types of self-control may be complementary. In the example just described, the dialysis patient decides to adhere to the fluid-intake restrictions (i.e., reformative self-control) and at the same time she engages in redressive self-control in order to reduce the emotional tension involved in her efforts to restrict fluid intake. Thus, if reformative self-control precedes redressive self-control, the two behaviors are likely to complement each other. Furthermore, we assume that someone's persistence in a self-change program (such as dieting or exercising) is highly dependent on whether she simultaneously engages in redressive self-control to reduce the pain and anguish involved in any self-change program (Rosenbaum, in press b).

To summarize, redressive self-control consists of a set of behaviors by which a person self-regulates internal responses, such as emotions, pain, and cognitions that interfere with the smooth execution of an ongoing behavior. These behaviors are directed at achieving homeostasis and the resumption of activities that were disrupted. On the other hand, reformative self-control consists of a set of behaviors that guide the person through the process of change. Any change entails a self-initiated interference with the smooth execution of well-established behaviors and the adoption of new kinds of behavior. These responses are directed at achieving heterostasis rather than homeostasis. However, since the process of change may be interfered with internal responses, redressive self-control may function in conjunction with reformative self-control.

Learned Resourcefulness and Self-Control Behavior

In order to engage in self-control behavior, one must have the necessary skills and behaviors in one's basic behavioral repertoire. Once this assertion is made, one needs to define the kind of skills and behaviors that are required for the successful execution of both redressive and reformative self-control behaviors. To do so, I looked into Meichenbaum's stress inoculation program in which he trains and instructs individuals in the use of different skills and behaviors to self-control their behavior in such a way that they could cope effectively with stressful events. The major components of the stress inoculation program are (a) self-monitoring of maladaptive thoughts, images, feelings, and behaviors; (b) problem-solving skills; and (c) emotion-regulation and other self-control skills (Meichenbaum, 1985). Meichenbaum (1977) found that persons who have acquired these skills develop a sense of "learned resourcefulness," i.e., the belief that they can effectively deal with "manageable levels of stress."

The personality repertoire that I call "learned resourcefulness" consists of beliefs plus self-control skills and behaviors. Underlying assumptions are that most people acquire these behaviors and skills even without any formal training; that the amount of learned resourcefulness varies from one person to another, and that for any one person, learned resourcefulness is fairly stable over time.

As our model of self-control proposes, having the necessary behavioral repertoire for self-control behavior does not automatically guarantee its utilization under the appropriate circumstances. The person has first to follow through specific cognitive processes (PRC) in which he or she assesses the situation at hand and evaluates his or her capabilities of coping with it. Nevertheless, the person's personality repertoires influence the judgmental processes. More specifically, learned resourcefulness is not expected to affect the person's perceptions of the situation at hand (i.e., whether it is stressful or not or whether it is "good" or "bad" for the person's well-being), but it is hypothesized to influence the person's self-efficacy beliefs (i.e., whether he or she can effectively cope with the situation). Saying that, I do not mean to say that learned resourcefulness is a sufficient source for self-efficacy expectations. In novel situations, a person may judge his or her self-efficacy on the basis of other sources [such as verbal persuasion and observing other people (Bandura, 1977)] and not on the basis of his or her learned resourcefulness. However, after a successful application of one's self-control skills, one is more likely to believe in his or her self-efficacy when faced again with a similar situation (Rosenbaum & Ben-Ari Smira, 1986).

Learned resourcefulness is also expected to influence the person's causal attributions. Previous research (Rosenbaum & Ben-Ari, 1985) indicated that high-resourceful (HR) individuals are more likely to attribute successful outcomes to their own efforts even on tasks in which their outcome was independent of the subjects' efforts.

In the next part of the chapter, I will discuss the assessment of learned resourcefulness and how this personality repertoire affects various health behaviors that are related to self-control behavior.

Assessment of Learned Resourcefulness

The main instrument used for the assessment of learned resourcefulness is the Self-Control Schedule (SCS) (Rosenbaum 1980a). The SCS is a self-report instrument directed at assessing individual tendencies to apply self-control methods to the solution of behavioral problems. It covers the following content areas: (a) use of cognitions and self-instructions to cope with emotional and physiological responses, (b) application of problem-solving strategies (e.g., planning, problem definition, evaluating alternatives, and anticipation of consequences), (c) ability to delay immediate gratification, and (d) a general belief in one's ability to self-regulate internal events. Items that were drawn from the first content area clearly relate to redressive self-control (e.g., "When I am feeling depressed I try to think about pleasant events"), whereas items drawn from areas (b) and (c) are more closely associated with reformative self-control (e.g., "Facing the need to make a decision, I usually find out all the possible alternatives instead of deciding quickly and spontaneously"). Since, redressive self-control skills are needed for successfully executing reformative self-control, more items relate to the skills required for reformative self-control.

The schedule (see Appendix A) consists of 36 items rated on a 6-point scale that indicates the extent to which the subjects evaluate the item as characteristic of themselves. Evidence on the psychometric adequacy of the schedule can be found in a number of previous publications (Redden, Tucker, & Young, 1983; Richards, 1985; Rosenbaum, 1980a; 1988) in addition to evidence on its construct validity, which is presented in the studies cited throughout this chapter. In a factor analysis performed on the SCS by Gruber & Wildman (1987), the following three factors have emerged: (a) problem-focused coping (which corresponds to skills needed for reformative self-control); (b) mood and pain control (which corresponds to skills related to redressive self-control); and (c) externality (e.g, "I need outside help to get rid of some of my bad habits"), which negatively corresponds to one's general belief in one's ability to self-control. Rude (1989) in a factor analysis of the SCS found a major factor which she has labeled "thought management" that accounted for nearly half of the total variance. This factor corresponds closely to the first content area of the SCS that is mentioned above. The other 4 factors found in her study were labeled: helplessness, systematic and planful approach, external control of habits, and impulsivity.

In all the studies that have used the SCS, a wide range of scores was obtained, which indicates that there are large individual differences in learned resourcefulness even in rather homogeneous populations. In the studies that are cited in this chapter, the subjects who scored above a certain cutting point on the SCS (usually the median score) are referred to as high-resourceful (HR) persons and those who score below that point are referred to as low-resourceful (LR) individuals.

Correlation of SCS with Other Scales

Evidence for convergent and discriminant validity of the SCS can be found in studies in which subjects' scores on the SCS were correlated with their scores on various other scales. Rosenbaum (1980a) reports that the SCS had low but statistically significant correlations with the following scales: Rotter's Internal-External Locus of Control Scale (Rotter, 1966; see also Richards, 1985), the Irrational Beliefs Test (Jones, 1968), and the G Factor ("Self-Control") of Cattell's 16 Personality Factors (Cattell, Eber, & Tatsuoka, 1970). In addition, the SCS was found to correlate with Fitz's Self-Esteem Scale (Michelson, 1985) and with the Bachman and O'Malley Self-Esteem Inventory (MacLachlan, 1985).

Kadner (1987) correlated the SCS with the Jaloweic Coping Scale (JCP) (Jaloweic, Murphy & Powers, 1984), which assesses the person's ways of coping with stressful events. This scale has three factors: confrontive coping, emotive coping behavior, and palliative coping. The highest correlation ($r= 0.49$) was found between the SCS and the confrontive factor of the JCS, whereas emotive and palliative coping factors were negatively correlated with the SCS ($r= -0.29$ and $r= -0.27$, respectively). Kadner (1987) also reported a moderate size correlation between the SCS and Barron Ego Strength Scale (Barron, 1953). Keinan and Melamed (1987) reported that the SCS did not correlate with a measure of Type A behavior. We have also unpublished data indicating that the SCS does not correlate with Type A behavior. Lewinsohn and Alexander (Chapter 8) have found that the SCS did not correlate with the Crowne-Marlow Social Desirability Scale, yet Rosenbaum (1980a) reports a low ($r= 0.21$) correlation with this scale.

Gintner, West, and Zarski (1989) compared responses on the SCS with those on Folkman and Lazarus's (1980) Ways of Coping Scale. Eighty graduate students completed the SCS 3 weeks prior to a midterm exam. HR and LR groups were created from the upper and lower thirds of the distribution. On the day of the exam (prior to taking the test) and a week later (prior to receiving results), subjects completed the Ways of Coping Scale and a measure of stress symptomatology. HR subjects reported using significantly more problem-focused coping during the preparation week than did LR subjects but not during the waiting week after the examination. In contrast, LR individuals reported more wishful thinking and distancing during the preparation week than did the HR subjects, and more wishful thinking and self-blame during the waiting week. For both measurement weeks, HR subjects reported significantly fewer stress symptoms than did LR subjects.

Learned Resourcefulness and Health Behavior

Self-control behavior is important mainly in two areas of medical psychology: (a) coping with the physical discomforts that are caused either by illness or by painful medical procedures and (b) adoption of and adherence to health behaviors. Successful coping with the adverse consequences of illness and medical treatment call for redressive self-control, whereas the successful execution of health behaviors requires reformative self-control. Both kinds of self-control behaviors require, among other things, a repertoire of self-control skills and habits (i.e, learned resourcefulness). In the following sections, I will discuss research findings on the role of learned resourcefulness in the above two areas of medical psychology.

Coping with Physical Discomforts

Laboratory Studies of Pain

Our initial studies with the SCS attempted to demonstrate that HR subjects (high scorers on the SCS) could tolerate a painful stimulus longer than LR subjects (low scorers on the SCS). In two experiments (Rosenbaum, 1980b), we asked subjects to immerse their nondominant hand in ice cold water (the pain stimulus) as long as they could (the targeted behavior). As expected, we found that HR subjects were able to endure the cold stressor longer than were LR subjects, but as predicted from our model they did not differ in their subjective evaluation of the pain. HR subjects also reported using self-control methods (mostly thought diversion) more often than did LR subjects. Specific instructions on a coping strategy ("think of a pleasant event") equally increased pain tolerance among HR and LR subjects in comparison to a control group that did not receive such instructions. Thus, HR did not differ from LR in their ability to benefit from instructions in the use of self-control methods in coping with pain.

Barrios (1985) who also used the cold pressor as the pain stimulus failed to find differences between HR and LR subjects in the time they were willing to endure the ice water. Similarly, Asikri (1988) was able to replicate our findings in only one of the three experiments he conducted with the cold pressor. Motivation appears to be a major problem in studying pain endurance in contrived laboratory settings (Rosenbaum, 1989). Why should subjects who volunteered for a psychological study endure a painful stimulus for a long period? There are no clear-cut benefits for laboratory subjects in going through a painful experience. In fact, subjects who are using problem-solving skills may well conclude that there is no advantage at all for them in enduring a needless pain for a long period. Hence, the effects of learned resourcefulness on redressive self-control of pain could best be studied in situations in which the individual has to cope with real-life physical discomforts.

Nonlaboratory Studies

Our first study on the use of redressive self-control in a real-life situation was on navy soldiers who had to cope with symptoms of seasickness (Rosenbaum & Rolnick, 1983). Seasickness is a major problem for individuals who have to work on relatively small high-speed missile boats in a stormy sea. The typical physiological symptoms of seasickness include malaise, pallor, cold sweating, nausea, and vomiting. Our findings indicated that although the performance of seasick sailors was in general worse than that of nonseasick sailors when sailing in a stormy sea, HR seasick sailors still showed significantly less performance deficits in a stormy sea than LR seasick sailors. Further, HR sailors reported using more extensively specific self-control methods in coping with seasickness, than LR seasick sailors. There were no relationship between learned resourcefulness and the propensity to develop seasickness as our model would predict the abscence of such a relationship.

Three additional studies on coping with stress-related medical problems provide evidence that HR subjects more frequently use self-control methods during stress than LR subjects. The first study examined the effects of learned resourcefulness on coping with epilepsy. In this study (Rosenbaum & Palmon, 1984), HR epileptics who experienced low and medium ranges of epileptic seizures were found to cope more effectively with their seizures than LR epileptics under the same conditions. HR epileptics reported that they have used more self-control methods during their coping with the psychological consequences of an epileptic seizure than LR epileptics. In a second study, Groves (1986) compared the reactions of HR women with those of LR women during natural childbirth (i.e., without anesthesia). As expected, HR women in comparison to LR women reported that they had more control over the delivery process, engaged more often in breathing-relaxation exercises, and used more self-encouraging statements during delivery. In a third study by Gruber and Wildman (1987), it was found that among women who suffered from dysmenorrhea, those who were HR functioned better in their daily activities than LR women.

Going through surgery is probably the most threatening medical procedure that calls for the subjects' coping abilities. Piamenta (1987) studied the combined effect of two personality repertoires on the level of state anxiety of patients who were about to undergo surgery. These repertoires included learned resourcefulness and Miller's personal coping style (Miller, Chapter 4). According to Miller, there are two main modes for coping with aversive events: monitoring and blunting. Monitors are individuals who are highly alert for and sensitized to threat-relevant information (i.e., they seek information about the threatening situation). Blunters are those who cognitively avoid or transform threat-relevant information. Piamenta divided her subjects into four groups: HR-monitors, HR-blunters, LR-monitors, and LR-blunters. She found interesting interaction effects on the patients' preoperative anxiety level between these two personality repertoires. HR-Blunters were significantly more anxious than HR-monitors whereas the reverse was true for LR-blunters and LR-monitors patients. For HR patients, a monitoring personal coping style was more effective for anxiety reduction than a blunting coping style. On the other hand, for LR patients, having the capability to blunt the threatening information was more anxiety reducing than for LR-monitors, who were sensitized to the threats of the surgery. In other words, patients who have a rich repertoire of self-control skills (i.e., HR) benefit more by confronting the threatening situation than by avoiding it, whereas LR subjects may benefit more by avoiding any threatening information.

In the above study, all the patients underwent the same kind of minor surgery, but half of them were completely anesthetized during surgery whereas the other half received only local anesthesia and were quite awake during surgery. The best postoperative adjustment was observed among HR patients who received only local anesthesia and thus were given the opportunity to employ their self-control skills during and immediately after surgery. For LR subjects, having the opportunity to be awake during surgery had no beneficial effects.

These findings are in line with a recent laboratory study by Weisenberg et al. (in press) in which they found that HR subjects showed less physiological arousal than LR subjects under conditions in which the subjects could decide on the number of electric shocks they would receive during the experiment. Thus, there is some evidence to indicate that one's repertoire of self-control skills is best utilized when the person has maximal information on the situation that he or she has to cope with it. On the other hand, for persons with low levels of learned resourcefulness, information about stressful medical procedures may be either useless or harmful.

To summarize, HR in comparison to LR individuals were found to employ more extensively redressive self-control methods when faced with physical pain and discomfort. This finding was more evident in real-life situations than in contrived laboratory conditions. Further, the use of redressive self-control by HR individuals may be enhanced by information on the medical procedures and by personal dispositions to monitor such an information.

Adherence to Health Behaviors

The adoption of and the adherence to health-promoting behavior often requires breaking with well-established habits and stressful interruptions in daily living. Individuals adopt health behaviors for the prevention of illness as well as for improving their physical fitness in the long run. Individuals who are already afflicted with a certain illness are also often ordered by their physicians to adopt health behaviors. Without the use of reformative self-control, health behaviors cannot be learned. The person must have the ability to delay immediate gratifications, and to engage in problem solving and planful behavior. In short, being highly resourceful is hypothesized to be a necessary but not a sufficient condition for the acquisition of health behavior. As our model of self-control proposes, the person must also accept the need for such behaviors and believe that he or she can acquire them through his or her own efforts.

It has been consistently found that HR subjects are more capable of adopting healthful behavior. HR subjects were found to be more successful in giving up smoking on their own (Katz & Singh, 1986), in changing their eating habits (Leon & Rosenthal, 1984; Rosenbaum, 1980a; Smith, 1979), and in curbing their intake of alcohol (Carey, M.P., Carey, K. B., Carnrike, & Meisler, 1988).

In a number of studies, my students and I have examined the psychological factors that enable people who are already afflicted with a disease to adhere to health-promoting practices. The first reported test of our self-control model was in the study of dialysis patients who were required to adherence to a strict regimen of fluid intake (Rosenbaum & Ben-Ari Smira, 1986). As I have already mentioned in this chapter, the dialysis patients face a typical situation that calls for reformative self-control behavior. In this study, we found a very strong association between the patients' level of learned resourcefulness and their ability to restrict their fluid intake. HR dialysis patients adhered more closely to fluid-intake restrictions than did LR patients. There was no difference in their understanding of the adverse consequences of failure to adhere, nor in their stated motivation to adhere. The path analysis performed on the data revealed that subjects' expectations that they could resist drinking even on a hot day were the function of how they had evaluated their own skills as well as their past success in fluid-intake restrictions. Those who believed that they were successful in the past in keeping up with the fluid-intake restrictions, attributed their past success to their own efforts and were highly resourceful. Thus, high resourcefulness, positive self-evaluations of past performance, and efficacy expectations enhanced the employment of self-control behavior, which contributed to the subjects' adherence behavior.

In line with our findings with dialysis patients, Amir (1985) reported that HR diabetics were more successful in controlling sugar intake than were LR diabetics. In a longitudinal study of heart attack patients and their spouses, Fuller (1987) found that HR subjects used significantly more problem-focused coping strategies when under the stress of a major illness. He also found that the patients' level of learned resourcefulness, combined with a low state of anxiety, was the best predictor of ability to plan rehabilitation goals and maintain an effective attitude toward their implementation.

In conclusion, there is strong research support to suggest that learned resourcefulness is one of the major personality repertoires that enables the individual to acquire health-promoting behaviors provided the person believes that these behaviors are important for his well-being and that he believes that he is capable of executing them.

Resourcefulness and Response to Cognitive Therapies

Cognitive therapies such as those suggested by Beck (1976) and Meichenbaum (1977) partially train individuals in the skills and the behaviors that are assessed by the SCS-the measure of learned resourcefulness. Hence, it can be expected that individuals who are already high on these skills (i.e., HR) would benefit more from such therapies than LR individuals. For these individuals, cognitive therapy may just provide a "reminder" for the application of these skills to their problems. In at least three studies (Achmon, 1987; Simmons, Lustman, Wetzel, & Murphy, 1985; Smith, 1979), it has been found that HR subjects were more capable of implementing behaviors they acquired in therapy that emphasize cognitive and self-management techniques.

Smith (1979) found that a weight-reduction program based on self-management techniques was more effective with HR women than with LR women both in terms of weight and eating habit changes. Furthermore, fewer HR women dropped the program than LR women. A study by Simons et al. (1985) suggests that subjects' resourcefulness could be used for matching patients with treatments. In this study, HR subjects who were clinically depressed benefited more from cognitive-behavior therapy than LR depressed patients. However, pharmacotherapy was more effective with the LR patients than with HR patients. Simons et al. (1985) explained their findings by suggesting that cognitive therapy was more effective with HR patients since it made use of their self-control skills and abilities. Furthermore, whereas cognitive therapy was more congruent with the HR expectations of therapy, pharmacotherapy fulfilled the LR expectations of treatment.

Achmon (1987) also studied the differential effects of cognitive-behavioral treatment on HR and LR individuals. The subjects were 97 people who suffered from hypertension. They were randomly assigned to the following experimental groups: cognitive therapy, biofeedback training, and a placebo-attention control group. The cognitive therapy consisted of training subjects to control and express their anger in line with Novaco's (1975) stress inoculation of anger training program. The biofeedback treatment consisted of training subjects in reducing their heart rate. The control group was exposed to discussions and lectures on hypertension. All subjects attended their respective treatment groups for 17 1-hour weekly sessions. Both treatments were more effective in reducing the patients' blood pressure than the control group. As predicted and in line with previous studies, HR subjects benefited more from cognitive therapy than LR subjects. Unexpectedly, however, HR hypertensives did worse on the biofeedback treatment than the LR hypertensives. The latter finding may be explained by the role of attentive processes in increasing or decreasing heart rate. It has been reported (cf., Sandman, 1986) that heart rate decreased during tasks requiring environmental attention, whereas tasks demanding cognitive efforts led to heart rate acceleration. HR subjects probably made cognitive efforts to self-control their heart rate, whereas LR just focused their attention on the feedback.

The above studies suggest that cognitive therapies may be particularly suitable for HR persons, whereas LR individuals may benefit more from noncognitive therapies such as pharmacotherapy (when it is appropriate) and biofeedback. An assessment of a client's level of learned resourcefulness can provide guidelines for choosing the most appropriate therapy for that particular client. For HR clients, cognitive therapies may be sufficient; for LR clients, they are not. For LR clients, these therapies may produce short-term gains, but the probability of relapse will be high. Therefore, therapy for LR clients calls for the development of techniques that help them acquire the basic personality repertoire needed for self-control.

Are LR individuals less capable in learning self-management skills than HR persons? The answer is probably not. Asikri (1988) found no differences in how HR and LR subjects benefited from a 30-minute training session on coping with painful stimuli (cold pressor and ischemic pain). Asikri's training, based on Meichenbaum's (1977) stress inoculation program, was equally effective for LR and HR subjects in increasing tolerance to a painful laboratory stimulus. Thus, it appears that HR and LR individuals do not differ in their ability to learn self-control skills. They do differ, on the other hand, in their ability to implement these skills on a long-term basis.

The successful implementation of what is learned in various stress inoculation and cognitive therapies requires the ability to resist the habitual ways of responding by ignoring thought and rushing into action. As many clinicians could attest (cf., Rosenbaum, 1989), clients often show good problem-solving skills in the calm atmosphere of a therapy session where they are capable of defining the problem, generating alternative responses, weighing the appropriateness of various solutions, and arriving at the optimal course of action. But when the clients are faced with real-life situations, they often find themselves saying the wrong thing, unable to inhibit what they know is a wrong reaction, and feeling emotionally aroused over trivial things. In short, they are incapable of self-imposing a delay in their responses and hence fail to use the problem-solving skills that they have been taught. Because HR individuals are better at self-controlling their responses under stress, they are also better at utilizing the skills they acquired during cognitive therapy.

Learned Resourcefulness and Illness Proneness

Our research on learned resourcefulness has so far focused on the role of learned resourcefulness in coping with the adverse consequences of physical illness and in the acquisition of health behaviors. However, learned resourcefulness may also play an important role in reducing the risks of specific illness such as coronary heart disease and cancer.

Eysenck and colleagues (Eysenck, 1988; Grossarth-Maticek, Eysenck, & Vetter, 1988) in three prospective studies have identified two personality types that predicted cancer and coronary diseases (Type 1 and 2, respectively). These personality types were defined in terms of the persons' differential ways of coping with interpersonal stress. Stress is defined in terms of a loss of an emotionally highly valued object (a person, an occupational goal, or any other goal in life). Failure to achieve disengagement from the object and feeling of dependency on it leads to feelings of helplessness and hopelessness. However, whereas the Type 1 persons cope with these feelings by repressing their emotional reactions and developing a seemingly stoic attitude, the Type 2 persons experience a reaction of anger, aggression, and arousal. According to Eysenck (1988), under stressful conditions the Type 1 persons are prone to develop cancer (see also Levy, 1985) and the Type 2 persons are prone to develop coronary heart disease. The Type 2 personality disposition is similar to the hostility factor of the Type A coronary prone personality (Williams et al., 1980).

The healthy counterpart of the Type 1 and Type 2 personalities is according to Eysenck (1988) the Type 4 personality type, who is relatively protected against cancer and coronary disease. "Failure in relation to emotionally highly valued people and/or life goals is experienced by persons of Type 1 and 2 as *unavoidable,* whereas persons of Type 4 posses the ability to cope with the situation, and hence stress is *avoidable*" (Grossarth-Maticek et al., 1988, p. 480). Eysenck and colleagues also emphasize the strong tendency of Type 4 persons toward autonomy and independence from the social environment. In the theoretical framework of the present discussion, the behavior of Type 4 persons is less under the control of environmental contingencies and more under their own self-control. Furthermore, Type 4 individuals are hypothesized to have the necessary skills and abilities to cope with disruptions in their habitual goal-directed behaviors. Therefore, on pure conceptual grounds, the Type 4 person corresponds quite closely to our HR person.

Eysenck (1988a) reports of a study that was done in Heidelberg, Germany on 91 cancer-prone (i.e., Type 1) and 82 coronary-prone (i.e., Type 2) individuals. They were randomly divided into an experimental and a control group. According to Eysenck (1988a), "the experimental group received a special type of cognitive behavior therapy attempting to change the behavior of the individuals involved in a direction away from the characteristics of the cancer prone or coronary prone person"

(p. 460). Elsewhere, Eysenck (1988) described this treatment as training in how to cope with stressful situations. The control group did not receive any treatment. In a 13-year follow-up, it was found that very significantly fewer of the experimental group, as compared to the control group, died of cancer or coronary heart disease. These data suggest that individuals can acquire the appropriate cognitive self-control skills that will change their proneness to cancer or coronary heart disease.

The studies reported by Eysenck and colleagues have clear implications on the relationship between learned resourcefulness and proneness to cancer and heart diseases. Although there is not a perfect correspondence between the Type 4 personality and learned resourcefulness, it can be speculated that HR individuals are less prone to develop cancer and coronary heart disease. This supposition awaits confirmation in future prospective studies.

Summary and Conclusions

The evolution of the human species during the past ten thousand years is characterized by an ever-increasing movement toward autonomy from the physical and social environment. Ancient humans were highly affected by changes in their immediate physical environment, and for their survival they were highly dependent on the social group. By using cognitive capabilities, humans have learned to solve problems, develop plans for the future, and self-control behavior. Over the centuries humans have not been fully successful in controlling the physical environment, but we have learned to control our own behavior. Humans never learned to control the weather, but we have learned to protect ourselves from the harsh effects of the weather. Humans have not been able to completely eliminate diseases from our lives. In fact, once we conquered the infectious diseases by controlling some aspects of our social and physical environment, other diseases (e.g., heart diseases and cancer) became prominent, partially because we inadvertently developed an environment that is conducive for such diseases. Nevertheless, we can protect ourselves from diseases by taking charge of our own behavior, emotions, and cognitions.

Understanding the process by which people take charge of their own behavior is undoubtly the biggest challenge of contemporary psychology and medicine. In the present chapter, I presented a theoretical model that guides our research to unravel the mystery of the self-control process. There are four basic assumptions underlying the model: (a) that human behavior is goal directed; (b) that self-control behavior is called for when individuals encounter obstacles in the smooth execution of goal-directed behavior; (c) that self-control behavior is always associated with certain process-regulating cognitions (PRC); and (d) that there are multiple and interactive factors that influence the PRC and the self-control behavior.

I have distinguished between two kinds of self-control behavior: redressive and reformative self-control. Whereas in redressive self-control the person's efforts are directed at resuming normal functioning that was disrupted, in reformative self-control the person's efforts are directed at disrupting his or her customary way of functioning and adopting a new behavior. Redressive self-control assists the person in coping with the physical discomforts caused by illness or by painful medical procedures. Reformative self-control facilitates the acquisition of health behaviors. According to our model, certain PRC foster self-control behavior. Under the rubric of "PRC," I have included cognitive processes such as the self-evaluation of disruptive events in terms of what it means to the person ("primary appraisal") and whether the person believes he or she can cope with it ("secondary appraisal"). Under that rubric, I include also causal attributions for past events and expectations for self-efficacy.

Situational, physiological, and personality factors influence both the PRC and the self-control behavior. In the present chapter, I have focused on one personality variable: learned resourcefulness. Learned resourcefulness refers to an acquired repertoire of skills and behaviors necessary for the successful execution of self-control behavior. It is assessed by the SCS (Rosenbaum, 1980a; Appendix A). I have presented research evidence on the effect individual differences in learned resourcefulness has on people's ability to cope with physical discomfort as well as on their ability to adopt and adhere to various health practices. Among other findings, research on learned resourcefulness has so far indicated that people who are HR benefit more from self-management therapies than LR individuals. For LR clients, these therapies produce short-term gains, but the probability of relapse will be high. Therefore, therapy for LR clients calls for the development of techniques that help them acquire the basic personality repertoire needed for self-control.

Since learned resourcefulness appears to be an important personality variable that promotes health, the question remains: How is it acquired? Cognitive-behavioral programs as those suggested by Meichenbaum (1985) may be the way in which adults acquire it through formal training. However, my basic premise is that resourcefulness is acquired from early childhood and throughout life by informal training (Rosenbaum, 1988). How do parents train children to become resourceful? What kind of life experiences foster the development of resourcefulness? In order to start answering some of these questions, we need to develop instruments that are capable of assessing children's resourcefulness and their parents' training practices. Further, one needs to embark on longitudinal studies that will follow the person through his or her various stages of development. Such studies are likely to shed further light on the relationship between learned resourcefulness and health.

References

Achmon, J. (1987). *The role of cognitive and physiological personality characteristics in self-regulatory processes.* Unpublished doctoral dissertation, Tel Aviv University, Tel Aviv.

Amir, S. (1985). *Prediction of compliance and control in juvenile diabetes through self-control, perceptions and assertive behavior determinants.* Unpublished master's thesis, Tel Aviv University, Tel Aviv.

Asikri, D. (1988). [The generalization of self-control training]. Unpublished raw data, Tel Aviv University.

Antonovsky, A. (1979). *Health, stress, and coping.* San Francisco: Jossey-Bass.

Bandura, A. (1977). Self-efficacy: Toward a unifying theory of behavior change. *Psychological Review, 84,* 191–215.

Bandura, A. (1978). The self-system in reciprocal determinism: *American Psychologist, 33,* 344–358.

Bandura, A. (1982). Self-efficacy mechanism in human agency. *American Psychologist, 37,* 122–147.

Barrios, F. X. (1985). A comparison of global and specific estimates of self-control. *Cognitive Therapy & Research, 9,* 455–469.

Barron, F. (1953). An ego-strength scale which predicts response to psychotherapy. *Journal of Consulting Psychology, 17,* 327–333.

Beck, A. T. (1976). *Cognitive therapy and the emotional disorders.* New York: International Universities Press.

Buss, A. H. (1980). *Self-consciousness and social anxiety.* San Francisco: Freeman.

Carey, M. P., Carey, K. B., Carnrike, Jr., C. L. M., & Meisler, A. W. (1988, November). *Learned resourcefulness, drinking, and smoking.* Paper presented at the annual meeting of the Association for the Advancement of Behavior Therapy, New York, NY.

Carver, C. S., & Scheier, M. F. (1982). An information processing perspective on self-management. In P. Karoly & F. H. Kanfer (Eds.). *Self-management and behavior change: From theory to practice* (pp. 93–128). New York: Pergamon Press.

Cattell, R. B., Eber, H. W., & Tatsuoka, M. M. (1970). *Handbook for the 16 PF questionnaire.* Champaign, IL: Institute for Personality and Ability Testing.

De-Nour, A. K., & Czaczkes, J. W. (1972). Personality factors in chronic hemodialysis patients causing noncompliance with medical regimen. *Psychosomatic Medicine, 34,* 333–344.

Eysenck, H. J. (1988). Personality, stress and cancer: Prediction and prophylaxis. *British Journal of Medical Psychology, 61,* 57–75.

Eysenck, H. J. (1988a). The respective importance of personality, cigarette smoking and interaction effects for the genesis of cancer and coronary heart disease. *Personality and Individual Differences, 9,* 453–464.

Folkman, S., & Lazarus, R. S. (1980). An analysis of coping in a middle-aged community sample. *Journal of Health and Social Behavior, 21,* 219–239.

Folkman, S., Lazarus, R. S., Gruen, R. J., & DeLongis, A. (1986). Appraisal, coping, health status, and psychological symptoms. *Journal of Personality and Social Psychology, 50,* 571–572.

Fuller, S. R. (1987). *Learned resourcefulness and other predictors of planning and beliefs in self-efficacy of cardiac patients and their spouses.* Unpublished master's thesis, Tel Aviv University, Tel Aviv.

Gintner, G. G., West, J. D., & Zarski, J. J. (1989). Learned resourcefulness and situation-specific coping with stress. *Journal of Psychology, 123,* 295–304.

Grossarth-Maticek, R., Eysenck, H. J., & Vetter, H. (1988). Personality type, smoking habit and their interaction as predictors of cancer and coronary heart disease. *Personality and Individual Differences, 9,* 479–495.

Groves, S. (1986). *The effect of "learned resourcefulness" and birth "expectancies" on coping with the birth process.* Unpublished master's thesis, Tel Aviv University, Tel Aviv.

Gruber, V. A., & Wildman, B. G. (1987). The impact of dysmenorrhea on daily activities. *Behavior Research and Therapy, 25,* 123–128.

Jalowiec, A., Murphy, S., & Powers, M. (1984). Psychometric assessment of the Jalowiec Coping Scale. *Nursing Research, 33,* 157–161.

Jones, R. G. (1968). *A factor measure of Ellis' irrational belief systems.* Whichita, KS: Test Systems.

Kadner, K. D. (1987). Resiliency in nursing: The relationship of ego strength, social intimacy, and resourcefulness to coping. Unpublished doctoral dissertation, The University of Texas, Austin.

Kanfer, F. H. (1977). The many faces of self-control, or behavior modification changes its focus. In R. B. Stuart (Ed.), Behavioral self-management: Strategies, techniques and outcomes (pp. 1–48). New York: Brunner/Mazel.

Kanfer, F. H., & Hagerman, S. (1981). The role of self-regulation. In L. P. Rehm (ed.), *Behavior therapy for depression: Present status and future directions* (pp. 143–179). New York: Academic Press.

Kanfer, F. H., & Schefft, B. K. (1988). *Guiding the process of therapeutic change.* Champaign, IL: Research Press.

Katz, R. C., & Singh, N. (1986). A comparison of current smokers and self-cured quitters on Rosenbaum's Self-Control Schedule. *Addictive Behaviors, 11,* 63-65.

Keinan, G., & Melamed, S. (1987). Personality characteristics and proneness to burnout: A study among internist. *Stress Medicine, 3,* 1–9.

Kobasa, S. C. (1979). Stressful life events, personality, health: inquiry into hardiness. *Journal of Personality and Social Psychology, 37,* 1–11.

Lazarus, R. S., & Folkman, S. (1984). *Stress, Appraisal, and Coping.* New York: Springer Publishing Co.

Leon, G. R., & Rosenthal, B. S.(1984). Prognostic indicators of success or relapse in weight reduction. *International Journal of Eating Disorders, 3,* 15–24.

Levy, S. M. (1985). *Behavior and Cancer.* San Francisco: Jossey-Bass.

MacLachlan, I. M. (1985). Learned resourcefulness, depression and self-esteem. *IRCS Medical Science, 13,* 816–817.

Mahoney, M. J., & Gabriel, T. J. (1987). Psychotherapy and the cognitive sciences: An evolving alliance. *Journal of Cognitive Psychotherapy, 1,* 39–59.

Mandler, G. (1982). Stress and thought processes. In L. Goldberger & S. Breznitz, *Handbook of stress* (pp. 88–120). New York: The Free Press.

Meichenbaum, D. (1977). *Cognitive-behavior modification: An integrative approach.* New York: Plenum.

Meichenbaum, D. (1985). *Stress inoculation training.* New York: Pergamon Press.

Michelson, S. (1985). Private self-consciousness interactive effect on the causation of anxiety and depression: Three possible mediating variables. Unpublished MA dissertation, Tel-Aviv University.

Nerenz, D. R., & Leventhal, H. (1983). Self-regulation theory in chronic illness. In T. G. Burish & L. A. Bradley (Eds.). *Coping with chronic disease: Research and applications* (pp. 1–37). New York: Academic Press.

Novaco, R. W. (1975). *Anger control: The development and evaluation of an experimental treatment.* Lexington, MA: Heath.

Pearlin, L. I., & Schooler, C. (1978). The structure of coping. *Journal of Health and Social Behavior, 19,* 2–21.

Peterson, C., & Seligman, M. E. P. (1984). Causal explanations as a risk for depression: Theory and evidence. *Psychological Review, 91,* 347–374.

Piamenta, R. (1987). The effect of learned resourcefulness and style of coping (blunter vs. monitor) on adjustment to surgery under local or general anesthesia. Unpublished master's thesis, Tel aviv University, Tel Aviv.

Redden, E. M., Tucker, R. K., & Young, L. (1983). Psychometric properties of the Rosenbaum Schedule for Assessing Self-Control. *The Psychological Record, 33,* 77–86.

Richards, P. S. (1985). Construct validation of the Self-Control Schedule. *Journal of Research in Personality, 19,* 208–218.

Rosenbaum, M. (1980a). A schedule for assessing self-control behaviors: Preliminary findings. *Behavior Therapy, 11,* 109–121.

Rosenbaum, M. (1980b). Individual differences in self-control behaviors and tolerance of painful stimulation. *Journal of Abnormal Psychology, 89,* 581–590.

Rosenbaum, M. (1988). Learned resourcefulness, stress, and self-regulation. In S. Fisher & J. Reason (Eds.). *Handbook of life stress, cognition and health* (pp. 483–496). Chichester, UK: John Wiley & Son.

Rosenbaum, M. (1989). Self-control under stress: The role of learned resourcefulness. *Advances in Behavior Research and Therapy, 11,* 249–258.

Rosenbaum, M. (1990). A model for research on self-regulation: Reducing the schism between behaviorism and general psychology. In G. H. Eifert & I.

M. Evans (Eds.): *Unifying behavior therapy: Contribution of Paradigmatic Behaviorism.* New York: Springer Publishing Co.

Rosenbaum, M., & Ben-Ari, K. (1985). Learned helplessness and learned resourcefulness: Effects of noncontingent success and failure on individuals differing in self-control skills. *Journal of Personality and Social Psychology, 48,* 198–215.

Rosenbaum, M., & Ben-Ari Smira, K. (1986). Cognitive and personality factors in the delay of immediate gratification of hemodialysis patients. *Journal of Personality and Social Psychology, 51,* 357–364.

Rosenbaum, M., & Palmon, N. (1984). Helplessness and resourcefulness in coping with epilepsy. *Journal of Consulting and Clinical Psychology, 52,* 244–253.

Rosenbaum, M., & Rolnick, A. (1983). Self-control behaviors and and coping with seasickness. *Cognitive Therapy and Research, 7,* 93–98.

Rotter, J. B. (1966). Generalized expectancies for internal versus external control of reinforcement. *Psychological Monographs, 80,* No. 1.

Rude, S. S. (1989). Dimensions of self-control in a sample of depressed women. *Cognitive Therapy and Research, 13,* 363–375.

Sandman, C. A. (1986). Cardiac afferent influences on consciousness. In R. J. Davidson, G. E. Schwartz, & D. Shapiro (Eds.), *Consciousness and self-regulation (Vol. 4)* (pp. 55–85). New York: Plenum.

Schefft, B. K., Moses, J. A., Jr., & Schmidt, G. L. (1985). Neuropsychology and emotion: A self-regulatory model. International Journal of Clinical Neuropsychology, 7, 207–213.

Schwartz, G. E. (1984). Psychobiology of health: A new Synthesis. In B. L. Hammonds & C. J. Scheierer, *Psychology and Health* (pp. 145–193). Washington, DC: American Psychological Association.

Seligman, M. E. P., Castellon, C., Cacciola, J., Schulman, P., Luborsky, L., Ollove, M., & Downing, R. (1988). Explanatory style change during cognitive therapy for unipolar depression. *Journal of Abnormal Psychology, 97,* 13–18.

Simmons, A. D., Lustman, P. J., Wetzel, R. D., & Murphy, G. E. (1985). Predicting response to cognitive therapy of depression: The role of learned resourcefulness. *Cognitive Therapy & Research, 9,* 79–90.

Smith, T. V. G. (1979). *Cognitive correlatives of response to a behavioral weight control program.* Unpublished doctoral dissertation, Queen's University, Kingston, Canada.

Staats, A. W. (1975). *Social behaviorism.* Homewood, IL: Dorsey.

Weisenberg, M., Wolf, Y., Mittwoch, T., & Mikulincer, M. (in press). Learned resourcefulness and perceived control of pain: A preliminary examination of construct validity. *Journal of Research in Personality.*

Wickramasekera, I. (1986). A model of people at high risk to develop chronic stress-related somatic symptoms: Some predictions. *Professional Psychology: Research and Practice. 17,* 437–447.

Williams, R. B., Jr., Haney, T. L., Lee, K. L., Kong, Y., Blumental, J., & Whalen, R.E. (1980). Type A behavior, hostility, and coronary atherosclerosis. *Psychosomatic Medicine, 42,* 539–550.

2

Pathways Leading to Successful Coping and Health

Aaron Antonovsky

At any one time, at least one-third and quite possibly a majority of the population of any modern industrial society is characterized by some morbid, pathological condition, by any reasonable definition of the term. Illness, then, is not a relatively rare deviance. There are two ways of looking at this phenomenon. A pathological orientation seeks to explain why people get sick, and why they enter a given disease category. A salutogenic orientation focuses on the origins of health and poses a radically different question: Why are people located toward the positive end of the health-ease/dis-ease continuum? Or, why do they move toward the health end, whatever their location at any given time?

In my book *Health, stress, and coping* (Antonovsky, 1979), I have developed the salutogenic model. I noted that it is in the very nature of human existence that stressful circumstances are omnipresent. Yet even with a high stressor load, many people (though far from most) survive and even do well. Barring stressors that directly destroy the organism, people's health outcomes are unpredictable. This is the mystery the salutogenic orientation seeks to unravel. Confronting a stressor results in a state of tension with which one must deal. Whether the outcome will be pathological, neutral, or salutary de-

The material for this chapter has been adapted, with permission, from Antonovsky, A. (1987). *Unraveling the mystery of health: How people manage stress and stay well.* San Francisco: Jossey-Bass. (Chapter 6 was reproduced as a whole with only few omissions and changes. Approximately five pages were reproduced from Chapter 2).

pends on the way one manages the tension. The study of factors determining tension management then becomes the key to health sciences.

I expressed my tentative answer to why some people remain healthy despite circumstances of stress in the concept of generalized resistance resources (GRRs)-money, ego strength, cultural stability, social supports, and the like-that is, any phenomenon that is effective in combatting a wide variety of stressors. Reviewing the literature on such resources, I discussed a very wide range of them, from elements that lead to a stronger immune system to magic. But what was lacking was a culling rule by which one could identify a phenomenon as a GRR without having to wait to see how it worked, or, better still, a rule by which one could understand how a phenomenon served as a GRR.

The answer to the salutogenic question that I developed was the sense of coherence concept (SOC). What is common to all GRRs, I proposed, is that they help to make sense out of the countless stressors with which we are constantly bombarded. In providing one repeatedly with the experience that the world makes sense, they generate, over time, a strong sense of coherence.

In this chapter, I start with a formal definition of the SOC and its three components: comprehensibility, manageability, and meaningfulness. Following that, I focus on the pathways through which the SOC and health are related. After identifying the dual issue involved in coping with stressful life events, instrumental problem solving and the regulation of emotion, a three-stage primary appraisal process is delineated, which then takes us to the selection of an appropriate coping strategy, action, and feedback evaluation. GRRs are defined as *potential* resources, which the person with a strong SOC can mobilize and then apply, seeking a solution to the instrumental problem. The subsequent section focuses on the ways in which the strength of the SOC is central to regulation of the emotional tension generated by confrontation with stressors. The theme throughout the article is the process of preventing the transformation of tension into stress. In the last section, I turn directly, though with some trepidation, to neurophysiological, endocrinological, and immunological mechanisms through which the SOC influences health outcome.

Sense of Coherence Concept

Initially, I had defined the sense of coherence as "a global orientation that expresses the extent to which one has a pervasive, enduring though dynamic feeling of confidence that one's internal and external environments are predictable and that there is a high probability that things will work out as well as can reasonably be expected" (Antonovsky, 1979, p. 123).

Although this definition was tentatively satisfying, I did not feel ready to operationalize it without further clarification. A series of in-depth, largely unstructured interviews with a wide variety of persons, 51 in number, was initiated. All the people interviewed had experienced major trauma. The question that guided the interviews was how they saw their lives. Analysis of the protocols led us to classify 16 persons as having a strong SOC and 11 as being at the other end of the scale.

I then searched the protocols of these two extreme groups, looking for themes consistently found in one group and markedly absent in the other. Repeatedly, I was able to identify three such themes, which I now see as the core components of the SOC: comprehensibility, manageability, and meaningfulness. The persons we had identified as having a strong SOC were high on these components, in stark contrast to those whom we had identified as having a weak SOC. The details of the pilot study and quotes from the interviews are given elsewhere (Antonovsky, 1987).

Definition of the SOC and Its Components

As a consequence of our research my new definition of the SOC includes its three core components:

> The sense of coherence is a global orientation that expresses the extent to which one has a pervasive, enduring though dynamic feeling of confidence that (a) the stimuli deriving from one's internal and external environments in the course of living are structured, predictable, and explicable (comprehensibility); (b) the resources are available to one to meet the demands posed by these stimuli (manageability); and (c) these demands are challenges, worthy of investment and engagement (meaningfulness).

To fully explicate the meaning of the SOC concept, I expand on the definitions of the three core components: "Comprehensibility" refers to the extent to which one perceives the stimuli that confront one, deriving from the internal and external environments, as making cognitive sense, i.e., as information that is ordered, consistent, structured and clear, rather than as noise-chaotic, disordered, random, accidental, inexplicable. The person with a high sense of comprehensibility expects that stimuli he or she will encounter in the future will be predictable or, at the very least, when they do come as surprises, they will be orderable and explicable. It is important to note that nothing is implied about the desirability of stimuli. Death, war, and failure can occur, but such a person can make sense of them.

"Manageability" is defined as the extent to which one perceives that resources are at one's disposal that are adequate to meet the demands posed by the stimuli which bombard one. "At one's disposal" may refer to resources under one's own control or to resources controlled by legitimate others-one's spouse, friends, God, history, the party leader, a physician-whom one feels one can count on,and whom one trusts. To the extent that one has a high sense of manageability, one will not feel victimized by events or feel that life treats one unfairly. Untoward things do happen in life, but when they do occur one will be able to cope and not grieve endlessly.

"Meaningfulness" refers to the extent to which one feels that life makes sense emotionally, that is that at least some of the problems and demands posed by living are worth investing energy in, are worthy of commitment and engagement, and are challenges that are welcome rather than burdens that one would much rather do without. This does not mean that someone high on meaningfulness is happy about the death of a loved one, the need to undergo a serious operation, or being fired. But when these unhappy experiences are imposed on such a person, he or she will willingly take up the challenge, will be determined to seek meaning in it, and will do his or her best to overcome it with dignity.

Although all the three components of the SOC are necessary, they are of unequal centrality. Meaningfulness seems most crucial. Without this motivational component, high comprehensibility and manageability are likely to be temporary. When a person is committed and caring, however, the way is open to gaining understanding and resources. Comprehensibility is next in importance; high manageability is contingent upon understanding. This does not mean that manageability is unimportant. If one does not believe that resources are at one's disposal, meaningfulness will be affected and coping efforts weakened. Successful coping, then, depends upon the SOC as a whole.

The SOC and its three core concepts are assessed by a self-report questionnaire. The SOC scale and details on its psychometric properties can be found elsewhere (Antonovsky, 1987).

SOC, Successful Coping, and Health

Social supports, ego strength, and cultural stability, provide life experiences that promote development and maintenance of a strong SOC. On the other hand, deficits in any of these GRRs provide experiences that vitiate one's SOC. The crucial question remains, although it is now moved to the next link in the chain: How and why does a strong SOC promote health?

Before turning to that discussion, however, the question must be linked to the reconceptualization of stressors (Antonovsky, 1987). I distinguish between stressor life situations, viewed as resistance deficits, that is, as providing life experiences conducive to a weak SOC, and stressor life events as the concept is more generally used, that is, as demands to which there are no readily available or automatic adaptive responses. If our goal is to understand the formation of the SOC, then it is useful to think in the former terms, in which the stressor, the counterpart to the resource, has negative implications. If our goal is to understand the resolution of tension, then the stressor is open-ended; it cannot automatically be assumed that the consequences will be negative. In other words, the young adult, having known in his or her life a given pattern of life experience generated by a resource/ deficit balance, will have arrived at a given location on the SOC continuum. He or she will continue to be confronted, over and over again, with stressor events, whether these are daily hassles or derive from potentially stress-inducing acute or chronic situations. Children are born; loved ones die; significant job changes occur (or do not occur; we tend to forget that "nonevents" such as not being promoted or not being able to have a child are no less stressors); one moves to a new community. How and why does having a strong or a weak SOC make a difference in confronting these stressors?

Stressors and Tension

The fundamental philosophic view of the human organism as prototypically being in a dynamic state of heterostatic disequilibrium is at the heart of the salutogenic orientation. Whether the source of the stressors is the internal or external environment, whether they are daily hassles, acute or chronic and endemic, whether they are imposed upon one or freely chosen, our lives are replete with stimuli to which we have no automatic, adequate adaptive response and in the face of which we must respond. The message to the brain, unless sensors have been damaged, is clear: You have a problem. The nature of the problem is dual, consisting of (a) the problem-solving or instrumental issue and (b) the issue of the regulation of emotion. Tension, then, reflects the recognition in the brain that some need one has is unfulfilled, that a demand on one has to be met, and that one must do something if one is to realize a goal.

Let us take some examples. A 40-year-old male steel worker is informed that his plant is to be closed down. A 20-year-old female junior executive believes that unless she submits to her boss's sexual harassment and sleeps with him, any promotion is out and her job is endangered. The morning after, a man's wife informs him of the crude and brutal remarks he made while drunk at the party the night before. In each case, one is confronted by the dual question: What am I to do? What am I worth? Stressors can also be happy events. A woman gives birth to her first child, a lovely, healthy infant. A widower meets an attractive woman, and the chemistry is right. A woman professor is elected chair of her department. The instrumental and emotion-regulating problems come to the fore of one's agenda, whether the stressors are unpleasant or pleasant events. One has entered a state of tension. Whatever the stressor, then, one must act, much as in a state of cognitive dissonance. Let us trace this process of action.

There are, unfortunately, contradictory stands in the many seminal and significant contributions of Lazarus to the study of coping. These may be summed up by reference to the use of two words: taxing and endangering. I have followed the definition of stressor (Lazarus and Cohen, 1977) that focuses on a stimulus that "tax[es] or exceed[s] the resources of a system, (p. 109)." But elsewhere (Lazarus and Folkman, 1984), Lazarus writes "Psychological stress is a particular relationship between the person and the environment that is appraised by the person as taxing or exceeding his or her resources and endangering his or her well-being" (p. 19). Thus, stimuli that are appraised as benign, positive or irrelevant are excluded from the category of stressors. Moreover, in discussing daily hassles and distinguishing them from daily uplifts (Lazarus, 1984a), Lazarus writes of the former that "what makes them harmful or threatening is that they involve demands that tax or exceed the person's resources" (p. 376). I find the first definition most useful. The failure to extend the definition of stressors to all stimuli that are taxing, whether or not they are appraised as endangering, underlies the widespread failure to distinguish between tension and stress (and derives from a pathogenic orientation).

Lazarus himself, by use of his concept of the appraisal process, has opened the way to solution of the problem. The stimulus that reaches the brain is indeed defined initially as a stressor or nonstressor. Let us call this "primary appraisal-I." If defined as a nonstressor, then the appropriate system resources are brought into play to respond to the stimulus. If, however, it is defined as a stressor, then we are witness to the creation of a state of tension, manifested in increased psychophysiological activity and emotion. The reader is asked to keep in mind the six examples given two paragraphs earlier. In each case, the chances are that most of us would define the stimulus as a stressor.

This is not to say, of course, that the same stimulus would be defined by all of us as stressor or nonstressor. Called upon unexpectedly at an international meeting of experts to make spontaneous remarks is likely to put a graduate student into a tizzy; I would not be fazed. Approached seductively at a party, one person would react with easy delight, another with intense tension.

The very first mechanism through which the SOC operates, I propose, is related to this primary appraisal-I. By and large, I hypothesize, the person with a strong SOC is more likely to define stimuli as nonstressors, and to assume that he or she can adapt automatically to the demand than one with a weak SOC. In this way, the former will not experience tension, nor see it transformed into stress.

But there are the daily hassles and, of greater significance, the acute life events and those engendered by chronic-endemic situations that none can, without considerable distortion, perceive as nonstressors. In Western cultures I cannot imagine any driver who has just stopped inches short of hitting a child who had suddenly run into the street as responding with equanimity. Nor can I imagine anyone confronting the six situations above (even though I have only experienced one personally and a second vicariously) who, in primary appraisal-I, does not enter a state of tension. Similar examples could be given for other cultures. The point is that primary appraisal-I, for all human beings, cannot, a good part of the time, prevent many stimuli from being defined as stressors.

The next step, "primary appraisal-II," then, is the judgment of the nature of the stimulus-now perceived as a stressor- as endangering one's well-being, positive, benign, or irrelevant. The terms "benign" and "irrelevant", however, are a bit problematic. To perceive a stressor as benign or irrelevant is to define it as of little consequence for one's life, to assume that whether one mobilizes the resources to deal with the demand matters little. It is assumed that the tension will soon be dissipated; in essence, it is taking cognitive action toward redefining the stressor as a nonstressor. "I didn't, after all, hit the child, and I had been driving carefully. My heart will soon stop racing." Or the British voter, after painfully deliberating whether to vote Labor or Social Democratic, and casting the ballot, says "Oh, well, the important thing is that I voted against the Tories." Once again, the strong-SOC person, having considerable experience in encountering stimuli that initially seem to be stressors but soon turn out not to be problematic, without any particular investment of energy on his or her part, is more likely, at the primary appraisal-II stage, to define a stressor as benign or irrelevant, to feel confident that the tension will quickly dissipate.

Why is the person with a strong SOC more likely than one with a weak SOC to define a stimulus as a nonstressor or, when it is appraised as a stressor, to define it as irrelevant or benign? Because he or she has confidence that, as in the past, by and large things will work out well, that what seems to be a problem will turn out not to be much of a problem and is reasonably soluble, and that the dissonance is only seeming. As I sit and write this article, I am confronted with the questions: Am I saying something new and worthwhile? Will it make sense to my colleagues who read it before it goes to press? If I have a strong SOC, I can, without resistance, let these questions come to mind. And, as I call up the many occasions in the past when such questions have been answered positively, the tension dissipates and I can go on working. If not, then I repress the question, go on writing, and only later have it brought to my attention that what I have written is worthless. Or I discover something else, "urgent" to be done and escape, neither solving the instrumental problem nor resolving the tension.

This approach has much in common with Bandura's (1977) self-efficacy theory. As he has noted, "Perceived self-efficacy influences choice of behavioral settings" (pp. 193-194). That is, the strong-SOC person is more likely to voluntarily choose to enter situations, not having appraised them as tension-inducing. Or if a situation is seen as tension-inducing, no unusual calling up of resources is needed, for the stressor is defined as irrelevant or benign. Bandura would, I think, concur that no particular coping behavior need be mustered. When one has "the conviction that one can successfully execute the behavior required to produce the (desired) outcome" (p. 193), tension is not much of a problem.

It is most important, particularly with respect to health matters, to qualify the hypothesis that persons with a strong SOC are more likely to define stimuli as nonstressors or as irrelevant or benign. In a detailed study of the trajectory from symptom perception to hospital care in the case of coronary artery disease (CAD), Alonzo (1986) writes that "the time from acute symptom onset (ASO) to arrival at definitive medical care is critical for both morbidity and mortality. Since the highest mortality from CAD occurs within the first hour after ASO, individuals should be placed under definitive care as quickly as possible" (p. 1297). Defining chest, arm, shoulder, or jaw pains, shortness of breath, and perspiration as nonstressors or as irrelevant-the data indicate that such behavior is quite frequent-is life-threatening. The data on delay in detection of cancer point to a similar widespread problem. There is a danger that the strong-SOC person will at times deceive himself or herself.

By and large, this self-deception is less likely to be the case for the strong-SOC person than for the weak-SOC person. The former, with successful experience in coping with stressors, will tend to be realistic in not worrying about stimuli, but open to perceiving stimuli that are objectively threats to one's well-being as stressors to be coped with.

If, then, the strong-SOC person is advantaged in terms of primary appraisal I and II, such advantage is relatively unimportant. Given the nature of human existence, problems do not go away and tension is generated. Over and over again, particularly if the stimulus defined as stressor is a major acute or chronic-endemic stressor, one will be confronted with the true problem of the stress situation: How does one prevent tension from being transformed into stress?

Defining the Problem

Before we turn to the question of how the SOC works to resolve tension, preventing its transformation into stress (and hence reinforcing health and preventing disease), three issues should be raised: (a) defining the stressor as positive or negative; (b) clarifying the emotional parameters of the problem; and (c) clarifying its instrumental parameters.

First, it must be recalled that a stimulus defined as a stressor may be appraised as happy or unhappy-as positive or as endangering one's well-being. The literature overwhelmingly focuses on negative stressors, perhaps for good reason, since reduction of suffering may morally be taken as having higher priority than enhancement of well-being. But from a theoretical point of view, we are called upon to understand how happy tension, no less than unhappy tension, is resolved. Indeed, the basic concept of the Holmes and Rahe's (1967) original approach involved a rejection of this distinction, insisting that it was the life event requiring adaptation that predicted illness. True, most subsequent research has shown that the negative life events score was a more powerful predictor than total life events (Thoits, 1981). But this may well be because it is easier to solve the instrumental and emotional problems posed by happy events. We should be able to learn as much from studying such resolutions as from studying the resolutions of the problems posed by negative stressors. Further, we must take note of the fact that many stressors are not easily and cleanly appraised as either positive or endangering. Approach/approach and approach/avoidance conflicts are hardly unknown in human life. The woman who gave birth to a lovely first child may not have the good fortune to live in Sweden and be assured of a guaranteed year's income and keeping her satisfying job.

The person with a strong SOC, I suggest, is more likely to appraise a stressor as happier, as less conflictful, or less dangerous than one with a weak SOC. Once again, the underlying confidence that things will work out-that one has the resources to cope, that the confusing will become comprehensible, that the potential for tension-resolution exists-in and of itself is a relevant resource.

Second, such confidence may well be linked to the nature of the emotional problem engendered by a stressor. The same happy stressor will arouse different emotions. The widower who meets a woman attractive to him and has a strong SOC will feel hope and excitement; with a weak SOC, he will experience hopelessness and apathy. The stressor appraised as endangering will arouse, in the person with a strong SOC, sadness, fear, pain, anger, guilt, grief, and worry; in one with a weak SOC, anxiety, rage, shame, despair, abandonment, and bewilderment. What distinguishes these two sets of emotions is that the former provide a motivational basis for action, whereas the latter are paralyzing. Further, the former emotions are focused, the latter diffuse. Or, to put it in terms of the SOC construct, the same stressor is more likely to engage the meaningfulness component of the strong-SOC person than of one with a weak SOC. Focused emotions are clearly more consonant with the sense that problems are comprehensible. Moreover, the focused emotions are more likely to lead to coping mechanisms, whereas the diffuse emotions will lead to unconscious defense mechanisms (Kroeber, 1963; Haan, 1977). For a discussion of the role of awareness of the use of defense mechanisms in coping with stress, see Heilbrun and Pepe (1985).

Third, and this issue is parallel to the second, it must be determined how the instrumental problem involved is perceived when a stimulus has been defined as a stressor. Election to the chair of one's department, for the weak-SOC person, is likely to bring to the fore, even though the position had been wanted, a train of perceived and anticipated complex problems. Now, one has to interact directly with the dean, exercise disciplinary power over students referred by teachers, allocate resources instead of just fighting for them, invite visitors for dinner, and so forth. The strong-SOC person perceives the same problems, but with greater clarity, more specificity, and more precise differentiation. The problems, moreover, are not only seen as more comprehensible and manageable, but also as challenges rather than as burdens.

These two latter issues, involving the perception of the emotion-regulation and instrumental problems posed by a stressor, may well be termed "primary appraisal-III." Shalit and Carlstedt (1984), extending Lazarus's model, have adopted a very similar approach. In a series of studies that analyzed effective coping with stressors derived from the external environment (parachute jumping, military underwater operations), Shalit proposed that the first two stages of a sequential appraisal process consisted in, first, cognitive appraisal of the quality of structure and lack of ambiguity in the perceived situation, and, second, affective appraisal of emotional involvement in the situation. In order to cope well, Shalit (1982) argues, one must both have a clear picture of the situation ["One can view the incoherence of a perceived situation as the universal and primary stress factor" (p. 7)] and have given emotional meaning to the situation. The strong-SOC person, encountering a stressor, is more likely to be capable of introducing order and meaning into the situation.

Whether one calls these processes the first stage of the coping process or sees them as preliminary to coping, or whether one insists that they are sequential (as Shalit does) or not, does not seem to me to matter much. What I have proposed is that the extent to which one is capable of cognitively and emotionally ordering one's perception of the stressor and accepting a willingness to confront it is contributory to ultimate successful coping. Or, to put it in terms of the SOC construct, the extent to which one approaches the world with the generalized anticipation that stressors are meaningful and comprehensible lays the motivational and cognitive basis for managing and for preventing the transformation of tension into stress. The strong-SOC person, then, always has a head start. Before taking action, he or she has mobilized resources to confront the stressor. By contrast, the weak-SOC person, confused and devoid of the desire to cope, tends to give up at the outset.

We can now turn to the question of action or, rather, of response to the stressor. How does the strong-SOC person manage? How does he or she resolve the instrumental problem, and control the emotional and physiological parameters of the tension so that noxious consequences are avoided?

Resolution of Tension

The very first and fundamental point to be made is that a strong SOC is *not* a specific coping style. This is the heart of the matter. The stressors life poses are many and varied: positive or negative; brief, continuing, intermittent, or enduring; more or less objectively controllable; from within or from without; idiosyncratic, related to social roles or situations, or universal; chosen or imposed, and so on. To consistently adopt one pattern of coping-to fight, to flee, or to freeze; to depend on others or on yourself; to use denial or rationalization or sublimation; to depend on social support or money or intelligence, and so on-is precisely to fail to respond to the nature of the stressor and hence to decrease the chances of successful coping. What a person with a strong SOC does is to select the particular coping strategy that seems to be most appropriate to deal with the stressor being confronted. Or, as I would rather put it, he or she chooses from the repertoire of generalized and specific resistance resources at his or her disposal what seems to be the most appropriate combination.

The notion of choice points to a distinction that has largely been ignored in the literature, particularly in the large bulk of work done on coping, which deals with social supports. I refer to the distinction between a resistance resource as a potential and the actual mobilization and utilization of a resource. True, the very knowledge that one has a variety of potential resistance resources at one's disposal is in itself a valuable asset. And it is precisely the person with a strong SOC who is more likely to have a considerable armamentarium of resources at his or her disposal. But it is in the actual mobilization of what seems to be the most appropriate resource or combination of resources in the face of the given stressor that the true advantage of the strong-SOC person comes to the fore.

The crucial factor involved in the process of mobilizing resources is the strong sense of meaningfulness. Confronted with a stressor, the person with a strong SOC is more likely to feel a sense of engagement, of commitment, and of willingness to cope with the stressor. There tends to be an *a priori* assumption that dealing with it is worthwhile, and is a challenge to be welcomed rather than a burden to be escaped. The stressor may be very painful: being refused a job promotion one believes one has deserved; being fired; being turned down by one to whom one has proposed marriage; profound conflict and a rift with one's adolescent child; the death of a spouse; the election to national office of a candidate one believes is a catastrophe. Of course, we would rather these things did not happen. But they do. What is one to do, then, so that the damage is minimal and the pain assuaged?

One possibility is to define the development as being beyond the boundaries of what is meaningful in one's life. One of the hallmarks of the person with a strong SOC is that the boundaries of what is meaningful are flexible and can be narrowed (or broadened)-always with the proviso that they cannot be so narrowed as to exclude the crucial spheres in human existence: inner feelings, immediate personal relations, major activity, and existential issues. The orthodox Jew in the ghetto whose child married out of the faith would sit *shiva* (the period of mourning), defining the child as dead. Embarking on retirement after a long life of employment, one can say: "Well, paid work is no longer important in my life." The crucial questions are whether there are alternative sources of meaningfulness in one's life and whether the redefinition is an act of self-deception. It may not be.

Let us, however, assume that the problem posed by the stressor cannot be defined as beyond the boundaries of what one cares about or that to do so would involve self-deception, with repeated reminders that the problem has not gone away. The person with the weak SOC, seeing the stressor only in its burdensome aspects, will tend to focus on the emotional parameters, on handling the anxiety and unhappiness brought into being by the stressor. This is as true for a stressor deriving from the internal environment as for one externally or interactively derived. It is as true for a happy as for an unhappy stressor. The person with a strong SOC, by contrast, will tend to focus on the instrumental parameters of the problem, and will see as the challenge the question of what resources can be mobilized to meet the problem.

Before resources are mobilized, it is essential to define the nature and dimensions of the problem, to make sense of it. Is it simple and self-contained, or does it have extensive, ongoing ramifications? Does it involve only oneself, or are others involved? Is it analogous to problems that have been confronted previously? Does it involve moral issues? Is it likely to intensify or lose its force, irrespective of what is done? This is precisely where the comprehensibility component of the SOC comes into play. Believing that problems can be ordered and understood, the strong-SOC person can set about turning chaos into order, puzzlement into clarity. The weak-SOC person, persuaded that chaos is inevitable, gives up in advance at any attempt at making sense of the stressor. A half-hearted, ineffectual coping attempt results-or, more likely, a sole focus on dealing somehow with the emotional problem.

Although it has taken me many words to discuss the process that brings the person to the stage of what Lazarus calls "secondary appraisal", this does not necessarily reflect the time span involved in confronting a stressor from its appearance until the moment one acts (or does not act) directly to deal with it. Nor is the process anywhere near as rational or cognitive as it may sound. The process may be most rapid and very largely unconscious.

The proposal that the hallmark of the strong-SOC person is the ability to choose what seems to be the most appropriate strategy from among the variety of potential resources available does not mean that anything goes. We always cope with stressors within culture contexts, which define the canon. The American will use primary control, the Japanese, secondary control (Weisz, Rothbaum, & Blackburn, 1984). A confidant(e) may be one's spouse or one's blood brother or sister. But within these cultural constraints, the strong-SOC person will be flexible in choosing strategies.

The emphasis on flexibility in the choice of appropriate strategies resolves, I believe, the nonfruitful issue of whether the SOC is a personality trait or a disposition. To see coping as process and to insist on the importance of the concrete situation, the nature of the stressor, and the particular transaction in no way contradicts the possibility of identifying, for a given person, a consistent pattern of coping-not in terms of selection of a specific coping style, but in terms of flexibility.

The more recent literature has begun to demonstrate how the same coping style, the same behavior pattern, or the same defense mechanism can be highly functional or severely dysfunctional in health terms, depending on the problem. Cohen (1984) reviewing a substantial number of studies that linked coping patterns and disease outcome concludes that, "The key question may not be *which* coping strategies an individual uses but rather *how many* are in his or her repertoire or how flexible the person is in employing different strategies" (p. 269).

I should like to call the reader's attention to further studies that support Cohen's conclusion, but which broaden the picture. Orr (1983), in a longitudinal study of the adaptation of women who had a mastectomy, found that the best-adapted women were those who sought information primarily at the time of the third interview, some months after the operation. This, she proposes, is when information is most useful and manageable. Those who sought information constantly, as well as those who closed themselves off throughout, were less well-adapted. The strong-SOC person, I suggest, regards information as a potential resistance resource, to be sought when it can be useful, not when it is likely to provide overload, nor to be avoided consistently. In a similar vein, Strull, Lo, and Charles (1984) distinguish between patients' desire for information and discussion and their desire to participate in medical decision-making. Their data indicate that physicians underestimate the former and overestimate the latter.

The more general issue raised by these and other studies is discussed in Lazarus's (1981) brilliant article on denial. He points to the "apparent paradox that illusion or self-deception can be adaptationally sound *and* capable of eliciting a heavy price. The paradox is: How is it possible for self-deception to be at once healthy and pathogenic?" (p. 138). He goes on to discuss various criteria which indicate when it may be one or the other, asking questions like: Is reality being distorted? Is action possible? How salient is the emotional distress? For present purposes, what is important about Lazarus's article is that he subjects to close scrutiny the dominant assumption in much of psychology for many years (and, one may add, the current ethos in the culture of the United States) that one must always actively confront reality in full and head on. Whatever philosophical validity this position may have, its health consequences are problematic.

But this is not to say that anything works well. In a study of adults with four diseases that have different levels of danger and controllability (hypertension, diabetes, rheumatoid arthritis, and cancer), Felton, Revenson, and Hinrichsen (1984) investigated the consequences of using different coping strategies. Although their study is cross-sectional and the results equivocal, there is some indication that "greater positive affective states . . . were associated with primarily cognitive strategies, that is, incorporating relevant information or changing the nature of one's cognition," whereas "coping strategies of wish-fulfilling fantasy, emotional expression and self-blame are not altogether positive" (p. 896).

In a more sociological vein, Seeman, Seeman, and Sayles (1985) point to the importance of making distinctions between different kinds of potential resistance resources. In a year-long study of physical illness and illness behavior, they focused on two variants in each of two resources often regarded as homogeneous. They distinguish between the denial of luck as a determinant of health and the sense of personal control, suggesting that the former is the important facet of the locus of control, whereas the latter may well be harmful, in that it may boomerang as a form of false consciousness. Similarly, in stressing the importance of how a social network is used, they suggest that using it instrumentally is helpful, whereas high consulting behavior is more likely an expression of dependence and may be of more harm than good.

Dressler's study (1985) takes us a step further, in showing "that the efficacy of a particular coping style cannot be assessed apart from the specific socio-cultural setting in which an individual lives" (p. 504). Its focus was on the relationship between health, and the use of active coping (aimed at dealing directly with the stressor) and passive coping (avoiding the stressor and dealing primarily with emotional parameters). The study was done among Southern black women and men. "Scoring more in the direction of active coping," he found, "is beneficial to the psychological and physical health of women and deleterious to the psychological and physical health of men" (p. 502). Black men, he argues, in the context of southern racism, get into trouble when active, whereas women, whose major role is that of the homemaker, cope successfully when active.

The historical situation may, of course, change, and the coping style that was once effective can become less so, or even pathogenic. In many years of discussion with young Israelis troubled by the profound question of the Holocaust and "Why did Jews let themselves be led to the slaughter?," I have—after making very clear that the extent of active Jewish resistance in World War II is almost unbelievable, given the circumstances-sought to lead to an understanding of Jewish history, which is unfamiliar to many Israelis. Given the historical circumstances of 2,000 years of exile, the Jewish culture pattern of turning inward, of maintaining one's own culture and social structure, of readiness to rebuild constantly, proved to be the most effective coping strategy for survival. In the face of the inconceivable Nazi program for a "final solution," the strategy failed.

Finally, I should like to refer to a study that, although it does not deal directly with health, is germane to the issue of selection of a coping strategy in coping with stressors. Unruh (1983) considers the social situation of the elderly in American culture and proposes the construction of a "social world" as a highly effective way of coping with a situation that is a chronic-endemic stressor for many. He defines a social world as "an extremely large, highly permeable, amorphous, and spatially transcendent form of social organization wherein actors are linked cognitively through shared perspectives arising out of common channels of communication" (p. 14). The social world is, for Unruh, first and foremost a mental construction, a way in which "people organize their life-rounds, perceptions and action" so as to make "sense of that which occurred throughout their lives and rendering life meaningful" (pp. 48-49). Whether it is ballroom dancing or gleaning, two of the worlds Unruh analyzes, the construction of a social world is a choice from a variety of potentials.

Reference to these studies and to those by Cohen (1984) has been made in order to stress two points. First, the search for the personality type of coping strategy that is universally effective in successfully dealing with stressors is not only useless; any such concrete type of coping is bound to be self-defeating. But second, not anything goes. There are times and places, and situations, and people where it is possible to say that this behavior is more likely to be successful than that, and that behavior is likely to be self-defeating and boomerang. Cohen, having recognized these points, avoids the underlying question, however, namely, can we generalize about the character of the person who has many alternative coping strategies as potentials and uses them flexibly and appropriately? This is, I suggest, the person with a strong SOC. Motivated to cope, and having clarified the nature and dimensions of the problem and the reality in which it exists, he or she is well on the road to managing, by selecting the most appropriate resources to the problem at hand.

About two decades ago, Shanan (1967) proposed the concept of an adaptive coping style, which he saw as a response set that individuals characteristically adopt in stressful situations. He pointed to four features of this set; the availability of free cathectic energy for directing attention to the sources of potential difficulty; clear articulation of the perceptual field, distinguishing between the internal and external environments as potential sources of difficulty; confronting rather than avoiding complexity and conflict in the external environment; and maintenance of an optimal balance between the demands of reality and of the self. In a recent study, Steinglass, De-Nour, and Shye (1985) used Shanan's concept of adaptive coping style (unfortunately, they call it "active coping") and the instrument he developed to measure it, in order to analyze coping with the stressor of geographical relocation. The active coping and self-image scores, they write, "appear to reflect aspects of what Antonovsky has called a 'sense of coherence' . . . active coping reflects confidence about one's external environment; positive self-image reflects the same about one's internal environment" (p. 525).

But once this confidence is established—in my terms, once the generalized view of the world as meaningful and comprehensible is focused on the specific situation-one is ready to act. Such action can be directed, simultaneously or sequentially, at solving the instrumental problem and the emotional load. What does this mean, in terms of one of the examples given earlier, for the 40-year-old male steel worker informed that his plant is to close and he is to lose his job? Consider the following variety of resources that might be activated by the person with a strong SOC: insisting that his union keep very careful track of any attempt on the company's part to appropriate any or all of the legitimately earned severance pay, pension benefits, or vacation and sick leave rights; making it clear that neither he nor his workmates, but rather incompetent management or general social conditions, were to blame for the plant's failure; examining the family budget, calculating what cuts can be made and how long savings might last; considering, with his wife who has preferred to stay home, whether she should look for a job, and how the kids can pitch in; taking the opportunity to reexamine whether this is not a good chance for a career shift and skill retraining; doing some of the things he'd wanted to do for a long time, without interfering with job hunting, now that some leisure time can be expected; contacting his uncle or an army buddy for new job leads; rejoining the church choir and singing to let the pain ease. And looking not only for another job, but for one that will give him reasonable gratification, in all ways. After all, we are talking about the way he is going to spend the next 25 years.

There are no guarantees in life, and reality may go on tearing away at one's heart, one's time, and one's pocket. One may well bark up the wrong tree, make mistakes, and deceive oneself. One begins to blame oneself, to nag at the spouse and kids, to drink. But the chances that the strong-SOC person will take maladaptive coping actions are fewer. Whatever potential reality does offer, there is a better chance that he or she will transform it into actuality.

Fagin (1985), in a valuable summary article of the illness consequences of unemployment, writing in a pathogenic vein, closely analyzes the psychological, social-psychological, and sociological characteristics of unemployment that facilitate illness. In a brief passing remark, however, he notes that "a period of unemployment may be a useful turning point for a few individuals," but the question raised is nowhere pursued (p. 36). My point, of course, is not that unemployment is a happy experience; quite the contrary. But, for the person with a strong SOC, it may be less damaging than usually thought and may even prove to be salutary.

Reference to making mistakes brings us to the final stage of the coping process: feedback and correction of course. The stage of *secondary appraisal* involves selection of the appropriate resources for coping with the stressor. Transforming this potential into reality, one begins to get feedback. The friend whom one has asked for a loan is strapped. The confidant(e) to whom one has turned is too burdened with his or her own problems to listen. The self-help group turns out to be dominated by someone interested only in power. The union is run by entrenched politicians. Or, in happy contrast, one's judgment is vindicated, and the resources one has tried to activate turn out to be both available and appropriate. Tertiary appraisal is the making of such assessments.

At this stage, too, the strength of the SOC plays a significant role. As Cassel (1974) pointed out, in analyzing the significance of the lack of social support, "The actor is not receiving adequate evidence (feedback) that his actions are leading to anticipated consequences" (p. 477). The person with a strong SOC, long familiar with looking for feedback, will both elicit it and be capable of assessing it. With a weak SOC, once one's course is set, one tends to disregard signals that contradict the wisdom of the action chosen. There is no motivation to relinquish a course leading to a dead end and search for alternative courses of action. One goes on one's way blindly.

In seeking to understand how the SOC works, it may be that I have oversimplified matters in discussing the process of coping with a single stressor. But, as Mechanic (1974) long ago pointed out, it is valuable to view coping with stress as a process-a complex set of changing conditions that have a history and future. The very act of coping with a stressor may give rise to new stressors, as coping involves role modifications, mobilization of hitherto potential resources, shifting perceptions of the coper by others, and so on. Thus, for example, in the case of our unemployed steel-worker, the process of coping may cata-pult him into union leadership, his wife may take on paid employment, his children may see more of him, or he may be offered a temporary, unattractive job by his uncle, with whom relations have been distant. This is what real life is like. But putting matters in this context only reinforces my initial position that stressors are ubiquitous in human existence, and that we are required to cope all the time. If anything, it only becomes clearer that the person with a weak SOC will be over-whelmed and that one with a strong SOC has a chance to cope suc-cessfully.

Three reminders must be noted. First, though I have throughout referred to persons with a "strong" or with a "weak" SOC, I trust it has been obvious that this was simply a parsimonious way of saying that, "The higher one is on the SOC continuum, the more likely it is . . ." Second, the actual content of behavior, of the resource chosen to cope with stressors, is always shaped by one's culture. The concept may be cross-cultural, but its concrete translation will vary widely. Thus, the confidant(e) may be a relative of the older generation, a holy person, a spouse, God, or a friend. Similarly, one's culture defines which re-sources are appropriate and legitimate in a given situation. Culture sets limits; within these limits, the SOC matters. Third, I hope it has not been inferred from what I have written that a strong SOC is a magic bullet, enabling one to fully solve all the problems in life posed by stressors. Not only do very few of us have a very strong, authentic SOC, many of the problems in life are intractable, not amenable to full solution no matter how strong one's SOC. What I have proposed is that people with a strong SOC will do better than those with a weak SOC in coping with these problems; that when a problem is not soluble, they will be able to go on living with it more adequately; and that they will be able to live less painfully.

Coping with Emotions

In introducing the issue to which this chapter is devoted, I noted that the nature of the problem posed by a stressor is dual: the instrumental issue and the regulation of emotion. Even when the source of the stressor is the internal environment, the problem is still instrumental. Demands that come from within—unfulfilled aspirations, approach-avoidance conflicts, cognitive dissonance, and the like-are no less in-strumental problems than are demands that come from interpersonal relations, cultural and structural sources, or life events. Throughout the discussion, I have focused on how the SOC facilitates coping with the instrumental demand. There is, however, no demand or problem, that does not also raise the issue of the regulation of emotion. Tension, the response to a stressor—is an emotional phenomenon (as well as a physiological phenomenon, an aspect to be discussed below). Thus, even though emotion is viewed as a secondary phenomenon, as a response to a stressor, it becomes a first-order problem in itself. Resolution of the instrumental problem posed by the stressor does not mean that the problem of emotion regulation is automatically solved.

In a fascinating exchange, Lazarus (1984b) and Zajonc (1984) debate the question of the primacy of cognition versus the primacy of affect. Although Lazarus does not dispute the existence of sensory states and preferences, he argues that these are usefully excluded from the concept of emotions. The latter, he states, should always and only refer to a cognition about the implication of a stimulus for one's well-being. It is in this sense that I see the problem of regulation of emotion. Having appraised a stimulus as a stressor, as having implications for our well-being, a set of feelings emerges. How does the SOC allow us to cope successfully with emotions?

Part of my answer has already been given. Discussing what I called "primary appraisal-II," I suggested that the person with a strong SOC is more likely to define a stimulus as a happy rather than a dangerous stressor, as a challenge rather than a burden. I used words like "hope" and "excitement" compared to "hopelessness" and "apathy." I further distinguished between focused and diffuse emotions. My concern above was to suggest that the former provided a more adequate motivational and cognitive basis for action in dealing with the instrumental problem. But what of the emotion itself?

First, the human organism cannot, without consequent damage, remain at a high and intense level of emotional tension, even if the emotion is pleasurable. One must relax, if one is not to become exhausted. The central hypothesis I would propose is that persons with a strong SOC are more likely to experience different emotions than those with a weak SOC, emotions which, by virtue of a number of characteristics, are more amenable to regulation. A focused emotion is one in which the feeling is linked to a relatively clear target. One is angry about something someone has done or some event that has happened. The dimensions of the anger are delimited, as are its perceived consequences. Rage is qualitatively different; its target is the world, life, and people in general. One boils in anger, and the steam dissipates; one seethes in rage, endlessly. Similar contrasts exist between fear and anxiety, or grief and feelings of having been abandoned. In each case, it is easier to figure out what to do about the one emotion than about the other.

Second, another distinguishing characteristic of the emotions is the extent to which they are at the level of the unconscious. The strong-SOC person is more likely to be aware of his or her emotions, can more easily describe them, and feels less threatened by them than the weak-SOC person. They are more likely to be personally and culturally acceptable, hence there is less of a need to disregard their existence. They are more appropriately responsive to the reality of the situation one is in.

Third, there are the many stressors that raise the attributional question of blame. The weak-SOC person is more likely to blame someone or something else, often a vague "they or bad luck." than the strong-SOC person. (Several of the items on the SOC questionnaire raise this question directly.) But this expresses the often ineffectual defense mechanism of projection, a frightened escape from assuming responsibility, and leaves a nagging sense of unease. The strong-SOC person will not hesitate to blame others when reality makes this appropriate. In studies of occupational stress and underlying many programs of stress management at work, the assumption is often made that the job demands are reasonable and the problem is to train the worker to adjust to the stressors, conveying the message that he or she is to blame. [See Schwartz, 1980, who devotes part of one paragraph to "procedures . . . geared toward helping people change their environment to be more healthful" (p. 101), referring largely to assertiveness training and anger control, and more than three and half pages to procedures "geared toward helping people cope with an environment that can not be changed" (pp. 101-102).] The weak-SOC person, deeply unsure of his or her own competence, will often buy this approach, in contrast to the strong-SOC person, capable of placing the blame where it belongs.

We may take the issue of attribution one step further. When one does blame oneself, the target may be characterological or behavioral. In a study of women who came to an abortion clinic, Major, Mueller, and Hildebrandt (1985) made the distinction between women who attributed their unwanted pregnancy to not being strong or responsible people and those who focused on more concrete behaviors. The character-blamers, who would, I expect, be low on the SOC, were found to cope significantly less well with the abortion than women who did not blame their characters. Guilt, I suggest, is more easily manageable when it is linked to what one has done than to whom one is.

I trust that the foregoing makes it clear that the difference between the person with a strong and with a weak SOC is not that the former does not, in response to negative stressors, have strong feelings of emotional distress. If anything, he or she is more likely to allow them to come to the surface and to express them in overt behavior, rather than to repress them. In this way, one can more easily both act to deal with the instrumental problem and manage the problem of emotion regulation. Tension is much less likely to be transformed into stress. Silver and Wortman (1980), in an otherwise excellent review of the literature on coping with stressors, fail to make this distinction in their discussion of emotion regulation. They note that the evidence suggests that controlling one's emotions is not necessarily salutary. But they do not adequately make the distinctions among emotions I have noted, nor are they aware of the significance of ongoing entrapment in the intense emotions. Intense emotional distress among the recently bereaved, to take their example, will be manifested no less, and possibly more, by persons with a strong SOC. Nor will their pain and sadness disappear for a long time, if ever. But if the distress continues to be acute, sharp, blinding, shutting out other emotions, and dominating one's life-if the tensions become stress-the consequence will be pathology.

Effects on Health

Up to this point, the chapter has been concerned with explicating how the SOC lowers the probability that tension will be transformed into stress. The concept of the health-ease/dis-ease continuum has not even been mentioned. Yet the whole point of the discussion has been that by managing tension well, the person with a strong SOC will indeed reinforce or improve his or her health status. But as Kaplan (1984) warns, "a study that focuses on coping strategies is of little value unless we know that these strategies mediate health" (p. 756). It is to this issue that I now turn directly.

When Snow urged closing the Lambeth Company's Broad Street pump in order to contain the cholera epidemic in London in 1853, he had formulated the hypothesis that cholera could be transmitted by discharge of fecal wastes into water supplies (1855). He was very far from understanding the mechanisms by which using water into which sewage had been dumped led to cholera. But the epidemiologic basis for his recommendation was sound. Similarly, there seems to be sufficient evidence that stressors, unless adequately coped with, are pathogenic and at least some evidence that when coping is successful the outcome is salutary. What are the pathways to which we can point? The discussion can, at the best, be no more than specification of hypotheses, for I know of no data that point directly to the link between the SOC, coping, and health.

Cohen (1984) proposes that there are five "mechanisms by which coping can affect the etiology of and recovery from disease" (p. 265).

Three of these are on the level of direct behavioral coping: (a) habits that directly interfere with or reinforce health, for example, smoking, excessive drinking, or exercise; (b) adaptive behaviors that could lessen the severity of illness,for example, seeking early treatment, openness to cardiac rehabilitation information; and (c) transactions with health professionals, for example, compliance.

Although Cohen's article is ostensibly devoted to stressors, the issues to which she refers cover the entire gamut of behaviors that presumably have a direct relationship to health. I make no claim that persons with a strong SOC are more likely to engage in those behaviors that evidence indicates are good for the health-not eating between meals, not smoking, regular physical activity, and so on (Berkman & Breslow, 1983). These behaviors are far more determined by social structural and cultural factors than by the way one sees the world, and I do not wish to confuse the two. It may well be that the same socio-cultural factors that decrease smoking rates (for example, social class) also influence the emergence of a strong SOC, so that the chances that a strong-SOC person will not smoke are greater. But one must be cautious about attributing a spurious causality. In this case, social class would be the causal factor, leading to both rates of smoking and SOC levels. The latter two variables would then be related, but not causally.

If, however, we limit our focus to coping with stressors, and ask: "Confronted with an acute or chronic stressor, who is more likely to respond behaviorally with maladaptive health behavior, such as increased smoking or drinking, denial of symptoms, and nonadherence to medical regimens, and who is more likely to respond behaviorally with adaptive health behavior, such as cutting down smoking or drinking, alertness to symptoms, and exercising?" then I would say that the advantage would be in the hands of those who have a strong SOC. The reasoning underlying this hypothesis has been detailed above. The person with a strong SOC is more likely to accurately identify the nature and dimensions of the instrumental problem; more likely to approach it as a challenge; and more likely to select from his or her repertoire of resources those which are appropriate to the problem and employ them rationally.

Thus, returning to our example of the male steelworker about to lose his job, one would predict that, with a strong SOC, he will not start drinking heavily, for this would interfere with job hunting; he will try to talk to his wife about his feelings of anger at management; he will turn to a doctor if he feels disturbing chest pains; and he will exercise to keep in shape.

From this point of view, there is indeed a basis for anticipating a causal sequence between the SOC, health behaviors, and health. That is to say, persons with a strong SOC will engage in adaptive health behaviors more often than those with a weak SOC, all other things being equal. This would be equally true for the three behavioral coping mechanisms discussed by Cohen. But my position is that there is a more direct relationship between the SOC and health, one that is linked to Cohen's other two mechanisms. As she puts it, "First, coping may increase hormonal levels, causing direct tissue damage or influencing bodily resistance to illness . . . others have suggested that positive morale and the will to live may have positive physiological consequences" (p. 265). My hypothesis, then, is that the strength of the SOC has *direct* physiological consequences and, through such pathways, affects health status.

I must grant, at the very outset, that in discussing this hypothesis I may well commit that second-most serious scientific crime (the first being fabricating data), not knowing what I'm talking about, and entering a field about which I know next to nothing. Moreover, even experts in the field grant that there is as yet very little definitive knowledge available. Nonetheless, if any progress is to be made, social and biological scientists must learn to talk to each other. We cannot become experts in the other's field. But we can make suggestions, which others may exploit. It is in this spirit that I venture to make the following remarks.

The most powerful and profound (as well as most readable, for the social scientist) general paradigm within which my approach fits is Schwartz's (1979) conceptualization of the brain as a health care system. His quotation from von Bertalanffy (1968, p. 23), unknown to me at the time I developed the salutogenic model, is crucial:

> Concepts and models of equilibrium, homeostasis, adjustment, etc., are suitable for the maintenance of systems, but inadequate for phenomena of change, differentiation, evolution, negentropy, production of improbable states, creativity, building up of tensions, self-realization, emergence, etc.; as indeed Cannon realized when he acknowledged, beside homeostasis, a "heterostasis" including phenomena of the latter nature. (p. 23)

Schwartz's model derives from general systems theory, his central concern being: What happens when there is disregulation in normal integrated, self-regulatory systems such as the human organism? This organism, as an open system, generally maintains a steady state, which is distinct from equilibrium. When the entire system is functional and intact, there is a neat chain of complex, self-regulatory processes of which the person need not even be aware. The external environment provides input stimulation to the system; through sensory receptors, these inputs are registered in and processed by the brain (the information-processing subsystem); the brain, in turn, transmits orders to "peripheral organs" designed to cope adequately with the demand which has been made on the system; and most crucial, there are numerous "input devices (biological transducers) that detect the status of the stage 3 (peripheral organ) behavior and feed this information back to the brain (Stage 2) in a closed-loop fashion" (Schwartz, 1979, p. 559). If there is any indication that the problem has not been solved, the brain continues in some way to deal with it (including seeking to ignore it).

"A normally self-regulatory system," Schwartz (1979) writes "can become disordered when communication of essential information between specific parts of the system is, for whatever reason, disrupted" (p. 563). Disregulation can occur at any stage in the chain: the sensory receptors or the brain can distort the input information; inappropriate information can be given to the peripheral organs; and as Schwartz greatly emphasizes, the feedback information provided by the sensory organs to the brain can be distorted or misinterpreted. Given such disregulation, the disorder creates the possibility for the initiation of a disease process. The organism has failed to mobilize adequate or appropriate resources to cope with the threat.

Schwartz goes on to note what, in the present context, is a crucial issue: the recovery time following the response to a stressor. "A more dramatic effect of disregulation," he writes, "would be seen as a deficit in recovery time" (p. 567). This relates most directly to my distinction between tension and stress. The brain may register disturbance or pain, physical or emotional: the pain of a broken limb or stomach ache; the fear of the loss of a job; or the ecstasy of taking part in a great military victory with its accompanying physiological deviations from a steady state. With adequate feedback loops and regulatory processes, no train of damage will ensue. But if information is distorted or disregarded, and inadequate resources available, the disorder lasts, that is, the organism enters a state of stress and damage begins. Introduction of the time dimension allows us to focus not on the response to the acute stressor, which arouses physiological deviations from a steady state but can be handled expeditiously, but on the repeated acute or chronic stressors, inadequately handled, that are the source of damage.

The strength of the SOC, I propose, is a crucial determinant of the likelihood of preventing disregulation. This is true at all but one stage of the functioning of the system. As I have noted, the person with a strong SOC is more likely to avoid entering environmentally induced stressor situations, or more likely to define stimuli as nonstressors. Given the nature of human existence, however, this is a peripheral contribution to health. Once in a stressor situation, he or she is less likely to ignore or distort the nature of the problem, that is, the information received by the brain. Accurate messages are more likely to be transmitted to the peripheral organs. The feedback loop to the brain will be carefully attended to. And most important of all, the brain will select the most appropriate resources, both from among the wide variety of subsystems within the organism and from extraorganismic environment. Note that I have ignored one stage in the circuit; the adequacy of information reception, processing, and transmission of peripheral organs.

In a fascinating aside, in which Schwartz asks about possible neuropsychological mechanisms which could cause disregulation, he writes, "One plausible theory applies research linking patterns of lateralization of brain function to patterns of cognitive and affective processes" (p. 565). He notes the possibility of a functional disconnection syndrome in the brain. "By the inhibition of neural transmission across the cerebral commissures, which connect the two hemispheres, each half can become disregulated by the other" (p. 565). In this way, adequate integration of cognitive and affective processes in coping with stressors is impeded. Henry (1982), who has made a significant contribution to the study of the interaction of social and biological processes, has suggested to me (personal communication, 1983), that at a biological substrate, the SOC is expressed in a balanced integration between the two hemispheres. The reader will perhaps recall the phrase I used referring to the comprehensibility and meaningfulness components of the SOC: "making sense." I suggested that, for the strong-SOC person, the world makes sense both in cognitive terms (it is ordered, understandable, predictable) and in emotional terms (its demands are worthy of engagement, one cares about the world). The two hemispheres are on the same wavelength.

There is no doubt that at this very early stage of our knowledge about the working of the human brain, the preceding paragraphs may well not be much more than speculation. But they are not wild speculations; they do not violate the little that is known. Most important of all, they give us a way of thinking that generates hypotheses to be tested.

This brings us, finally, to a more precise focus on the relationship between adequate regulation and the maintenance of health (though, as always, the emphasis in the literature is on disregulation and disease processes). In the past two decades, there has been a most exciting explosion in a field that is coming to be called psychoneuroimmunology. All those involved would agree that "the concept that the immune system, operating via the central nervous and neuroendocrine systems, may act as a 'transducer' between experience and disease" (Solomon, 1985, p.7) is no longer an alien, speculative concept, even though knowledge is just at the beginning stage.

In his recent review of the field, Solomon (1985) proposes fourteen hypotheses on the linkages between the central nervous system and the immune system, four of which are particularly germane to the present discussion. Hypothesis I is put as follows: "Enduring coping style and personality factors (so-called trait characteristics) should influence the susceptibility of an individual's immune system to alteration by exogenous event, including reactions to events" (p. 87). Solomon arrives at the "tentative conclusion that there is . . . an 'immunosuppression-prone' personality" which, in interaction with particular pathogens and/or genetic predispositions and/or weak links, leads to disease (p. 8). This approach, then, in contrast to the type A behavior pattern, would not predict to specific diseases, but to disease. Cannot we then infer that there is also an "immunoenhancement-prone" personality? Is not a person with a strong SOC a candidate for the kind of person who, confronted with challenge to the integrity of the organism, mobilizes immunological competence?

Solomon's (1985) second hypothesis refers to the consequences of emotional upset and distress for "the incidence, severity, and/or course of diseases that are immunologically resisted . . . or are associated with aberrant immunologic function" (p. 9). In discussing this hypothesis, he refers to the possibility that Kobasa's (1979) concept of hardiness is relevant to understanding why some are protected against the immunological effects of emotional distress.

Hypothesis VIII proposes that "hormones and other substances regulated or elaborated by the central nervous system should influence immune mechanisms" (p. 12). In this hypothesis as well as in Hypothesis XIII, which relates to thymic hormones, Solomon considers indirect impact of central nervous system functioning on immunocompetence via neuroendocrines under the direction of the central nervous system. His question relates to "the effects of psychological events" (p. 12), but it might just as well relate to the processing of these events by the brain.

Finally, Hypothesis XIV raises the question of "whether behavioral intervention can enhance immunity" (p. 14). But Solomon is unclear about the goals of interventions designed to be immunoenhancing, referring to "happiness, security, sense of control, relaxation and other positive emotions." And why only positive emotions? Is it not conceivable that fear, grief, uncertainty, excitement and other emotions characterizing tension-if confronted by the conviction that they make sense, are challenges and can be managed-can be immunoenhancing?

This very issue is raised in Corson and Corson's (1983) discussion of

Anokhin's (1965/1974) work, which fits neatly into Schwartz's conception of the brain as a health care system. Anokhin "postulated the operation in the central nervous system of a series of feedback loops that eventually include an 'action acceptor' involving the hippocampus and frontal areas of the cerebral cortex. The operation of this action acceptor leads to the development of integrated somatic-behavioral and visceral-endocrine adaptive responses, at which point the hippocampal electrical desynchronization disappears. The information deficit is thus eliminated" (p. 293). Insoluble problems, Corson and Corson (1983) suggest, conditions in which an adaptive consummatory response cannot be achieved, open the way to disease. But if the brain can indeed direct the achievement of such a response-or, in my terms, prevent tension from being transformed into stress-immunocompetence can be enhanced.

Borysenko's (1984) brief review of psychoneuroimmunology notes this possibility, citing studies that "have even found an enhancement of outcome measures as a function of stress" (p. 250). The same point is made in an empirical study by Dillon, Minchoff and Baker (1985-86), who conclude that the mechanism by which "positive emotional states in disease prevention and cure . . . may be found in enhancement of the immune system" (p. 17). A behavioral intervention study of geriatric residents of independent-living facilities, using relaxation training, showed a significant increase in natural killer-cell activity and other immunocompetence changes (Kiecolt-Glaser et al., 1985). But for the most part, the work in this young field has concentrated on "the complex ways in which the nervous, endocrine and immune systems interact to affect the occurrence of disease" (Jemmott, 1985, p. 507).

In a sense, one may point to Cannon's (1942) article on "Voodoo Death," as the progenitor of serious study of the mechanisms linking emotions and pathology. Cannon speculated that the emotional trauma generated by violation of a profound taboo led to overactivation of the sympathicoadrenal system, hypovolemic shock, and rapid death. But autonomic arousal is rarely so extremely intense and sustained as to directly abrogate vital functions and lead to death. Even in Auschwitz, the central nervous system mediated chronic trauma and sometimes made a difference. Radil-Weiss (1983), a survivor of Auschwitz and professor at the Institute of Physiology, Czechoslovak Academy of Sciences, writes:

> Under these exceptional conditions, where the stress was maximum and the reserves were subject to maximum depletion, it was more apparent than under normal circumstances to what an extent the neural and neurohumoral regulation of internal processes in the organisms depends on the psychic processes. (p. 259)

And further, in terms surely consistent with the SOC concept:

> Men of strong will, convinced of the importance of the principles they consistently followed, and imbued with a unified world conception, endured better than persons who vacillated in their points of view. (p. 259)

We must, then, once we accept the plausibility that central nervous system functioning is a decisive determinant of the link between stressors and disease, maintain awareness of a process-a process that takes time, a process during which tension may not be transformed into stress and may even have healthy outcomes. It is within this mode of thought that the SOC hypothesis has been proposed.

One final issue: Heretofore, the thrust of the argument has been that stressors pose a dual instrumental/emotional problem. The person with a strong SOC mobilizes emotional and cognitive intra- and interpersonal and material resources to cope with problems. He or she also mobilizes, through the central nervous system, neuroimmunological and neuroendocrinological resources to prevent damage to the organism. The SOC, in this model, is an attribute of the person or, if one wills, of the brain, a characteristic way of relating to stimuli. This seems to imply a one-way relationship between psychology and biology, were it not for the insistence on feedback loops. But the recent work of Krantz and his colleagues on Type A behavior raises an important possibility: that the SOC might reflect an underlying biological substrate.

The preponderance of research on Type A has followed the line of thought described by Krantz and Durel (1983): "Situations perceived as psychologically stressful or challenging are thought to elicit Type A coping behaviors in susceptible individuals and in turn, evoke sympathetic neuroendocrine responses that act upon the cardiovascular system to promote or precipitate ischemic heart disease" (p. 384). Studies of surgery patients under general anesthesia, however, showed increased cardiovascular responses "under conditions where conscious perceptual mediation is minimized" that is, "the impatience, hostility, and speech patterns exhibited by Type A individuals may, in part, *reflect* an underlying sympathetic nervous system responsivity" (p. 401). Subsequent studies of the effect of beta blockers, drugs which attenuate sympathetic reactivity, in lowering Type A behavior, support the physiological substrate hypothesis. In other words, rather than the central nervous system controlling peripheral physiologic responses and being sensitive to feedback, the responses to stimuli are initiated directly, and subsequent information processing of these responses may allow the resolution of the emotional problem. Krantz and

Durel do not, however, totally reverse the directionality. Rather, they propose that Type A behavior is the outcome of the interaction of constitutional sympathetic responsiveness and central nervous system processing of peripheral sympathetic responses that include one's psychological set and cognitive reactions to a particular situation (p. 405).

Might it be, then, that the SOC too reflects an underlying biological substrate, a prototypical pattern of responses of various physiological systems of the organism which, in *interaction* with central nervous system information processing, predisposes the person to cope well with stressors and the problems they raise in ways which effectively prevent tension from being transformed into stress? This approach does not necessarily commit one to accept a genetically determined predisposition. It is equally compatible with a view that emphasizes the repeated set of experiences over the life course.

This chapter has been devoted to tracing the pathways through which the SOC leads to health. But one's state of health in itself is a significant life situation and, as such, plays a role in strengthening or debilitating the SOC.

References

Alonzo, A. A. (1986). The impact of the family and lay others on care during life-threatening episodes of suspected coronary artery disease. *Social Science and Medicine, 22,* 1297–1311.

Anokhin, P. K. (1974). *Biology and neurophysiology of the conditioned reflex and its role in adaptive behavior* (S. A. Corson, Trans.). New York: Pergamon. (Original work published in 1965)

Antonovsky, A. (1979). *Health, stress, and coping: New perspectives on mental and physical well-being.* San Francisco: Jossey-Bass.

Antonovsky, A. (1987). *Unraveling the mystery of health: How people manage stress and stay well.* San Francisco: Jossey-Bass.

Bandura, A. (1977). Self-efficacy: Toward a unifying theory of behavioral change. *Psychological Review, 84,* 191–215.

Berkman, L. F., & Breslow, L. (1983). *Health and ways of living: The Alameda county study.* New York: Oxford University Press.

Borysenko, J. (1984). Stress, coping, and the immune system. In J. D. Matarazzo et al. (Eds.), *Behavioral health: A handbook of health enhancement and disease prevention.* New York: Wiley.

Cannon, W. B. (1942). "Voodoo" death. *American Anthropologist, 44,* 169–181.

Cassel, J. (1974). Psychological processes and 'stress': theoretical formulation. *International Journal of Health Services, 4,* 471–482.

Cohen, F. (1984). Coping. In J. D. Matarazzo et al. (Eds.), *Behavioral health: A handbook of health enhancement and disease prevention*. New York: Wiley.

Corson, S. A., & Corson, E. O. (1983). Biopsychogenic stress. In H. Selye (Ed.), *Selye's guide to stress research (Vol. 2)*. New York: Van Nostrand Reinhold.

Dillon, K. M., Minchoff, B., & Baker, K. H. (1985-86). Positive emotional states and enhancement of the immune system. *International Journal of Psychiatry in Medicine, 15,* 13–18.

Dressler, W. W. (1985). The social and cultural context of coping: Action, gender, and symptoms in a southern black community. *Social Science and Medicine, 21,* 499–506.

Fagin, L. (1985). Stress and unemployment. *Stress Medicine, 1,* 27–36.

Felton, B. J., Revenson, T. A., & Hinrichsen, G. A. (1984). Stress and coping in the explanation of psychological adjustment among chronically ill adults. *Social Science and Medicine, 18,* 889–898.

Haan, N. (Ed.). (1977). *Coping and defending: Processes of self-environment organization*. Orlando, FL: Academic Press.

Heiburn, A. B., Jr., & Pepe, V. (1985). Awareness of cognitive defences and stress management. *British Journal of Medical Psychology, 58,* 9–17.

Henry, J. P. (1982). The relation of social to biological processes in disease. *Social Science and Medicine, 16,* 369–380.

Holmes, T. H., & Rahe, R. H. (1967). The social readjustment rating scale. *Journal of Psychosomatic Research, 11,* 213–218.

Jemmott, J. B. (1985). Psychneuroimmunology: The new frontier. *American Behavioral Scientist, 28,* 497–509.

Kaplan, R. M. (1984). The connection between clinical health promotion and health status: A critical overview. *American Psychologist, 39,* 755–765.

Kiecolt-Glaser, J. K., et al. (1985). Psychosocial enhancement of immunocompetence in a geriatric population. *Health Psychology, 4,* 25–41.

Kobasa, S. C. (1979). Stressful life events, personality, and health. *Journal of Personality and Social Psychology, 37,* 1–11.

Krantz, D. S., & Durel, L. A. (1983). Psychobiological substrates of the Type A behavior pattern. *Health Psychology, 2,* 393–411.

Kroeber, T. C. (1963). The coping functions of the ego mechanisms. In R.W. White (Ed.), *The study of lives*. Hawthorne, New York: Aldine.

Lazarus, R. S. (1981). The costs and benefits of denial. In B. S. Dohrenwend & B. P. Dohrenwend (Eds.), *Stressful life events and their contexts*. New York: Prodist.

Lazarus, R. S. (1984a). Puzzles in the study of daily hassles. *Journal of Behavioral Medicine, 7,* 375–389.

Lazarus, R. S. (1984b). On the primacy of cognition. *American Psychologist, 39,* 124–129.

Lazarus, R. S. & Cohen, J. B. (1977). Environmental stress. In I. Altman and J. E. Wohlwill (Eds.), *Human behavior and environment (Vol. 2.)* New York: Plenum.

Lazarus, R. S., & Folkman, S. (1984). *Stress, appraisal, and coping.* New York: Springer.

Major, B., Mueller, P. & Hildebrandt, K. (1985). Attributions, expectations, and coping with abortion. *Journal of Personality and Social Psychology, 48,* 585–599.

Mattarazzo, J. D., et al., (Eds.), *Behavioral health: A handbook of health enhancement and disease prevention.* New York: Wiley

Mechanic, D. (1974). Social structure and personal adaptation: Some neglected dimensions. In G. V. Coelho, D. A. Hamburg, & J. E. Adams (Eds.), *Coping and adaptation.* New York: Basic Books.

Orr, E. (1983). Life with cancer: Patterns of behavior and affective reaction during the first year after mastectomy. Unpublished doctoral dissertation, Department of Psychology, Hebrew University, Jerusalem.

Radil-Weiss, T. (1983). Men in extreme conditions: Some medical and psychological aspects of the Auschwitz concentration camp. *Psychiatry, 46,* 259–269.

Schwartz, G. E. (1979). The brain as a health care system. In G. C. Stone, F. Cohen, N. E. Adler, et al. (Eds.) *Health psychology-a handbook: Theories, applications, and challenges of a psychological approach to the health care system.* San Francisco: Jossey-Bass.

Seeman, M., Seeman, T., & Sayles, M. (1985). Social networks and health status: A longitudinal study. *Social Psychology Quarterly, 48,* 237–248.

Shalit, B. & Carlstedt, L. (1984). *The perception of enemy threat: A method for assessing the coping potential.* FOA report C 55063-H3. Stockholm: Forsvarets Forskningsanstalt.

Shanan, J. (1967). Active coping. *Behavioral Science, 16,* 188-196.

Schwartz, G. E. (1980). Stress management in occupational settings. *Public Health Reports, 95,* 99–101.

Silver, R. L., & Wortman, C. B. (1980). Coping with undesirable life events. In J. Garber & M. E. Seligman (Eds.), *Human helplessness.* Orlando, FL.: Academic Press.

Snow, J. (1855). *On the mode of communication of cholera.* (2nd ed.) London: Churchill. Reproduced in *Snow on cholera* (1936). New York: Commonwealth Fund.

Solomon, G. F. (1985). The emerging field of psychoneuroimmunology. *Advances: Journal of the Institute for the Advancement of Health, 2,* 6–19.

Steinglass, P., De-Nour, A. K., & Shye, S. (1985). Factors influencing psychosocial adjustment to forced geographical relocation: The Israeli withdrawal from Sinai. *American Journal of Orthopsychiatry, 55,* 513–529.

Strull, W. M., Lo, B., & Charles, G. (1984). Do patients want to participate in medical decision making? *Journal of the American Medical Association, 252,* 2990–2994.

Thoits, P. A. (1981). Undesirable life events and psychophysiological distress: A problem of operational confounding. *American Sociological Review, 46,* 97–109.

Unruh, D. R. (1983). *Invisible lives: Social worlds of the aged.* Beverly Hills, CA: Sage.

von Bertalanffy, L. (1968). *General system theory.* New York: Braziller.
Weisz, J. R. Rothbaum, F. M., and Blackburn, T. C. (1984). Standing out and standing in: The psychology of control in America and Japan. *American Psychologist, 39,* 955–969.
Zajonc, R. B. (1984). On the primacy of affect. *American Psychologist, 39,* 117–123.

3

Does Hardiness Moderate Stress, and How?: A Review

Emda Orr
Mina Westman

The concept of hardiness as a personality construct that moderates stress–illness relationships was first introduced by Kobasa (1979). Within 10 years, by January 1989, it had been cited in hundreds of papers published in 103 different journals and had been featured in the research design of 52 studies. Publications by Kobasa, Maddi and their colleagues, and other groups, reported the findings of independent studies that both replicated the hardiness model and expanded it to a wide variety of populations, men and women, young and old, healthy and sick, United States citizens and Israelis, in a wide range of settings such as white- and blue-collar working locations, universities, the army, and hospitals. The interest in the concept of hardiness, to our mind, stems from some of its main facets: it embraces the perennial mind–body enigma; optimism is its basis, as expressed in its focus on health instead of illness, and in its image of the person as an active, daring but circumspect and caring person. It would seem that it was this attractive blend that captured the attention and even imagination of social scientists, bringing about this proliferation of productive research. The purpose of the current review is to evaluate this body of research. Our first goal in this evaluation is an examination of the operational definitions of hardiness, which includes a comparison between the various hardiness scales, a discussion of whether hardiness should be treated as a single constellation or as the three separate phenomena of commitment, control, and challenge, and the issue of the current status of challenge. Our second goal is to clarify *whether, when,* and *how* hardiness works, and, finally, hardiness will be discussed in comparison to other similar concepts.

Hardy Personality

The concept of the hardy personality emerged from an existential theory of personality (Kobasa & Maddi, 1977). Three personality concepts were introduced as especially relevant to hardy orientation: commitment, control, and challenge. Commitment is the belief in the truth, importance, and value of who one is and what one is doing, and is thereby related to the tendency to involve oneself fully in one's total life space as a social being. Control is the tendency to believe and act as if one can influence the course of events within reasonable limits; it entails the responsibility to act, but excludes the tendency to manipulate others. Challenge is based on the belief that change rather than stability is the normative mode of life; change is, therefore, expected in everyday life and not viewed as an adventurous rare occasion. Change is anticipated as an opportunity and an incentive for personal growth (Kobasa, 1982a).

The concept of hardy personality appears to have developed out of the existential concept of the authentic personality. Both concepts are considered a complex continuum ranging from hardy authentic to nonhardy unauthentic personalities. But for purposes of clarity and ease of communication, the continuum is dichotomized into two general types. According to the existential view, a person has as a goal the finding of meaning in life and is defined by his or her subjective attitudes and goals. The existential personality theory contends that the authentic person has a meaningful life-style. It suggests a long list of attitudes and goals that signify an authentic versus an unauthentic style, and the hardy personality is defined in part by these attitudes.

The hardy personality is indexed, as described earlier, by commitment, control, and challenge. Commitment captures the authentic positive state of caring. "Caring is not a passive comfort, but rather an active, involving, and strenuous matter which takes into account the need and resources of one's self, one's environment, and the other" (Kobasa & Maddi, 1982a, p. 403). Control and challenge assess another major element of authentic being: courage. A common element of existential thinkers' views is that life is by its nature chaotic and threatening, and that persons live at their best if they react courageously. By courage, existential personality theory means recognizing hard facts, the personal belief that one is able to exert control on external and internal events, and attributing to stress the meaning of challenge (Kobasa & Maddi, 1982a, p. 413). The hardy personality appears, then, as having characteristics very similar to those of the authentic personality. The term "hardiness," however, emphasizes the outcome rather than the authentic experience.

Hardiness is hypothesized to moderate (or buffer) the deleterious effects of life stress on physical, psychological, and social health. Moderation is the specific effect of a variable under the condition of high stress, versus the effect brought about independent of level of stress. The hardy personality is hypothesized to moderate the effect of stress by activation of transformational coping. This is a series of activities, hypothesized by existential personality theory, as undertaken by the hardy (authentic) person when facing stress, thereby reaching well-being. Transformational coping includes interpretations of situational events, activating imagination to produce new possible ways of confronting the stressful situation, decisions on worthwhile and possible ways of dealing with such events, mobilizing resources, and performing other activities for carrying out these decisions (Kobasa, Maddi, Puccetti, & Zola, 1985).

In sum, the uniqueness of hardiness is displayed in presenting a global existential personality theory versus an isolated list of variables, the terms of which are transformed into operational definitions and workable hypotheses, thereby rendering it susceptible to empirical testing. The hardy image is of an active optimist organizing his or her ever-changing social context. Instead of being on the watch and only reacting to stress when confrontation is inescapable, the hardy person seeks out change and, thereby, stress; instead of suffering negative effects of stress, the hardy personality thrives on it (Kobasa, 1982a).

The following review of personal hardiness literature includes 31 studies published in journals from January 1979 to December 1988, 12 dissertations published during this period, and nine presentations at conferences. The inclusion of dissertations is considered especially important, since they contain supportive and nonsupportive data, whereas published material has a bias toward supportive material.

Is Hardiness Reliably and Validly Measured?

Kobasa and colleagues offered several versions of hardiness scales. The first instrument used to assess hardiness was a questionnaire, composed of all, or parts of, several standardized and newly constructed instruments, selected according to the criteria of tapping the three components of control, commitment, and challenge (Kobasa, 1979). Kobasa relied mainly on previously reported psychometric properties of the instruments and used discriminant analysis in order to identify scales that discriminated between groups of persons who, under conditions of high stress, were healthy, and those who were not.

Only two studies reported the use of the resultant battery of six scales (Kobasa, 1979; Ganellen & Blaney, 1984). Subsequent research on hardiness, however, used somewhat different sets of instruments. The most popular version consisted of 71 items within six scales, two for each of the three basic dimensions: commitment was measured by the Alienation From Self and Alienation From Work Scales (Maddi, Kobasa & Hoover, 1979); control was measured by the Locus of Control Scale (Rotter, 1966) and the Powerlessness Scale of the Alienation Test (Maddi et al., 1979); challenge was measured by the Security Scale of the California Life Goals Evaluation Schedule (Hahn, 1966) and by the Cognitive Structure Scale of the Personality Research Form (Jackson, 1974). The Cognitive Structure Scale was not correlated with the other measures and appeared as a separate factor in a principal-component factor analysis. The other five scales formed one factor accounting for 46.5% of the variance. As a result, the authors suggested that subsequent studies should form the composite hardiness score by computing Z scores for the five measures, excluding Cognitive Structure and assigning a double weight to the Security Scale that measured challenge (Kobasa, Maddi, & Kahn, 1982). The intercorrelations between the five scales were around 0.60 ($p < 0.001$) when the Cognitive Structure scale was excluded. The stability over time was 0.61 for a 5-year period (Kobasa & Puccetti, 1983).

Before long, the authors offered two other shorter versions of the hardiness scale consisting of 36 and 20 items. The specific items chosen were those that had the highest factor load in the factor analysis performed on the original longer version. Later, a 50-item version was devised in order to solve some of the problems of the previous versions. That is, the items in the older versions of the scale were specifically selected for tapping hardiness within the context of executive work; and the items were negatively keyed to indicate *lack* of hardiness. The items in the new 50-item version were phrased with a broader social context in mind, the direction of items was balanced, and hardiness was indicated positively by the total score (Kobasa, 1987, personal communication).

The following data are a summary of findings across a long list of studies (e.g., Hull, Van Treuren, & Virnelli, 1987; Funk & Houston, 1987; McNeil, Kozma, Stones, & Hannah,1986; Okun, Zautra, &

Robinson, 1988; Rich, & Rich, 1987; Kahn, 1987). Internal consistency and stability over time of the four scales of hardiness are acceptable across the versions. The internal consistency is highest in the 50-item and lowest in the 20-item scales (*Alpha* = 0.90, 0.67, respectively), whereas the stability over time is best for the long 71-item and lowest for the 50-item version (*r* = 0.89, 0.60, respectively). The correlations between the longer 71-item scale and the shorter 36-, 20-, and 50-item scales were 0.76, 0.89, and 0.78, respectively, indicating an acceptable agreement.

No systematic endeavor has been undertaken to compare convergent and discriminant hardiness validity across the four scales, though such an effort has been made for the first two scales (Hull et al., 1987). However, reviewing the data, one can confidently say that the four are very similar in their relations to other variables. For example, anxiety and depression were found to correlate in the range of 0.29 to 0.48 with each of the four scales (Funk & Houston, 1987; Hull et al., 1987; Kahn, 1987; Rhodewalt & Augustdottir, 1986; Schlosser & Sheeley, 1985). Positive affect was correlated minus 0.42 with the 36-item scale, and on average minus 0.29 with the 20-item scale (Schlosser & Sheeley, 1985; McNeil et al., 1986, respectively). Hardiness (the 71- and 36-item scales) was correlated − 0.35 (average of several samples, Hull et al., 1987) with optimism, i.e., generalized expectations for positive outcomes, (Scheier & Carver, 1985). The findings indicate that high hardiness is negatively related to constructs of negative affect and positively related to those of positive affect. The correlations, though modest, indicate distinctive elements.

Type A, on the other hand, was insignificantly correlated with hardiness, when the 71- and 36-item scales and some other modifications were used (Contrada, 1985; Lang & Markowitz, 1986; Kobasa et al.,1983; Nowack, 1985; Schmied & Lawler, 1986). It was only very modestly correlated with it (*r* = 0.16; *p* < .05) when the 20-item scale was used (Rhodewalt & Augustdottir, 1986). The lack of correlation with Type A clearly indicates that hardiness is a distinct personality construct, related differentially to health. The discriminant validity of hardiness was also established by its insignificant correlation with Scholastic Aptitude, within a homogeneous group of male students (Hull et al., 1987).

Establishing the discriminant validity of hardiness is also possible by inspecting findings about its relationships with demographic variables. The relationships between hardiness and demographic variables have been reported by only a few studies. Lack of reports may stem from the homogeneous nature of the samples (undergraduates and only one gender). In mixed-gender studies, men were found to have significantly higher scores on hardiness than women in samples consisting of elderly people (McNeil et al., 1986) and chronically ill respondents (Pollock, 1986).

Inconsistent results were found for age and education. Three studies report very low and insignificant correlations between age and hardiness for both men (Kobasa et al., 1982) and women (Rhodewalt & Zone, 1989; Schlosser, 1986). However, significant positive correlations were found in several studies (Hannah et al., 1988; Kobasa, 1982b; Nowack, 1986; Rich & Rich, 1987; Schmied & Lawler,1986), but negative correlation in another (Okun et al., 1988). Similarly, contradicting results concerning the independence of education and hardiness were found in two studies (Kobasa et al., 1982; Okun et al., 1988), but significant positive correlation was found in two others (Pollock, 1986; Schmied & Lawler, 1986). Although the findings are inconclusive as to the relations of gender, age, education, and hardiness, the inconsistency of the relationships between hardiness and each of these variables is indicative of its distinctiveness. The findings about the psychometric properties of hardiness scales lead to the conclusion that all of them measure the same construct with acceptable reliability and stability. By devising the 50-item scale, shortcomings of previous scales such as unidirectionality and negative indication have been overcome.

Hardiness as a Constellation

Hardiness was introduced as a constellation of three subconcepts. The three components of the constellation are presupposed to interact with each other, producing a unique effect on health, which is different from the separate effect of the three subconcepts. Now, after extensive use of the hardiness scales, it is time to evaluate whether the findings support the constellation hypothesis.

The hypothesis that hardiness is a single concept, tapped by three subscales, could be tested by regressing health outcomes on interaction scores derived from the three subscales. Unfortunately, this procedure has yet not been undertaken by any researcher. An alternative, although weaker confirmation, is the finding of moderate to high correlations between the scores of the subscales and the total score, and moderate intercorrelations between subscales. The correlations of the subscales with the total score were satisfactory, in the seventies for the 71-, 36-, and the 50-item scales (Hull et al., 1987; Okun et al., 1988; Kahn, 1987). The only exception was challenge, with the low correlation of 0.46 with the total hardiness score in the 36-item scale. Inspection of the intercorrelations among the subscales reveals a picture of moderate correlations between commitment and control, but unacceptable low and even nonsignificant correlations between these two and challenge on the 71- and 36-item scales (Hull et al., 1987). On the 50-item scale, the intercorrelations were satisfactorily moderate (Kahn, 1987; Okun et al., 1988; an ongoing research project conducted by Orr). The intercorrelations between the subscales and between them and the total concept were not reported for the 20-item scale.

An additional way of testing the unity of the hardiness construct is by performing factor analysis on the entire set of items. This was done on five versions of hardiness scales, and similar results were obtained for both varimax and oblique procedures. The results unanimously confirmed the commitment component as a distinct factor. However, challenge and control comprised one factor on the 90-item scale[1] (Hull et al., 1987), and control was merged with the other two components as one factor of three on the 50-item scale, commitment and challenge being the other two factors (Kahn, 1987). A principal-factor analysis performed on five subscales of the 71-item scale revealed one factor in one sample (Kobasa et al., 1982) and two in another one (Funk & Houston, 1987). The factor analyses performed on the 20-item scale (Hannah & Morrissey, 1987; McNeil, Kozma, Stones, & Hannah 1986) showed in two independent studies of adolescents and elderly respondents (respectively) the best agreement with the notion of the hardiness constellation: on the first-order analysis, three factors appeared vaguely comparable to the three hypothesized components (within the adolescent group emerged a fourth factor not related to the concept of hardiness). On the second-order analysis, one factor appeared representing the unitary hardiness construct.

To sum up, the findings concerning the 20- and 50-item scales indicate that they measure three subscales, and that each of the subscales is related to one unitary concept of hardiness. The 71- and 36-item subscales seem to tap two related concepts: commitment and control. Challenge appears as a distinct and salient concept in these two scales.

Status of Challenge

The findings presented in the previous section show that commitment has the most consistent status across the hardiness scales. It appears as a factor for each of the four versions of the scale, is intercorrelated

[1] The 90-item scale analyzed by Hull, Van Treuren, and Virnelli (1987) on a sample of undergraduate students was the 71-item scale with the addition of the Cognitive Structure Scale (Jackson, 1974) as an additional measure of challenge.

with control, and contributes most of the explained variance to the criteria (see also Hull et al., 1987). The findings about control appear somewhat less consistent. Its intercorrelations with commitment and its correlations with the total score are appropriate, but it does not emerge as a distinct factor in any of three versions of hardiness (71-, 36-, and 50-item scales). Moreover, it has no independent significant contribution (beyond commitment) to the criteria in the 71- and 36-item scales. Challenge does not appear as a factor in the 71-item scale, its correlations with commitment and control are low or nonsignificant; the correlation with the total score is relatively low; and it has had discriminant predictions of several criteria in the 36- and 71-item versions of the scale (Hull et al., 1987; Magnani 1986; Rich & Rich, 1987; Schmied & Lawler, 1986; Wiebe & McCallum, 1986). On the basis of results from the 36- and 71-item scales, Hull and colleagues (1987) suggest that the challenge subscale should be eliminated from the hardiness scale. This conclusion, according to the entire set of available results, is premature. Challenge appears as a distinctive factor in regard to the 20- and the 50-item scale (Kahn, 1987; McNeil et al., 1986), and in the 50-item scale the intercorrelations and correlations with the total score are appropriate.

In addition, the operational definition of hardiness as measured in the 71- and 36-item scales is incongruous with its theoretical definition. This has happened, in our opinion, because challenge has been measured by existing scales that were constructed with a different concept in mind.

Examples taken from the Security Scale of California Life Goals Evaluation Schedules (Hahn, 1966) used by Kobasa and colleagues for tapping challenge in the 36- and 71-item scales illustrate our point. Agreement with these items is interpreted in these scales as low challenge: Public-supported medical care is the right of everyone. The young owe the old complete economic security. From each according to his or her ability, to each according to his or her needs.

These three excerpts show challenge to be conceived as equated with extreme liberalism. It seems from these examples that the hardy person is assumed not to rely on others or on social institutions for help in stressful situations. But, we contend, supporting social security for the weak members of society does not imply that persons embracing this ideology consider themselves weak and in need of social security. Neither does it preclude a personal belief that environmental change is the rule rather than the exception in life. In other words, we argue that the security test does not tap basic attitudes about the nature of the world or the motivation for self-change within this world. Neither does it measure the motivational and cognitive derivatives of these basic attitudes, such as seeking stimulation, risk taking, cognitive flexibility, tolerance for ambiguity, and, concomitantly, responsibility (Kobasa, 1979). In short, by using the Security Scale as a measure of challenge, the most important constituents of challenge were not assessed, and the assessed security construct was only weakly related to challenge, as presented by the authors themselves (see also Antonovsky, 1987, for similar arguments).

Interestingly, the two subscales discriminating between the sick and healthy groups of executives in the first hardiness study were two subscales of the Alienation Test, constructed by Kobasa and colleagues: Vegetativeness and Adventurousness (Kobasa, 1979). These same scales were found to predict depression in the only study using them as a challenge measure (Ganellen & Blaney, 1984).

To sum up, challenge is an essential component of existential personality psychology and, as such, deserves a second chance. We recommend the empirical testing of its reoperationalization before a final verdict is reached.

Hardiness as a Moderator

Hardiness was originally hypothesized as moderating (or buffering) the effect of stress on health. However, most studies report the main effects of hardiness as being that hardy people are generally healthier, no matter how stressful the situation (Cohen & Wills, 1985; Gore, 1985). In order to establish the moderating effect of hardiness on the stress-health relationship, findings indicating the stress-hardiness interaction effect on health of the are needed (Baron & Kenny, 1986), i.e., a significant difference between hardy and nonhardy persons under high stress should be found. Such a difference would mean that nonhardy persons are affected negatively by stress, whereas hardy persons are not. For the sake of clarity, the main effects of hardiness will first be reported, followed by findings of moderating effects.

In the original studies of Kobasa and colleagues, stress was measured by the Stressful Life Event Scale (Schedule of Recent Life Events; Holmes & Rahe, 1967), and health was assessed by the Seriousness of Illness Survey (Wyler, Masuda, & Holmes, 1968). The average number of respondents in each study was 175, selected out of 670 managers in a large firm. The specific study groups were selected randomly or on the basis of criteria of interest. Regression-based analyses (discriminant analysis, analysis of variance and covariance, and multiple regression analysis) were used in the research designs. The results reported by Kobasa and colleagues supported the hardiness main effect hypothesis (e.g., Kobasa, 1979; Kobasa et al., 1982). The effect of hardiness was found to be significantly independent of stress, social support, exercise, and constitutional predisposition (Kobasa, Maddi & Courington, 1981; Kobasa & Puccetti, 1983; Kobasa, Puccetti, & Zola, 1985).

In contrast to these findings, two studies (Funk & Houston, 1987; Schmied & Lawler 1986) failed to find significant correlation between hardiness and reported illness in a prospective and a concurrent designs performed on samples of 117 students and of 82 women working in a bank (respectively). However, Kobasa's findings of the main effect of hardiness on reported physical health (after controlling for stress) were supported by 12 studies performed on a wide array of populations. It was found concurrently on medium to large samples of teachers (Holt, Fine, & Tollefson, 1987), students' resident assistants (Nowack & Hanson, 1983), rabbis (Freedman, 1987), high school children (Wendt, 1982), students (Banks, & Gannon, 1988), women (Rhodewalt & Zone, 1989), and members of all ranks of employment (Padnick 1985). Further support was provided prospectively on bus drivers (Bartone, 1984), police-officer cadets (Herlich, 1985), and students of both genders (Schlosser & Sheeley,1985; Wiebe & McCallum, 1986), assigned helpers to bereaved families of United States' soldiers (stress measured by prolonged exposure to a bereaved family) (Bartone, Ursano, Wright, & Ingraham, in press).

The studies reported thus far used self-report measures for tapping physical health. Four studies used objectively measured health outcomes as their dependent variables (Okun et al., 1988; Pollock, 1986; Solomon & Temoshok, 1987; Tucker, 1987). Tucker failed to find a significant relationship between hardiness and postpartum complications. Pollock found hardiness main effect on health status rated by doctors for diabetes but not for hypertension and rheumatoid arthritis patients. Temoshok, on the other hand, in a preliminary study of AIDS patients, reported that the control subscale was significantly higher for an "alive" group of pneumocystis carinii pneumonia patients and commitment was significantly higher for an "alive" group of persons with symptoms of the AIDS-related complex than for the comparison groups of patients who died. It is difficult to interpret these results as the author of the first study did not provide a sufficiently detailed description of the study, and the two other studies employed weak methodologies. Stronger support for the hardiness hypothesis is provided by Okun and colleagues (1988), who report significant correlation between hardiness control subscale and percentage of circulating T cells in women with rheumatoid arthritis.

Three studies with concurrent designs reported contradictory results concerning the moderation effect on physical health. Confirmatory results were found in two studies on samples of male executives (Kahn, 1987) and highly educated women (Rhodewalt & Zone, 1989) using the 50- and 20-item hardiness scales, respectively. However, no stress-hardiness interaction was found in a study with female undergraduate students using a 36-item scale (Schlosser, 1986). One should bear in mind, however, that young people do not vary substantially on physical health, and the lack of a significant effect of hardiness on undergraduates' health may be attributed to a health ceiling effect.

Prospectively found moderation effects were reported only by Kobasa, Maddi, and Kahn (1982). Kobasa and colleagues found that under the conditions of high stress, high-hardy managers in the United States were healthier than the group low on hardiness.

To summarize, the hypothesis that hardiness affects reported physical health was strongly supported by the findings. The moderating effect of hardiness on reported health was found in two out of three concurrent studies. Support for prospective moderating effect was provided by one study. Hence, the hypothesis of the moderation effect of hardiness on the stress-health relationship should await further evidence. The information available to date about the relationships of hardiness with objectively measured health is also insufficient.

Stress, Hardiness, and Psychological Health

Hardiness was originally defined as moderating the stress–physical health relationships. However, the concept can be easily expanded to denote psychological health or other adjustment outcomes. Sixteen studies investigated the relationships between hardiness and psychological health. These studies, similarly to those investigating physical health, employed medium to large samples ($M = 213$) and used various instruments to assess strain or psychological distress. Stress was assessed by several versions of a life events scale, hassles, and perceived overload. The results were unequivocal: Psychological health was significantly predicted by the main effect of hardiness in studies employing concurrent (Freedman, 1987; Holt et al., 1987; Kobasa, 1982b; Nowack & Hanson, 1983; Schlosser, 1986; Schneider, 1986; Wendt, 1982) and prospective designs (Nowack, 1986). Moderating effects of hardiness were found by significant stress by hardiness interactions concurrently (Ganelen & Blaney, 1984; Kahn, 1987; Rhodewalt & Augustsdottir, 1986; Rhodewalt & Zone, 1989), prospectively (Funk & Houston, 1987; Hill, 1982; Lang & Markowitz,1986), and experimentally (Frohm, 1987).

Six studies tested the stress-moderating hypothesis concerning the relationships between hardiness and burnout. Burnout is one possible outcome of stress in work situations. In most studies, burnout was defined as a syndrome combining emotional exhaustion, a sense of lack of achievement, lack of fulfillment, and apathy towards others in the work area (Maslach & Jackson, 1981). Testing the effect of hardiness on the stress–burnout relationship followed the hypothesis that individual differences, in addition to situational work stress, account for the phenomenon of burnout. The results of two studies fully confirmed this hypothesis. Hardiness had significant negative, main, and interaction effects on burnout: concurrently on a sample of female teachers (Holt et al., 1987) and prospectively on a sample of employees in the human services (Nowack, 1986).[2]

Hardiness was also found to be related to a number of other adjustment outcomes: fathers' marital adjustment in a group of married couples (Barling, 1986), objectively assessed performance of officer cadets in the Israel Defense Forces and police academy cadets (Westman, in press; Herlich 1985, respectively), and, finally higher levels of general activity in a group of senior citizens (Magnani, 1986).

To sum up, the reported findings indicate that hardiness is related to a wide range of psychological adjustment outcomes. The degree of consistency among the findings is particularly impressive. The variety of measures, the substantial number of prospective designs, the findings of significant interactions of stress by hardiness, together with the diverse and large populations tested, underscore the generality of the hypothesis that hardiness moderates stress as applied to psychological well-being.

Differential Effects of Various Hardiness Scales

The findings reveal similar results for the variety of hardiness scales. For example, the significant main effect of hardiness on physical health was found by seven studies using the 71-item scale, five using the 36-item scale, two studies using the 20-item scale, two using the 50-item scale, and other studies using certain modifications. Most of the modifications consisted of rephrasing of items and adjusting them to special populations. A similar picture emerges when inspecting main effects of hardiness on psychological well-being. Moderating effects of hardiness were also found for each of the scales. A tentative

[2] Other studies revealed a set of significant negative correlations between hardiness and burnout in samples of school psychologists (Berger, 1983), nurses (Keane, Ducette & Adler, 1985; Lambert & Lambert, 1987; Rich & Rich, 1987), and student resident assistants (Nowack & Hanson, 1983).

conclusion of the different scales issue is that so far findings do not indicate meaningful differences among the various hardiness scales. It should be noted, however, that no prospective design with the 20- and only one with the 50-item scales have been reported so far.

How Does Hardiness Work?

The literature on hardiness suggests several options as possible processes by which hardiness moderates stress-outcomes relationships: (a) hardy persons tend to perceive or appraise positively their physical and psychological health; (b) they tend to perceive or evaluate positively their situational stress; (c) hardiness takes effect by the application of specific coping strategies; (d) hardiness takes effect by the active recruitment of social resources; (e) hardiness affects outcomes through the reduction of psychological strain; and (f) hardiness affects outcomes through the reduction of negative physiological outcomes. These alternative options are not mutually exclusive, and hardiness may operate via more than one of them or through additional ones.

Hardiness and Perception of Outcomes

Before trying to support the hypothesis that hardiness affects outcomes via positive perception or appraisal of outcomes, rival hypotheses of methodological artifacts must be ruled out. Such methodological artifacts may stem from two main sources. First, hardiness scales are negatively keyed, and persons who suffer from neurotic depression or anxiety most probably respond similarly to both hardiness scales and self-reports on psychological or physical health. In other words, nonhardy individuals tend to complain, but actually they are not sicker than the hardy (Funk & Houston, 1987). Second, hardy individuals may report better health, less depression, and less burnout, not because they are healthier, less depressed, and less exhausted by their work, but because reporting symptomatology is inconsistent with the hardy individual's self-image as a resilient person (Hull et al., 1987).

The problem of neurotic complaints can be eliminated by showing that hardiness has an independent effect on outcome after controlling for neuroticism. This task was undertaken by six independent studies. Hardiness-illness relationships remained significant after controlling for neuroticism in only one study out of four (Kahn, 1987). This study used the 50-item scale, which is balanced with respect to direction of items. Other outcomes displayed mixed results. Depression remained significantly related to hardiness after controlling for neuroticism (anxiety) in a prospective study of male students (Funk & Houston, 1987). However, the correlation between hardiness and depression was eliminated after controlling for trait anxiety in a concurrent study of female students (Schlosser & Sheeley, 1985). The findings indicate that clarification of the relationship between hardiness and neuroticism should await further findings from studies using a balanced hardiness scale.

Another way of overcoming the problem of both neuroticism and consistency is to use prospective designs. Controlling for initial levels of illness (or other outcomes) eliminates the response bias, because the hypothesized tendency to give negative or consistent responses is assumed to be a consistent personality trait and, hence, will be displayed in both the initial and later measurements. Thus, when the initial level of outcome is controlled, neuroticism or the tendency to appear consistent are also controlled. Actually, as noted previously, significant prospective effects of hardiness have been reported: on physical health (Bartone, 1984; Bartone et al., in press; Herlich, 1985; Kobasa et al., 1982; Wiebe & McCallum, 1986), psychological health (Funk & Houston, 1987; Lang & Markowitz, 1986; Nowack, 1986), and other outcomes (performance, Herlich, 1985; coping, Lang, 1987; activity, Magnani, 1986; growth, Nemiroff, 1986). Only two studies reported lack of significant results (Funk & Houston, 1987, on students' physical health, and Nemiroff, 1986, on growth in a sample of blue-collar subjects). Other indications that hardiness-outcome relations are not merely a response bias are (a) findings of 89% agreement between reported health and independent medical diagnosis (Kobasa et al., 1981), (b) correlations between hardiness and objectively measured evaluations of performance (Herlich, 1985; Nowack & Hanson, 1983; Westman, in press), and (c) lymphocyte counts among AIDS patients (Solomon & Temoshok, 1987) and average percentage of circulating T cell among women with rheumatoid arthritis (Okun et al., 1988).

Physiological measures are also "hard" parameters for measuring hardiness outcomes. However, the relations obtained to date between hardiness and a number of physiological measures are nondecisive (these measures will be discussed later on).

In sum, the findings indicate that hardiness affects outcomes and we can rule out the interpretation of an artifact of the methodology. The problem of the relationships between hardiness and neuroticism will be further pursued as a theoretical issue in its own right and not just in the context of methodological constraints.

The second rival hypothesis suggests that the positive effect of hardiness stems from the tendency of hardy people to report benevolent outcomes. Whereas the above-mentioned methodological interpretations attribute specific reported health to response bias, i.e., the interpersonal relationships between the respondents and the researchers, this second hypothesis focuses on intrapersonal processes. Van Treuren and Hull (1987) suggest that hardy people may be less conscious of their internal reactions and report better health because they deny their symptoms. In Van Treuren and Hull's experiment, hardy male students reported less anxiety than the low-hardy, and those high on commitment reported being less troubled by immersing their hands in ice water. Nevertheless, systolic blood pressure was higher for hardy students, and they did not keep their hands in the water longer than the nonhardy ones. These findings may indicate that hardy respondents used mechanisms of denial. However, an alternative interpretation is that hardy do not deny their internal reactions, but appraise them in a different way from nonhardy persons. Thus, the ability to withstand the pain in the hands may be appraised as a sign of persistence or courage and serve as a self-indication for self-esteem instead of anxiety. This line of reasoning was not considered by Van Treuren and Hull and merits further research. To sum up, the hypothesis that hardiness affects outcomes by the denial of negative aspects calls for further investigation and elaboration of findings.

Hardiness and Perception of Stress

Kobasa and colleagues suggested that hardiness affects health by use of transformational coping, defined as "optimistic cognitive appraisals, by which the stressful events tend to be perceived as natural changes, meaningful and interesting despite their stressfulness" (Kobasa et al., p. 525). Before discussing the hypothesis that hardiness moderates the stress-health relationship because the hardy individual appraises events more positively, we will try to rule out the competing hypothesis that hardy people somehow experience fewer stressful events. Recurrent findings show that when tested by reported recent life events, hardiness is not related to number or sort of events (Kobasa et al., 1982; Rhodewalt & Augustsdottir, 1986; Rhodewalt & Zone, 1989; Wiebe & McCallum, 1986). However, hardy individuals were less likely than their less hardy counterparts to perceive events as undesirable and uncontrollable (Banks & Gannon, 1988; Rhodewalt & Augustsdottir, 1986), and although high stress/high hardiness females were less depressed than the high stress/low hardiness group (stress measured by reported life events), physical illness was predicted only by the interaction of hardiness with appraisal of stress. The researchers found that under conditions of undesirable events, highly hardy females reported fewer symptoms than those low on hardiness. Hardiness was related to fewer experiences appraised negatively, but not to those positively appraised (Frohm, 1987; Rhodewalt & Zone, 1989; Schlosser & Sheeley, 1985).

So far, findings indicate that hardy respondents experience events in a similar way to the nonhardy, but appraise their life as less stressful. These findings, taken together with Van Trueren and Hull's (1987) findings of the hardy individual's lower awareness of physiological arousal and inconvenience on immersing their hands in ice water, may imply that hardy persons tend to deny their reactions, whereas nonhardy ones are of the sensitizer type. However, a study reported by Westman (in press) testing the relationships between hardiness and stress appraisal within several situations in an officer cadets' course in the Israel Defense Forces suggests a different interpretation. Westman explored the hardiness-stress relationships on a time series: (a) at the beginning of the cadet course while respondents were anticipating the difficulties of the course, (b) during the course while active coping was taking place, and (c) at the end, after the cadets knew how successful they had been. At the beginning, hardy cadets appraised the stress significantly higher, but toward the end of the course significantly lower than the nonhardy group. Interestingly, throughout the entire course, hardy cadets appraised their ability to cope with the stress as higher than did the nonhardy. These findings indicate that hardy cadets did not appraise stress in a consistent way and that their appraisals were dependent on the context. It is as if they tended not to deny or diminish the stress when they had to prepare themselves for effective coping. Retrospectively, after the project was over, they were prepared to appraise it more favorably, probably because no more active coping was needed.

To conclude, it seems that stress appraisal is an important component of hardiness-related processes, and there are some indications that hardy persons do not ignore the negative implications of stress, unless in situations of minor stress, when active coping is not important. It may be interesting to test the hypothesis that hardy persons use a positive interpretation of stress as a method of stress–health moderation when stress is low and does not necessitate change of habit, or when it is extremely high and change in behavior is unlikely to affect the outcome. With moderate to high stress, according to the present hypothesis, hardy persons will not resort to cognitive measures, but change their actual behavior in order to cope successfully.

Specific Coping Strategies

The studies cited in the last section support Kobasa's hypothesis that cognitive appraisal of stress is a strategy that hardy people use. The hypothesis about the role of such appraisals in the stress–health chain of relationships should be further supported. Additionally, however, Kobasa et al. (1985) suggests that "decisive coping actions will also be taken" especially those of "finding out more about the changes constituting the (stressful) events" (p. 525).

The relationships between hardiness and specific coping behaviors were investigated in several studies with both health and psychological strain as dependent variables: exercise (Kobasa et al., 1985), health-promoting behavior (Wiebe & McCallum, 1986; Schlosser & Sheeley, 1985), incompetent coping styles (Hill, 1982), and regressive coping style (Kobasa, 1982b). For example, in agreement with the transformational coping model, emotion-focused coping was negatively correlated with hardiness or some components of hardiness, but in contrast information-focused coping was unrelated to hardiness (Hill, 1982; Schlosser, 1985; Schlosser & Sheeley, 1985). Exercise, which may be a way of enhancing physical and emotional resilience, was shown in one study to contribute significantly to health independently of hardiness or stress (Kobasa et al., 1985), whereas in another it was shown to affect health as a mediator between hardiness and physical health (Wiebe & McCallum, 1986). The incompatibility between the studies can probably be resolved by a third moderating variable indicated by the finding that for those individuals with high concern for health hardiness was significantly related to health behavior, whereas for those with low concern no such relationship was found (Hannah, 1988).

A main effect of hardiness on active coping was found in a prospective study (Lang, 1987). The results reported by Lang indicate that in the context of an intensive academic evening course, hardy students used a coping strategy of planned task management more frequently than nonhardy students. However, this study did not test the moderating effect of coping on psychological or physical health. Allred & Smith (1987), using an experimental design, found that highly hardy male students in high stress conditions involved themselves in positive thinking more than students rated low on hardiness in similar conditions. Moreover, as the conditions became more stressful, the hardy students engaged more in positive thinking. The opposite was true for students rated low on hardiness. One should note, however, that the link between positive thinking and health is missing. The relationship between positive thinking and health, though established in previous research (Scheier & Carver 1985), has not been tested specifically in connection with hardiness. Generally, the results indicate that hardiness is connected with a variety of coping strategies, but the question of how they are associated with health and strain during stressful situations must await future study.

Recruiting Social Support

The concept of transformational coping relates to what a person does in order to transform a stressful situation into a desirable event. The same line of reasoning may be applied to social support. Recruiting support from family, friends, and community in order to transform an undesirable situation into a desirable one may be included in the category of transformational coping.

Both hardiness and social support are conceived of as resistance resources buffering the effect of stress on health. Empirical research indicates that social support is related to hardiness in an inconsistent way. Moderate correlations between the two were found in several studies (Hull et al., 1987; Kahn, 1987; Kobasa et al., 1985; Nemiroff, 1986; Westman, in press). However, whereas hardiness was related significantly to health in each of the studies utilizing both variables, a variety of relationships was found in regard to social support. The independent main effect of social support on health was found in one study (Kobasa et al., 1985), no significant social support main effects on strain and physical health were found in two others (Ganellen & Blaney, 1984; Kobasa & Puccetti, 1983), and a deleterious effect of social support on strain was found in a third study (Kobasa, 1982). The inconsistency is understandable if we note that social support is an umbrella concept that covers a number of qualitatively different interpersonal interactions (Cohen & Syme, 1985).

The hypothesis that hardiness affects an active component of support has received some support in findings that (a) quality and not quantity of support is correlated with hardiness (Schlosser & Sheeley, 1985), i.e., it is not the sheer availability of support that is related to hardiness, but the ability to perceive it as beneficial; (b) in the context of work stress, health is enhanced for hardy executives who get support from the boss independent of family support (Schneider, 1986; Kobasa & Puccetti, 1983). For those ranked low on hardiness, support from the boss is not related to better health and family support worsens the status of health (Kobasa & Puccetti, 1983). These findings indicate that hardy persons know which support to use in a specific situation, whereas the nonhardy do not.

In a recent study with path-analysis design on executives, main effects of social support on both physical and psychological health were eliminated after controlling for hardiness, but hardiness main effect remained significant after controlling for social support (Kahn, 1987). These findings provide support for the hypothesis that hardy persons keep healthy by the use of their social resources. However, it should be noted that Kahn's study was based on a concurrent design, hence, not establishing a causal effect between the relevant variables.

To conclude, it is clear that hardiness and social support are distinct concepts and not two sides of the same coin. The specific relationships between hardiness and social support should be further clarified. Prospective studies focusing on specific populations and systematic situational variability using three-way stress, hardiness, and social support interactions will be helpful in identifying the specific conditions under which social support does and does not moderate stress, and mediates the effect of hardiness on health.

Reduction of Psychological Strain as a Process Through Which Hardiness Affects Health

Kobasa and Puccetti (1983) suggest that social resources and coping are only one link in a chain of mediators between hardiness and health. Their model suggests that transformational coping affects a reduction in the emotional strain. Emotional well-being, in its turn, affects a reduction in physiological strain and, thereby, health. The findings reviewed previously show that psychological strain is an outcome of low hardiness, especially under conditions of high stress. The present section addresses the question of whether emotional strain moderates the hardiness–illness relationships and whether hardiness has an independent main effect after controlling for emotional strain. Six studies tested the effect of hardiness on outcomes after controlling for emotional strain. Findings show consistently that hardiness covaried with emotional strain to affect illness and other outcomes. The findings concerning the independent main effect of hardiness on illness, after controlling for the common variance with strain, are inconsistent. Frohm (1987), in a prospective design, found no independent effect of hardiness on reported symptoms, after controlling for anxiety. However, in the same study, when finger pulse served as the dependent variable, the stress by hardiness interaction was significant after controlling for anxiety. Findings from studies using concurrent designs are also inconsistent. Kahn (1987) reported an independent main effect of hardiness on illness after controlling for anxiety, but Schlosser and Sheeley (1985) reported elimination of the hardiness effect on illness and depression after controlling for anxiety. It is important to note that the findings of a significant main effect of hardiness on health, but insignificant hardiness effects after controlling for negative emotional affectivity, may have alternative interpretations. Either (a) hardiness and emotional strain are overlapping constructs, or (b) hardiness and strain are independent constructs and hardiness promotes health via one path, i.e., its influence on emotional strain. Research, so far, has not provided an answer as to which of these two possibilities is the correct interpretation, nor has it produced any other, perhaps better, explanation. We are not able to offer a satisfactory explanation for the inconsistency in the findings, and hope that further research will illuminate the presently vague picture.

Hardiness and Physiological Processes

In order to support the hypothesis (presented in the previous section) that hardiness promotes health through its effect on physiological strain, two conditions should be met. It must be shown that hardiness affects physiological reactions and that these reactions are health promoting. None of the studies reviewed accomplished this undertaking. However, the relationships between hardiness and several physiological processes, known to be health related, have been investigated in four studies. The designs (Allred & Smith, 1987; Contrada, 1985; Frohm, 1987; Van Treuren & Hull, 1987) were experimental, measuring students' diastolic and systolic blood pressure, finger pulse amplitude, heart rate, and skin conductance during task performance under several conditions of manipulated stress. No significant findings were found for heart rate or skin conductance. Diastolic blood pressure was found to be lower for highly hardy individuals in one study (Contrada, 1985), but independent of hardiness in the other three studies (Allred & Smith, 1989; Frohm, 1987; Van Treuren & Hull, 1987). Systolic blood pressure was related to hardiness in two studies (Allred & Smith, 1987; Van Treuren & Hull, 1987) but unrelated to it in the other two. Contrary to hypothesis, hardiness was related to higher rather than to lower systolic blood pressure. Allred and Smith (1987) attributed the enhanced physiological reactions to active coping and suggested that blood pressure during recovery rather than during performance would be a better criterion for health risk. This interpretation is supported by results of studies on finger pulse amplitude (Allred & Smith, 1989; Frohm, 1987). A significant interaction effect between hardiness and time was found in both studies; lower arousal was found for highly hardy individuals either before or after performing the task, but no difference in arousal level was found between individuals rated low and high on hardiness during the actual performance of the task. The findings are thus inconclusive in regard to the role of the physiological reactions in the process linking hardiness to promotion of health. Future investigators should focus on physiological reaction during recovery time and tap verbal reactions throughout task performance in order to understand the subjective experience concomitant to arousal. It is quite probable that highly hardy individuals will interpret their physiological reactions as positive affects such as excitement, whereas those rated low on hardiness will perceive them as negative affects.

In sum, more research is needed in order to support the hypothesis that hardiness affects health generally and specifically under high stress. It seems important to investigate these general hypotheses in a sophisticated way through hypotheses about the processes by which hardiness works. The hypothesis that high hardy persons appraise more favorably the stress they encounter was investigated more systematically than the other processes implied by the concept of transformational coping and the hardiness model. However, even this process was only concurrently tested. Other possible routs, e.g., the coping strategies and social supports used by high hardies should be studied more intensively and more systematically in the future.

The examination of the discriminant validity of a concept in comparison to similar constructs is an additional route for clarifying a theoretical concept. With this aim in mind, in the next section, the hardiness construct will be compared with three other concepts: sense of coherence, learned resourcefulness, and optimism.

Hardiness and Related Constructs

Sense of coherence (SOC) (Antonovsky, 1987; Chapter 2, this volume), learned resourcefulness (Rosenbaum, 1988; Chapter 1, this volume), and optimism (Scheier & Carver, 1987) are three health-related concepts that, similarly to hardiness, are hypothesized to explain what is there that helps a person to stay healthy under conditions of stress. The similarities among the three models are as follows: (a) a definition of stress as demands to which no automatic responses are readily available; (b) health is their outcome of interest; (c) the assumption that sociopsychological factors affect physical health; (d) an interest in personal resiliency; and (e) a construct of personality that consists mainly of conscious, cognitive, and acquired processes.

Empirical findings about the relationships between hardiness and the other constructs are very scarce. In our own ongoing studies, we obtained correlations of 0.52 between hardiness and SOC, and 0.34

between hardiness and resourcefulness. A similar correlation in the thirties was reported between hardiness and optimism (e.g., Hull et al., 1987). Unfortunately, no empirical investigation we know of has tested the effects of hardiness and any of the other constructs simultaneously across systematically varied situations, leaving us, at least for the time being, with our personal predilections for one rather than the other concept and its derived model. A theoretical comparison, however, may pave the way to effective research by clarifying whether the four concepts are actually four of a kind, or rather differential personality processes.

Sense of coherence (SOC) is a concept coined by Antonovsky (1979; Chapter 2) and defined as "a global orientation that expresses the extent to which one has a pervasive, enduring though dynamic feeling of confidence that (a) stimuli deriving from one's internal and external environments in the course of living are structured, predictable, and explicable; (b) the resources are available to one to meet the demands posed by these stimuli; and (c) these demands are challenges, worthy of investment and engagement" (Antonovsky, 1987, p. 19). The three components in the definition were conceived as interacting with each other and named "comprehensibility," "manageability," and "meaningfulness," respectively. Antonovsky devised a 29-item self-report questionnaire to tap this construct. Preliminary results show acceptable psychometric properties (Antonovsky, personal communication), but formal results have not yet been published.

Kobasa and Antonovsky explicate what they mean by the components of their constructs. Both refer to extensive and vigorous self-involvement in one's full life scope by the concepts of commitment as a component of hardiness and meaningfulness as a component of SOC (Antonovsky, 1987; Kobasa, 1979). Furthermore, in their theoretical description, Kobasa and Antonovsky underscore the point that control in hardiness and manageability in SOC are not identical to internal attribution of control. They include these aspects in their constructs: prediction as a way to manage the situation, delegation of control to others, individual limits of control, and exclusion of domination of others as a mode of adaptive control (Antonovsky, 1987; Kobasa, 1979). The two constructs differ most in their third component: Antonovsky considers that an internal sense of order and consistency (comprehensibility) is crucial for being resilient, whereas Kobasa conceives that an internal sense of change (challenge) is a predominant normative mode of life conducive to health. Interestingly, Antonovsky assumes that comprehensibility is the personal ability to construct ambiguous reality (Antonovsky, 1987). Existential personality theory, on the other hand contends that the personal ability to sustain change and ambiguity is a prerequisite of growth. Growth in this context means reconstruction or reorganization of the world in a new higher level of order (Kobasa & Maddi, 1982). Kobasa taps the beginning of the process, the perception of the chaotic unorganized situation; Antonovsky, its end product, its systematic organization. However, underlying the difference between comprehensibility and challenge is a more profound motivational difference. Kobasa assumes that individual search for meaning through active reconstruction of the ever-changing environment is the force motivating people to behave in a specific way, leading to well-being and health (Kobasa, 1982a). Antonovsky, (1987) as does Kobasa, thinks "that the way people construct their reality is a decisive factor in coping and health outcome" (p. 47). However, unlike Kobasa, Antonovsky suggests that persons are motivated to act coherently when sensing areas in their life as worthy of emotional involvement and commitment (Antonovsky, 1987). Meaningful goals are the motivational factors of the coherent person, whereas the attribution of meaning to life events is the motivational force of the hardy person. To conclude, the concept of challenge seems to be the most important difference between sense of coherence and hardiness, but as noted earlier, reoperationalization of challenge or, alternatively, more extensive research using the 50-item scale is the precondition of the empirical testing of challenge as a hardiness subconcept.

Learned resourcefulness is a personality repertoire that has been defined as a set of behaviors and skills by which individuals self-regulate internal responses that interfere with the smooth execution of an ongoing behavior (Rosenbaum, 1983; Chapter 1, this volume). The personality repertoire consists of a set of beliefs that one can effectively deal with specific stress situations, skills, and self-control behaviors. The main instrument for the assessment of learned resourcefulness is the Self-Control Schedule (SCS) (Rosenbaum, 1980). This is a self-report instrument directed at assessing individual tendencies to apply self-control methods to the solution of behavioral problems. It covers (a) the use of cognition and self-instruction to cope with emotional and physiological responses, (b) application of problem-solving strategies, (c) ability to delay immediate gratification, and (d) a general belief in one's ability to self-regulate internal events. Adequate psychometric properties of the scale were reported by the author (Rosenbaum, 1980; 1988).

Resourcefulness is clearly distinct from hardiness. Its uniqueness is apparent in its underlying motivation, its status within the stress-health model, and its domain-specific activity. Resourcefulness is an elaboration of social learning theory (Rosenbaum, 1988). Self-control behavior by the resourceful person is motivated by emotional and or cognitive strain aroused as a reaction to real or imagined changes within the self or within the environment. This automatically aroused strain disrupts habitual goal-directed behavior (Rosenbaum, 1988) and triggers a process of self-regulation consisting of conscious evaluation of the event and action that is aimed at regulating the automatic disruption. In comparison to the need of the hardy person to give meaning to the unstructured situation, termination of strain reactions is the motivational power underlying resourcefulness.

Transformational coping and not the set of beliefs is the concept analogous to resourcefulness in the hardiness model. However, whereas transformational coping is hypothesized to include processes of stress appraisal and problem-solving strategies (Kobasa, 1982b), the resourcefulness model consists, as noted earlier, of the latter strategies and additional self-regulating skills such as the ability to delay gratification and management of emotions.

Most importantly, only one of the characteristics of the resourceful person is a generalized belief. Its other three are beliefs in having specific skills. As such, they were hypothesized and found to be active under specific rather than under general stress. Hardiness, on the other hand, is hypothesized as a consistent belief affecting favorable outcomes without specification of situational conditions except the magnitude of stress.

The term "dispositional optimism" refers to a consistent general positive outcome expectancy. It was coined by Scheier and Carver and is measured by the Life Orientation Test (LOT). The scale consists of 12 items: four positively and four negatively phrased outcome expectancies, and four filler items. The authors report sound psychometric properties of the scale (Scheier & Carver, 1985). The reasoning with respect to the effects of optimism presumed by the authors is that when persons are confronted with impediments to goal attainment, the goal-directed activity is interrupted and the expected outcome is reevaluated. If optimism is defined as generalized expectancies for favorable outcomes, then optimism should instill a sense of confidence in dealing with whatever obstacles are encountered. The positive optimistic expectancies (versus the negative pessimistic ones) give rise to continued efforts to solve the problem, thus gaining a better chance to reach effective solutions. One should note that the benign sequel of outcome expectancy is independent of the optimistic outlook antecedents (Scheier & Carver, 1987).

Dispositional optimism, like resourcefulness, is rooted within the social learning approach. The dispositional optimism model is most parsimonious, suggesting one-trait theory, anticipated reward (expected positive outcome) as a determinant of personal resiliency. The approach of these authors differs from that of the radical behaviorism in that they assume, not unlike Kobasa, that internal generalized beliefs rather than actual rewards within specific situations affect outcomes. But the model of dispositional optimism is profoundly different from that of hardiness because (a) optimism ignores global personality contributions, and (b) although the search for meaningful experience (that is, the process of interaction with the physical and the social world) motivates hardy people, dispositional optimists are motivated to act persistently because they believe in attaining desirable outcomes. Although the two models differ in their basic assumptions, their alternative contributions to health can be empirically tested. It is not enough to demonstrate which of them affects health significantly after controlling for the other. The crucial test for optimism is demonstrating that the antecedents of the beliefs in positive outcomes (for example a defensive versus a realistic assessment of self-efficacy) do not affect differential health outcomes.

To conclude, hardiness was compared with three other theories of personal resiliency: sense of coherence, resourcefulness, and dispositional optimism. It was demonstrated that the four constructs are similar on a number of criteria, but each of them entertains a different image of the individual. Because no serious empirical comparison has been performed, further research is needed to rise to the challenge of investigating whether or not a general resiliency and model-specific factors can be found.

Further Research

Throughout this review, suggestions have been offered for further research. In this section, we would like to address three most important specific issues in need of clarification: hardiness as a constellation of commitment, control, and challenge, the problem of multiplicity of scales, and the relationship between hardiness and neuroticism.

The question of whether hardiness is a constellation of three concepts has not found an empirical answer to date. Whereas commitment and control seem to measure a single construct, challenge appears to measure a different construct. Our standpoint is, however, that challenge is not to be discarded until its reoperationalization has been undertaken. This is because items in previous challenge scales are not consistent with the construct described by theory of existential personality.

The hypothesis that the three subscales affect health as a constellation has not been investigated. Findings of significant multiple correlation between the scores of the three components and health outcome have been reported (e.g., Ganelen & Blaney, 1984). These findings support a linear hypothesis, but in order to demonstrate a constellation effect, an interaction hypothesis should be tested.

A new and interesting line of inquiry might be the issue of the relationships between social context and the relative importance of the three hardiness components. For example, it may well be that the need to be in control has a small and even negative effect on health in situations of objective helplessness such as severe illness. Challenge may have a negligible effect during advancing age, when, according to Erikson (1959), honorable resignation is the central mode of life.

Hardiness was measured by many different versions of the scale, making comparison difficult. However, as shown earlier in this review, the scales correlate appropriately with each other, and similar results were obtained from the various scales. The 50-item still seems a better scale than previous versions, because only part of its items are negatively keyed. Unfortunately, not enough studies using this scale have been reported. Therefore, we recommend the use of the 50-item scale in further research.

We feel that the most important theoretical problem is the issue of the relationship between hardiness and both negative and positive affect. However, comparing two constructs such as hardiness and neuroticism or negative affectivity is in itself problematical. Hardiness is a cognitive global concept, whereas low negative affectivity may be the emotional tone contingent on it. In order to test their relationship, one has to assess it in various situations and specifically look into the state/trait relations. Existential psychology postulates that hardy (authentic) persons usually experience low trait anxiety, but high state anxiety which dissipates quickly during threatening situations. Testing this hypothesis is one way of testing the confounding between the two concepts.

Conclusion

The findings lend strong support to the hypothesis that hardy persons are healthier, less depressed, and perform better than the nonhardy. The moderating effect of hardiness is supported for psychological health, but remains inconclusive with regard to physical health. The question of whether hardiness is a constellation of three distinct subconcepts has been tested by linear rather than by interactional designs, and, therefore, further research is needed to resolve this issue.

Only preliminary and partial treatment has been offered on the questions of how and under what conditions hardiness effects beneficial outcomes, what the processes by which it operates are, and how the processes are affected by the social context. Further research is recommended employing prospective designs and testing stress–hardiness interactional effects, especially with objective physical health criteria. We did not find any studies dealing with the development of hardiness, either naturally or through hardiness training. Research in this direction is urgently needed.

References

Allred, K. D., & Smith, T. W. (1989). The hardy personality: Cognitive and physiological responses to evaluative threat. *Journal of Personality and Social Psychology, 56,* 257–266.

Antonovsky, A. (1979). *Health, stress, and coping.* San Francisco: Jossey-Bass.

Antonovsky, A. (1987). *Unraveling the mystery of health: How people manage stress and stay well.* San Francisco: Jossey-Bass.

Banks, J. K., & Gannon, L. R. (1988). The influence of hardiness on the relationship between stressors and psychosomatic symptomatology. *American Journal of Community Psychology, 16,* 25–37.

Barling, G. (1986). Interrole conflict and marital functioning amongst employed fathers. *Journal of Occupational Behavior, 7,* 1–8.

Baron, R. M., & Kenny, D. A. (1986). The moderator-mediator variable distinction in social psychological research: Conceptual, strategic, and statistical considerations. *Journal of Personality and Social Psychology, 51,* 113–118.

Bartone, P. T. (1984). Stress and health in Chicago Transit Authority bus drivers. Unpublished doctoral dissertation. The University of Chicago.

Bartone, P., Ursano, R. J., Wright, K. M., & Ingraham, L. H. (in press). The impact of a military air disaster on the health of assistance workers: A prospective study. *Journal of Nervous and Mental Disease.*

Berger, H. (1983). An investigation of the relationship among burnout, hardiness, job and demographic characteristics, life event change and physical health in school psychologists. *Dissertation Abstracts International, 45,* 654–655-B.

Cohen, S., & Syme, S. L. (1985) Issues in the study and application of social support. In S. Cohen & S. L. Syme (Eds.), *Social support and health* (pp. 3–22). Orlando: Academic Press.

Cohen, S., & Wills, T. A. (1985). Stress, social support, and the buffering hypothesis. *Psychological Bulletin, 98,* 310–357.

Contrada, R. J. (1985). Type A behavior, hardiness, and the subjective and cardiovascular response to performance challenge. *Dissertation Abstracts International, 46,* 1733-B.

Erikson, E. H. (1959). Growth and crises of the healthy personality. *Psychological Issues, 1,* 50–100.

Freedman, L.R. (August, 1987). Psychological hardiness and demoralization among American Rabbis. Paper presented at the hardiness conference, CUNY, New York.

Frohm, K. D. (August, 1987). Hardiness effects on automatic reactivity: Psychological correlates of anxiety. Paper presented at the 95th Annual APA Convention, New York.

Funk, S. C., & Houston, B. K. (1987). A critical analysis of the hardiness scales' validity and utility. *Journal of Personality and Social Psychology, 53,* 572–578.

Ganellen, R. J., & Blaney, P. H. (1984). Hardiness and social support as moderators of the effects of life stress. *Journal of Personality and Social Psychology, 47,* 156–163.

Gore, S. (1985). Social support and styles of coping with stress. In S. Cohen & L. Syme (Eds.) *Social support and health* (pp. 263–278), New York: Academic Press.

Hahn, M. (1966). *California Life Goals Evaluation Schedule.* Palo Alto: Western Psychological Services.

Hannah, T. E. (1988). Hardiness and health behavior: The role of health concern as a moderator variable. *Behavioral Medicine, 3,* 59–63.

Hannah, T. E., & Morrissey, G. (1987). Correlates of psychological hardiness in Canadian adolescents. *The Journal of Social Psychology, 127,* 339–344.

Herlich, K. A. (1985). The use of hardiness and other stress-resistance resources to predict symptoms and performance in police academy trainees. *Dissertation Abstracts International, 46,* 2063-B.

Hill, L. A. (1982), Personality and coping style as mediators of the stress and mental health relationship of employed women. Unpublished doctoral dissertation. The University of Chicago.

Holmes, T., & Rahe, R. (1967). The social adjustment rating scale. *Journal of Psychosomatic Research, 11,* 213–218. Holt, P., Fine, M. J., & Tollefson, N. (1987). Mediating stress: Survival of the hardy. *Psychology in the Schools, 24,* 51–58.

Hull, J. G., Van Treuren, R. R., & Virnelli, S. (1987). Hardiness and health: A critique and alternative approach. *Journal of Personality and Social Psychology, 53,* 518–530.

Jackson, D. N. (1974). *Personality research form manual.* New York: Goshen, Research Psychologists Press.

Kahn, S. (August, 1987). Descriptive statistics and alpha coefficients for third-generation hardiness scale and subscales. Paper presented at the hardiness conference, CUNY, New York

Keane, A., Ducette, J., & Adler, D. C. (1985). Stress in ICU and non-ICU nurses. *Nursing Research, 34,* 231–236.

Kobasa, S. C. (1979). Stressful life events, personality, and health: An inquiry into hardiness. *Journal of Personality and Social Psychology, 37,* 1–11.

Kobasa, S. C. (1982a). The hardy personality: Toward a social psychology of stress and health. In J. Suls, & G. Sanders, (Eds.), *Social psychology of health and illness* (pp. 3–33). Hillsdale, NJ: Erlbaum.

Kobasa, S. C. (1982b). Commitment and coping in stress resistance among lawyers. *Journal of Personality and Social Psychology, 42,* 707–717.

Kobasa, S. C. O., & Maddi, S. R. (1977). Existential personality theory. In R. Corsini (Ed.). *Current personality theories* (pp. 243–276). Itasca, IL: T. F. Peacock.

Kobasa, S. C. O., & Puccetti, M. C. (1983). Personality and social resources in stress resistance. *Journal of Personality and Social Psychology, 45,* 839–850.

Kobasa, S. C., Maddi, S. R., & Courington, S. (1981). Personality and constitution as mediators in the stress illness relationship. *Journal of Health and Social Behavior, 22,* 368–378.

Kobasa, S. C., Maddi, S. R., & Kahn, S. (1982). Hardiness and health: A prospective study. *Journal of Personality and Social Psychology, 42,* 168–177.

Kobasa, S. C., Maddi, S. R., & Zola, A. (1983), Type A and hardiness, *Journal of Behavioral Medicine, 6,* 41–51.

Kobasa, S. C. O., Maddi, S. R., Puccetti, M. C., & Zola, M. A. (1985). Effectiveness of hardiness, exercise and social support as resources against illness. *Journal Psychosomatic Resources, 29,* 525–533.

Lambert, C. E., & Lambert, V. A. (1987). Hardiness: Its development and relevance to nursing. IMAGE: *Journal of Nursing Scholarship, 19,* 92–95.

Lang, D. (1987). The role of hardiness in effective coping with short-term role overload. Paper presented at the hardiness conference, August, CUNY, New York.

Lang, D., & Markowitz, M. (1986). Coping, individual differences, and strain: A longitudinal study of short-term role overload. *Journal of Occupational Behavior, 7,* 195–206.

Maddi, S. R., Kobasa. S. C., & Hoover, M. (1979). An Alienation Test. *Journal of Humanistic Psychology, 19,* 73–76.

Magnani, L.E. (1986). The relationship of hardiness and self-perceived health to activity in a group of independently functioning older adults. *Dissertation Abstracts International, 46,* 4184-B.

Maslach, C., & Jackson, S. (1981). *The Maslach Burnout Inventory, Research edition.* Palo Alto, CA: Consulting Psychologists Press.

McNeil, K., Kozma, A., Stones, M. J., & Hannah, E. (1986). Measurement of psychological hardiness in older adults. *Canadian Journal on Aging, 5,* 43–48.

Nemiroff, D.G. (1986). Stressful life events, personality hardiness, and psychological growth (adult development, change). *Dissertation Abstracts International, 47,* 1775-B.

Nowack, K. M. (1985). The relationship between stress, cognitive hardiness, and health coping behavior to psychological well-being. *Dissertation Abstracts International, 46,* 1737-B.

Nowack, K. M. (1986). Type A, hardiness and psychological distress. *Journal of Behavioral Medicine, 9,* 537–548.

Nowack, K. M., & Hanson, A. L. (1983). The relationship between stress, job performance, and burnout in college student resident assistants. *Journal of College Student Personnel, 24,* 545–550.

Okun, M. A., Zautra, A. J., & Robinson, S. E. (1988). Hardiness and health among women with rheumatoid arthritis. *Personality and Individual Differences, 9,* 101–107.

Padnick, S. H. (August, 1985). Relationship of daily hassles, major life event and personality hardiness to physical symptoms and employee absenteeism. Paper presented at the hardiness conference, CUNY, New York.

Pollock, S. E. (1986). Human responses to chronic illness: Physiologic and psychosocial adaptation. *Nursing Research, 35,* 90–95.

Rhodewalt, F., & Augustdottir, S. (1986). On the relationship of hardiness to the Type A behavior pattern: Perception of life events versus coping with life events. *Journal of Research in Personality, 18,* 212–223.

Rhodewalt, F., & Zone, J. B. (1989). Appraisal of life change, Depression and illness in hardy and nonhardy women. *Journal of Personality and Social Psychology, 56,* 81–88.

Rich, V. L., & Rich, A. R. (1987). Personality hardiness and burnout in female staff nursing. IMAGE: *Journal of Nursing Scholarship, 19,* 63–66.

Rosenbaum, M. (1980). A schedule for assessing self-control behaviors: Preliminary findings. *Behavior Therapy, 11,* 109–121.

Rosenbaum, M. (1988). Learned resourcefulness, stress, and self-regulation. In S. Fisher & J. Reason (Eds.). *Handbook of life stress, cognition, and health* (pp. 483–496). Chichester, UK: Wiley & Sons.

Rotter, J. B. (1966). Generalized expectancies for internal vs. external control of reinforcement. *Psychological Monographs, 80,* 609.

Scheier, M. F., & Carver, C. S. (1985). Optimism, coping, and health: Assessment and implications of generalized outcome expectancies. *Health Psychology, 4,* 219–247.

Scheier, M. F., & Carver, C. S. (1987). Dispositional optimism and physical well-being: The influence of generalized outcome expectancies on health. *Journal of Personality, 55,* 171–209.

Schlosser, M. B. (1985). Stress, coping, hardiness, and health-protective behavior. *Dissertation Abstracts International, 46,* 4028-B.

Schlosser, M. B. (August, 1986). Anger, crying, and health among females. Paper presented at the 94th annual convention of APA, Washington, DC.

Schlosser, M. S. & Sheeley L. A. (August, 1985). The hardy personality: Females coping with stress. Paper presented at the 93th Annual APA Convention at Los Angeles, California.

Schmied, L. A. & Lawler, K. A. (1986). Hardiness, Type A behavior, and the stress-illness relation in working women. *Journal of Personality and Social Psychology, 51,* 1218–1223.

Schneider, M. G. (1986). The boss and organizational stress. Unpublished doctoral dissertation. The University of Chicago.

Solomon, G. F., & Temoshok, L. (1987). Psychoneuroimmunology perspective on AIDS research: Questions, preliminary findings, and suggestions. *Journal of Applied Social Psychology, 17,* 286–308.

Tucker, E. R. (1987). The relationships of hardiness and stressful life events to obstetric risks. Unpublished doctoral dissertation. The University of Texas at Galveston.

Van Treuren, R. R., & Hull, J. G. (August, 1977). Hardiness and the perception of symptoms. Paper presented at the annual APA convention, New York.

Wendt, B.R. (1982). The role of hardiness as a mediator between stress and illness among adolescents. *Dissertation Abstracts International, 42,* 2042-B.

Westman, M. (in press). The relationship between stress and performance: The moderating effect of hardiness. *Human Performance.*

Wiebe, D. J., & McCallum, D. M. (1986). Health practices and hardiness as mediators in the stress-illness relationship. *Health Psychology, 5,* 425–438.

Wyler, A. R. , Masuda, M., & Holmes, T. H. (1968). Seriousness of Illness Rating Scale. *Journal of Psychosomatic Research, 11,* 363–374.

4

To See Or Not To See: Cognitive Informational Styles in the Coping Process

Suzanne M. Miller

Consider two patients about to undergo the identical aversive dental procedure. When the first individual arrives, he seeks out information about the details of the procedure from the receptionist. This includes information about exactly what the dentist will do, when and under what circumstances he can expect to feel pain, and what the aftereffects will be. The second individual prefers to avoid such information and instead distracts himself by alternately leafing through a magazine, singing along with the music, and thinking about other things altogether.

This example raises an intriguing question. Will the patient who tunes into and "monitors" the situation, or who fails to distract, show more—or less—stress and discomfort than the patient who is able to tune out and psychologically "blunt" the negative aspects of the event?

Attention to a coping dimension of this kind has preoccupied personality psychology throughout its history. Yet, despite previous research into individual differences, evidence on the effects of informational search and avoidance on human stress has been conflicting, with a morass of studies yielding contradictory results (Miller, Combs, & Stoddard, 1989a). Part of the confusion appears to stem from the failure to take simultaneous account of relevant personal dispositions and the specific properties of the situation. That is, a fine-grained analysis of the coping process requires attention to the separate and interacting effects of both individual dispositions *and* situational factors (Miller, 1989). This perspective dovetails with recent advances in personality theory, which endorse the value of viewing self-regulatory processes generally in interactional terms (Mischel, 1973, 1979). Applied to the dental example, this interactive approach suggests that the degree of stress exhibited by individuals should vary as a function of the fit between their dispositional styles and situational constraints. For the patient who seeks information and/or fails to distract, anxiety and arousal should be lower when voluminous information is made available by the dental staff than when it is withheld. Conversely, the information-avoiding and/or actively distracting patient should be less aroused when the staff does not impose unwanted information upon him or her.

The program of research presented in this chapter attempts to make sense of the inconsistencies in previous research, by adopting such an interactional framework. I begin by reviewing the traditional views on information and stress and then go on to present an alternative framework—"The Monitoring and Blunting Hypothesis"—that takes an interactive perspective on the coping process. Following this, the available evidence is reviewed and its fit to this framework is examined. Issues such as the identification of individual differences and the implication of such dispositional variables for adaptive coping are discussed. Finally, developmental considerations and clinical applications are highlighted.

Traditional Views

The major experimentally based theories all focus on the situational availability or unavailability of threat-relevant cues. These theories generally predict that information and knowledge about threat should be preferred and stress reducing. For example, the safety signal hypothesis postulates that when the occurrence of an aversive event is predictable, then its absence is also predictable and the individual can relax during periods of safety. In contrast, when the event is unpredictable, no one signal reliably predicts danger and hence no one signal reliably predicts safety. Therefore, the individual can never relax and remains in constant fear (Weiss, 1970).

To illustrate, if the dentist were always to provide a warning before turning on the drill, then the patient could at least relax as long as the dentist was quiet. In contrast, if the dentist were to provide no warning, then the individual could never relax because the drilling could begin at any moment. Thus, if given a choice, individuals should prefer information so that they can be exposed to acute periods of danger (and long periods of safety) rather than to chronic periods of danger.

While considerable data from the animal literature support this view, the relation between information and human stress is more complex than the traditional theories imply. Although information is sometimes preferred and found to decrease stress, it can also have the reverse effect (Bandura, 1979, 1981; Miller, 1980a, 1981). Moreover, distraction is often chosen and can have stress-reducing effects. One of the main problems of these theories in accounting for the evidence is that they fail to distinguish between the objective presence of danger signals and their psychological presence. That is, they focus on the physical arrangements of stimuli (e.g., the presence or absence of danger signals) without considering how such stimuli are psychologically processed and transformed by the individual. There is no reason to expect, for example, that an individual will become aroused when medical results show that he or she requires surgery but the patient does not yet know it. Arousal will be induced only when the information becomes psychologically present, that is, when the doctor explains what the tests mean and the necessity to operate.

Even when individuals have been faced with a real or objective danger signal that they have psychologically processed, they can still adopt a variety of cognitive strategies that eliminate or attenuate further psychological awareness of it. The use of such strategies will, in turn, moderate the level of arousal that is experienced. In other words, having been told by the doctor that the tests signal the need for surgery, the individual can then use various cognitive strategies to become removed psychologically from this state of affairs, and so perhaps reduce arousal, even though the danger signal remains objectively present.

A second problem with theories drawn from laboratory work on animals is that they fail to take account of individual differences in information-seeking preferences under threat. When faced with aversive events, some individuals will choose to distract themselves from and/or avoid threatening information. However, in these very situations, others will not. They will find it too difficult or undesirable to distract themselves. The stressfulness of threatening cues should be very different for these groups, and any adequate theoretical framework must be able to address the role of individual dispositions.

In direct contrast to the experimental theories, psychodynamically based views focus—almost exclusively—on dispositional differences in selective attention to threat-relevant cues. They postulate that individuals vary in their inclination to "repress" and avoid or to become "sensitized" to unconscious sources of anxiety. Within this framework, those who use repression as a basic coping mode are generally considered to handle threatening events in a more "primitive" fashion than those who use sensitization as a basic coping mode (Byrne, 1961, 1964). Although this approach highlights the role of individual difference variables, it is inconsistent with evidence showing that repressors are often found to fare as well or better in aversive circumstances than sensitizers (Averill & Rosenn, 1972; Cohen & Lazarus, 1973; Miller & Mangan, 1983). Further, it assumes that some individuals consistently engage repression as a coping strategy and suffer debilitating consequences, regardless of the nature of the threat (e.g., external versus internal) or the situational constraints that prevail (e.g., the presence or absence of threatening warning cues). Finally, it categorizes individuals as either repressors or sensitizers and, therefore, fails to take account of the multidimensional nature of the coping process (Folkman & Lazarus, 1985).

Not surprisingly, personality scales derived from this framework have proven to be of limited utility, both in predicting who actually seeks or avoids information under threat and in predicting level of anxiety in response to information or distraction (Averill & Rosenn, 1972; Cohen & Lazarus, 1973; Miller & Mangan, 1983). Instead, they have turned out to measure a wide variety of response sets and to correlate in the 0.9 range with social desirability (Byrne, 1961, 1964; Goldstein, 1959; Goldstein, Jones, Clemens, Flagg, & Alexander, 1965). Taken together, the problem called for new ways of looking at the coping process, focusing at a more molecular level on informational search and avoidance, without being locked into assumptions about the beneficial effects of informational safety signals on the one hand or the maladaptiveness and cross-situational pervasiveness of a repressive coping style on the other hand.

"Monitoring and Blunting" Hypothesis

Any satisfactory theoretical account must spell out the conditions under which information is stress-enhancing for individuals as well as the conditions under which it is stress-reducing for them. The monitoring and blunting hypothesis seeks to do this. It is basically an extension of the safety signal view, but broadens this framework by emphasizing the way in which individuals cognitively process information about aversive events to reduce concomitant stress reactions (Miller, 1989; Miller, in press; Miller et al., 1989a). It postulates that there are two main modes for coping with aversive events. The first mode, **monitoring**, is the extent to which the individual is alert for and sensitized to threat-relevant information. A second mode, **blunting**, is the extent to which the individual cognitively avoids or transforms threat-relevant information; it is called "blunting" because it helps individuals to blunt or attenuate the psychological impact of objective sources of danger. The main premises of the monitoring and blunting hypothesis attempt to specify when each coping mode is engaged and when each is adaptive.

Here is an overview of this framework. Arousal remains high in aversive situations, to the extent that an individual is tuned into and monitoring the negative aspects of the events. Arousal is reduced when he or she can cognitively avoid and/or psychologically blunt objective sources of danger. When an aversive event is controllable, high monitoring and low blunting are the main coping modalities. Although they heighten arousal, these tactics enable the individual to execute controlling actions. When an aversive event is largely uncontrollable, however, high monitoring and low blunting (which heighten arousal) have little instrumental value. Therefore, low monitoring and high blunting become the main coping modes on these occasions, since an individual without controlling actions can most effectively reduce stress by engaging in distraction and similar psychological techniques. Here, information will be dispreferred and arousal-inducing, since it forces the individual back into the psychological presence of a danger he or she cannot avoid (Miller, 1979a, 1979b, 1980a, 1980b).

To illustrate, consider a dental patient whose dentist warns him or her every time the drill goes on. The individual will be listening for the dentist's warning; and the dentist's voice itself is invasive and intrusive, even if the individual is trying to block it out. In contrast, if a patient were to receive no warning, threat-relevant information would be more diluted and less psychologically invasive and intrusive. This would make it easier for the individual to distract him or herself.

Two main conditions may make it difficult or inappropriate for individuals to distract themselves. The first is situational: that is, the threat may be too intense to allow distraction. For example, when it is of high probability, of high level, of long duration or imminent, the threat will be harder to distract than when it is of low probability, of low level, of short duration or remote (see Miller, 1980a, 1981; Miller et al., 1989a; Miller & Grant, 1979). The second is related to individual differences in the ability and inclination to monitoring and distraction. That is, the ability to successfully tune out and/or distract oneself from danger signals should be subject to wide individual differences. Some people should find it easy or desirable to tune out and/or distract, even under conditions providing minimal support; others should find it difficult or inappropriate to tune out and/or distract, even under conditions providing maximal support. People who believe themselves to be effective information avoiders and/or blunters should tend consistently to choose unpredictability, even under conditions that may not support distraction.

For individuals who find it undesirable or too difficult to tune out and distract, safety signal considerations apply, especially under conditions that do not support distraction. That is, information will be preferred and stress-reducing, because information provides them at least with external cues that reduce uncertainty and signal periods of safety. For example, if the dentist always provides a warning before the drill goes on, then the high monitoring/low blunting individual can at least relax as long as the dentist is silent (Miller, in press). Information also enables individuals to interpret bodily sensations in an accurate and nonthreatening manner (Leventhal, 1989).

This view predicts that if individuals are forced to their nonpreferred condition, they should show higher arousal than they did in their preferred condition. It is important, then, to be able to identify independently and in advance those disposed to distract or not distract and to monitor or not monitor for information. However, research in this area has been hampered by the lack of an easy-to-administer and well-validated self-report coping measure to assess coping preferences.

Identification of Individual Differences: The MBSS

One of the main problems with earlier measures of individual differences has been too much converging validity and too little discriminant validity among them (Byrne, 1961, 1964). To circumvent these problems, a self-report measure was devised and designed to be more closely tailored to the kinds of informational choices under study. The Miller Behavioral Style Scale (MBSS) divides individuals into coping style groups on the basis of their self-reported preferences for information and distraction in a variety of naturalistic stress situations (Miller, 1987).

The scale consists of four hypothetical stress-evoking scenes of an uncontrollable nature. For example, imagine that you are afraid of flying and must go somewhere by plane. Each scene is followed by eight statements, which represent different ways of coping with the situation. Half of the statements following each scene are of a monitoring variety (e.g., in the airplane situation: "I would listen carefully to the engines for unusual noises and would watch the crew to see if their behavior was out of the ordinary"; or "I would read and reread the safety instruction booklet"). The other half of the statements are of a blunting variety (e.g., "I would watch the in-flight movie, even if I had seen it before"). The subject simply marks all the statements following each scene that might apply to him or her.

Three measures are derived from this scale. The monitoring measure is the sum of all the items endorsed on the monitoring subscale. Subjects scoring above the median are high monitors, and those scoring below are low monitors. The blunting measure is the sum of all the items endorsed on the blunting subscale; and subjects are divided into high and low blunters. Finally, the monitor/blunter measure is obtained by subtracting the total number of items endorsed on the blunting subscale from the total number of items endorsed on the monitoring subscale. Using this difference score, subjects are divided into monitors and blunters. Originally, researchers tended to rely on the difference score. More recently, however, there has been an interest in exploring the distinctive effects of the separate monitoring and blunting dimensions.

This scale has been validated in a number of contexts. For example, in one laboratory study, subjects were threatened with a low-probability electric shock to the fingers and allowed to choose whether they wanted to listen for information about the shock or to distract themselves with music (Miller, 1987). This meant that on one auditory channel, subjects heard a warning signal that indicated possible shock onset, as well as a series of statements that described the shocks, the machinery used to deliver shock, and the sensations that shock produces. On the other channel, subjects heard distracting music. Subjects could switch back and forth between the two channels as often as they liked.

The results showed that the amount of time spent on the information channel on each of four trails could be predicted by an individual's MBSS score. Figure 4.1 shows how much time was spent listening to the information/tone channel on each trial, using scores on the blunting subscale. As can be seen, low blunters spent on average over twice as much time as high blunters listening for information. Indeed, low blunters listened on average about 50 seconds out of a maximum of 60 seconds per trial, whereas high blunters listened to the information only about 20.26 seconds per trial. So, low blunters almost exclusively opted for an information-seeking mode, whereas high blunters generally preferred to distract themselves. Moreover, this difference in

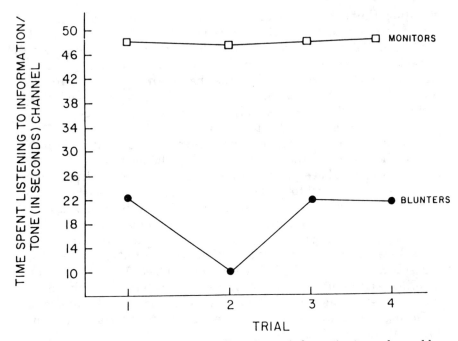

FIGURE 4.1. Amount of time spent listening to information/tone channel by coping style groups. (From S. M. Miller, *The Journal of Personality and Social Psychology,* © 1987, vol. 52, p. 348. Reprinted with permission.)

listening times was evident from the first trial on, reflecting a consistent divergence in strategy between the two coping style groups. Similar results were obtained with the other measures of coping style.

The MBSS also predicts informational search or avoidance in the face of an ego-threatening cognitive task (Miller, 1987). Subjects worked on a series of tests that presumably predicted success in college. They could attend as often as they wished to a light that signaled how well they were performing. The less time spent looking at the light, the greater the preference for distraction. MBSS scores accurately predicted attentional behavior. For example, using scores on the monitoring subscale, low monitors looked up at the light on average only 1.6 times during the session. In contrast, high monitors looked up at the light on average 11.2 times. Thus, the MBSS predicts information-seeking in response to both physical and psychological stressors and may represent a rather stable dispositional preference for coping with external threats of an uncontrollable nature.

In addition to predictive validity, the evidence shows the MBSS to be an acceptable psychometric instrument. For example, it has been found to be unrelated to demographic variables, such as sex, race, age, educational status, and marital status (Miller, 1987; Miller & Mangan, 1983). It has also been found to be unrelated to trait measures such as repression–sensitization, depression, anxiety, optimism, attributional style, and Type A (Caspi, 1987; Miller, Brody, & Summerton, 1988; Miller & Mangan, 1983; Miller, Lack, & Asroff, 1981; Steptoe, 1986). For example, in one field sample of women at risk for cervical cancer, the repressor–sensitizer scale correlated highly with trait anxiety, and both of these measures were related to education and race (Miller & Mangan, 1983). Specifically, as can be seen in Table 4.1, sensitizers tended to be highly trait anxious, less educated, and black. In contrast, there was no relation between being a monitor or blunter on the MBSS (as defined by the difference score) and repression-sensitization, trait anxiety, education, or race. This provides evidence that the scale may be measuring a distinctive dimension and parallels our results in other contexts (Miller, 1987; Miller, et al., 1988a; Miller & Mischel, in preparation; Steptoe, 1986). Further, high monitors/low blunters and low monitors/high blunters do not differ on state measures of anger, anxiety, and depression when not in an aversive situation (Miller & Mischel, in preparation; Phipps & Zinn, 1986).

The relation between the MBSS and Rosenbaum's (1983) Learned Resourcefulness Measure has been explored so far in only one study. In this study (see Chapter 1), it has been found that for High Resourceful surgery patients, a monitoring style was more effective in reducing anxiety than was a blunting style. For Low Resourceful patients, on the other hand, blunting was more effective than monitoring. (For a further discussion on the relationship of the MBSS and various coping strategies, see also Carver, Scheier, & Weintraub, 1989; Miller, in press).

Finally, test-retest analyses show the MBSS to be highly stable (in the 0.8 range) over a 3-month period (Miller & Mischel, in preparation). Thus, the scale appears to show good reliability as well as good

TABLE 4.1. Correlations among Miller Behavioral Style Scale (MBSS) Dispositional, and Demographic Measures ($N = 40$)

	TRAI	R-S	Ed	Race
(MBSS)	0.164	0.076	0.014	−0.103
Trait anxiety (TRAI)		0.932*	−0.370*	−0.343*
Repression-Sensitization (R-S)			−0.500*	−0.470*
Education (Ed)				0.426*

*$p < .01$.

From S. M. Miller & C. E. Mangan. *The Journal of Personality and Social Psychology,* © 1983, vol. 45, p. 228. Reprinted with permission.

predictive and discriminative validity and to represent a dimension that does not overlap with more traditional trait measures.

One might suspect, however, that although subjects who attend to information or who fail to distract are not more generally anxious, they may simply become more aroused or anxious by the prospect of the particular aversive event than the subjects who choose distraction. Contrary to this, various studies have shown that high and low monitors and high and low blunters do not differ from each other on initial measures of state distress or on initial measures of psychophysiological arousal, in both laboratory and field settings (Miller, 1979, 1987; Phipps & Zinn, 1986; Sparks & Spirek, 1988; Watkins, Weaver, & Odegaard, 1986). Thus, those who monitor under threat—or who fail to distract—are not simply made more anxious by the event than those who can tune out. Rather, the different modes appear to represent distinctive strategies for coping with aversive events of equivalent stress value. An obvious question arises: Which of these divergent strategies is the more adaptive for dealing with uncontrollable threats? In particular, which mode more effectively enables the individual to reduce stress and modulate arousal?

Alternative Modes of Response to Stress: Monitoring and Blunting

To explore differential arousal between high and low monitors and high and low blunters in the process of coping with aversive events, we have obtained measures of distress at various points during the stressful encounter. The results show that despite equally high levels of initial measures of state anxiety and physiological arousal, the different coping modes are sometimes accompanied by distinctive patterns of emotional responsivity over time. For example, as Figure 4.2 shows, when faced with the threat of electric shock, high and low blunters (as defined by their scores on the blunting subscale) do not differ in their self-reports of tension after the first trial (Miller, 1987). However, those who attend to information show sustained higher arousal and less habituation across trials than those who distract, who eventually decrease in arousal. This differential habituation is also evident using other self-report measures and physiological indices (Miller, 1979, 1987; Sparks & Spirek, 1988). Further, measures of behavioral arousal are consistent with this effect. Using the MBSS difference score, Efran, Chorney, Ascher, & Lukens (1989) found that blunters demonstrated greater pain tolerance (implying lower arousal and distress) on the cold pressor task than did monitors. As can be seen in Figure 4.3, blunt-

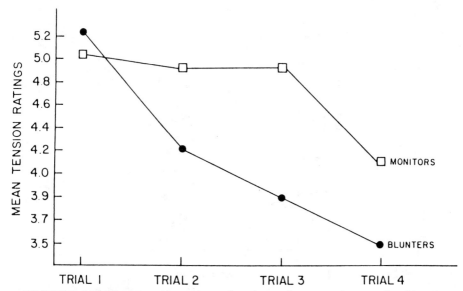

FIGURE 4.2. Mean tension ratings of coping style groups (on a scale of 1 to 7, where 1 = not at all tense and 7 = I am extremely tense) obtained after each trial. (From S. M. Miller, *The Journal of Personality and Social Psychology,* © 1987, vol. 52, p. 348. Reprinted with permission.

ers were able to keep their hands in ice water one and one half times as long as monitors were.

Similar findings have been obtained in field settings. For example, Miller and Mangan (1983) studied gynecologic patients at risk for cervical cancer who had to undergo an aversive diagnostic procedure ("colposcopy"). Again, with the difference score, results showed that monitors expressed more anxiety and discomfort than did blunters during the five days following the procedure. As can be seen in Figure 4.4, blunters showed a steady decrease in the amount of discomfort expressed. Monitors, on the other hand, showed a more gradual decline in pain and discomfort, and did not feel significantly better even at the third day. Following the exam, blunters reported that they were satisfied with the amount of information they had received, but monitors said they would have preferred to know more (see also Steptoe & O'Sullivan, 1986; Watkins et al., 1986). During the exam itself, a striking result emerged: The doctor rated the monitors to be significantly more aroused than the blunters as indexed by various overt signs of distress, such as muscular tension in the vaginal area (see Figure 4.5).

In a study of cancer patients undergoing chemotherapy, a significantly higher percentage of the monitors experienced nausea than the

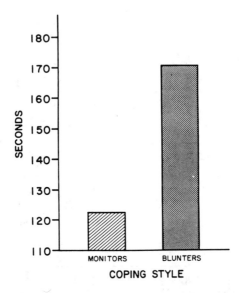

FIGURE 4.3. Mean pain tolerance scores of coping style groups during the cold pressor task. (Based on data from Efran et al., 1989.)

blunters (75% versus 41 %). In addition, monitors experienced signifi-cantly longer episodes of nausea than blunters did (an average of 15.31 hours versus 4.21 hours). Indeed, 9 of the 10 patients who experienced episodes of nausea that were greater than 12 hours in duration were monitors. These results were obtained despite the fact that a signifi-cantly larger number of monitors (87%) than blunters (45%) had re-ceived antiemetic medication, designed to reduce the severity of these side effects (Gard, Edwards, Harris, & McCormack, 1988).

Finally, Phipps and Zinn (1986) compared a group of at-risk preg-nant women, about to undergo amniocentesis, to a control group of pregnant women not at risk. Patients were divided into monitors and blunters on the basis of the difference score. Measures of distress were obtained after genetic counseling, after amniocentesis, and after obtaining the results (which were favorable in every case). Overall, the amniocentesis group showed more distress than the control group. However, this effect was largely due to the monitors in the amniocen-tesis group. As can be seen in Figure 4.6, monitors in the at-risk group showed greater anxiety than blunters—as measured by the Profile of Mood States (POMS)—after genetic counseling. This differential arousal was most heightened after the procedure itself. Arousal then dissipated after the results were announced.

Similar patterns were obtained for measures of depression and an-ger, with monitors evidencing far greater distress than blunters, both

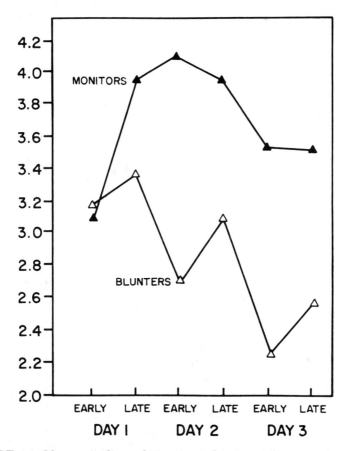

FIGURE 4.4. Mean pain/discomfort ratings of coping style groups (on a scale of 1 to 7, where 1 = I do not feel any pain/discomfort and 7 = I feel extreme pain/discomfort) for 3 days after the procedure. (Based on figure from Miller & Mangan, 1983.)

after genetic counseling and after amniocentesis (before knowing the results). Interestingly, no differences were observed between monitors and blunters at equivalent points in time in the control group. This supports the view that monitors are not overall more distressed than blunters. Rather, they become more distressed in response to threat—particularly uncontrollable threats—which activates their tendency to scan for threatening cues (see also Sparks, 1989; Sparks & Spirek, 1988).

Taken together, the studies reviewed thus far suggest that there are alternative modes for coping with aversive events—the extent to which the individual turns on or off threat-relevant information—and that the most adaptive modes for coping with uncontrollable threat

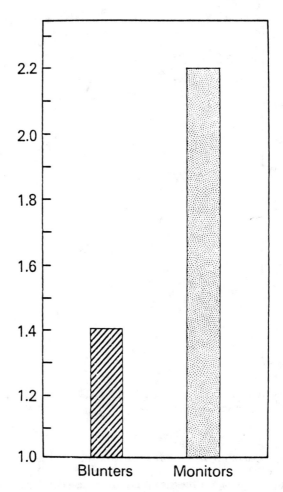

FIGURE 4.5. Mean doctor ratings of muscular tension of coping style groups (on a scale of 0 to 3, where 0 = no tension and 3 = extreme tension) during the examination. (From S. M. Miller and C. E. Mangan, *The Journal of Personality and Social Psychology*, © 1983, vol. 45, p. 230. Reprinted with permission.

may involve cognitive avoidance and blunting of threatening cues. These results raise an intriguing question: Are individuals suffering from chronic disorders such as hypertension—which are characterized by prolonged, high levels of physiologic and subjective arousal—prone to exhibit a high monitoring/low blunting style of coping?

In order to begin to explore this issue, we studied 50 individuals seeking outpatient treatment at a primary care facility for various acute medical problems (e.g., upper respiratory infection, muscle strains, etc.) (Miller, Leinbach, & Brody, 1989b). Twenty-five patients

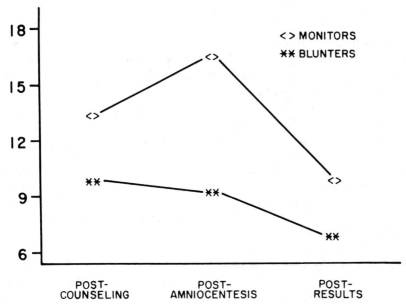

FIGURE 4.6. Mean anxiety ratings of coping style groups (on a 0 to 32 scale, where 0 = not at all anxious and 32 = extremely anxious) after counseling, after amniocentesis, and after hearing the results. (Based on figure from Phipps & Zinn, 1986.)

with a secondary or tertiary diagnosis of hypertension were chosen, and a control group matched on sex and age was selected. Subjects were divided into high and low monitors and into high and low blunters, based on their scores on the MBSS in each of the clinical groups (hypertensive, normotensive). Results indicated that hypertensives were twice as likely to be characterized by a high monitoring (low blunting) style than a low monitoring (high blunting) style. Conversely, normotensives were two and one-half times more likely to be characterized by a low monitoring (high blunting) style than a high monitoring (low blunting) style. Indeed, over two-thirds of the hypertensives were high monitors (low blunters), whereas close to three-fourths of the normotensives were low monitors (high blunters).

Although only preliminary in nature, these results indicate that hypertensives may be characterized by an information-seeking style that may take a physical and psychological toll. These individuals tend to monitor and scan for threat-relevant cues, even when the situation is uncontrollable. Previous research has shown that high monitoring/ low blunting produces acute or transient increases in subjective, behavioral, and physiologic arousal. This study extends these effects to a group suffering from chronic levels of elevated arousal and may implicate monitoring as a contributing factor in either the onset or exacerbation of the disorder. Alternatively, since hypertension is a symptomless yet life-threatening condition, information seekers may become alarmed at the emergence of even trivial symptoms and therefore may over-utilize medical services. Indeed, while hypertensives reported that their presenting medical problem was less serious than normotensives did, they nonetheless reported more concerns that it would last a long time, recur, or lead to more serious problems.

To summarize, the evidence shows that, at least in uncontrollable settings, to be a high monitor/low blunter is to have a more arousing coping style than to be a low monitor/high blunter. These results make sense, since the former typically seek out threat-relevant information about aversive events, whereas the latter typically cope with aversive events by distracting themselves from threat-relevant information. That is, individuals who voluntarily place themselves in the psychological presence of danger signals appear to suffer arousal consequences, compared with individuals who can psychologically avoid and transform such signals. This effect should be particularly heightened when information does not enable individuals to amplify the meaning of situational cues or to exclude threatening interpretations (Leventhal, 1989).

Interactive Effects of Coping Style and Situational Cues

In the studies reported above, subjects selected for themselves which strategies they would employ. Therefore, it is unclear whether the differential arousal observed between groups was due to characteristics of the individuals or to the efficacy of the strategies. Sustained high arousal on the part of high monitors/low blunters may have been the consequence of adopting an information-seeking strategy and actually receiving more information; or information-seekers may have been more anxious and arousable than information-avoiders, regardless of the level of information. Alternatively, there may be interesting person-by-situation interactions: information-seekers may show greatest anxiety when information is not readily available than when it is supplied; whereas information-avoiders may increase in anxiety when they cannot distract themselves. To systematically untangle these effects, arousal must be measured when individuals are exposed to both their preferred and nonpreferred strategies.

These interacting effects were explored in a study with gynecologic patients about to undergo an uncontrollable aversive diagnostic procedure for gynecologic cancer (colposcopy)(Miller & Mangan, 1983). Patients were divided into monitors and blunters, based on their difference scores on the MBSS. Half in each group were exposed to voluminous preparatory information, and half to the usual low level of information. Subjective, physiological, and behavioral measures of arousal and discomfort were obtained before, during, and after the procedure.

Results showed that individual differences in coping style interacted with and moderated the impact of threat-relevant information, with blunters benefiting more from distraction and monitors tending to benefit more from information about the procedure. This is reflected most dramatically on measures of physiologic arousal, as indexed by pulse rate. As Figure 4.7 shows, there were initially no differences among the groups. The only group to show a decrease in pulse rate

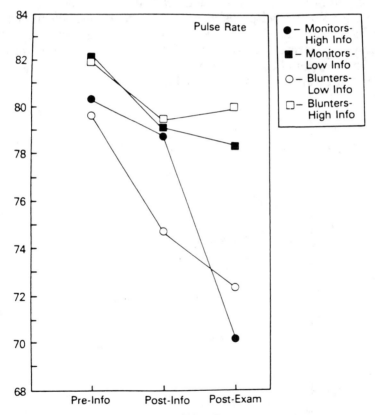

FIGURE 4.7. Mean pulse rate readings of coping style groups before information, after information, and after the examination. (From S. M. Miller and C. E. Mangan, *The Journal of Personality and Social Psychology,* © 1983, vol. 45, p. 230. Reprinted with permission.

immediately before the exam were blunters given low information, and they maintained this low pulse rate throughout. By the end of the exam, monitors who were given a large amount of information also showed reduced pulse rates, but low-information monitors and high-information blunters showed sustained higher pulse rates.

This general pattern of results has been replicated in other field settings. For example, similar findings were obtained on coronary patients undergoing cardiac catheterization. Watkins et al. (1986) found that monitors receiving high levels of preparatory information showed less physiologic and self-reported arousal throughout the procedure than those receiving low levels of information. Conversely, blunters receiving lower levels of information were less aroused than blunters receiving high levels of information. As can be seen in Figure 4.8, high-information blunters and low-information monitors showed more physiologic arousal, as measured by heart rate, during cardiac catheterization than low information blunters and high information monitors, who were less aroused. Similar results were found for pulse rate and ratings of state anxiety.

Finally, Efran et al. (1989) studied the performance of monitors and

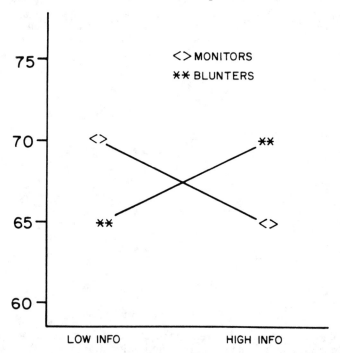

FIGURE 4.8. Mean heart rate readings of coping style groups during the examination. (Based on figure from Watkins et al., 1986.)

blunters on the cold pressor task in the laboratory. It was predicted that higher pain thresholds—that is time to perceive the stimulus as painful—would be found when subjects were induced to use coping strategies compatible with their coping style. As Figure 4.9 shows, blunters demonstrated higher pain thresholds—i.e., less sensitivity to pain—when they were induced to distract from the pain sensations in their hands ("Think about the fact that one of the good things about this experience is that it might help psychologists learn more about people . . ."). In contrast, monitors did not demonstrate significantly higher pain thresholds when they were encouraged to observe and focus on the sensations in their hands ("Think about how your fingers feel, where they experience cold, numbness, tingling . . ."), although the means were in the predicted direction (see also Lamping & Catechis, 1989; Lerman, Rimer, Blumberg, & Cristinzio, 1989; Sparks, 1989).

In summary, how well an individual copes is determined, in part, by the fit of his or her characteristic style to the individual situation. This helps to make sense of the conflict in results among previous studies, where information sometimes had a beneficial and sometimes a detrimental effect (e.g., Cohen & Lazarus, 1973; Langer, Janis, & Wolfer,

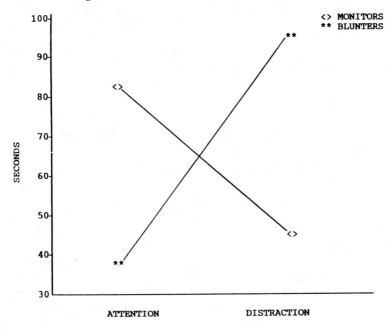

FIGURE 4.9. Mean pain threshold scores of coping style groups during the cold pressor task. (Based on data from Efran et al., 1989.)

1975; Miller, 1979a; Monat, 1976; Monat, Averill & Lazarus, 1972; Sime, 1976, versus Averill, & Rosenn, 1972; Egbert, Battit, Welsh, & Bartlett, 1964; Vernon & Bigelow, 1974). In ongoing work, we are varying the nature of the stressor (e.g., its severity and duration), type of information (e.g., procedural versus sensory), and type of blunting strategy (e.g., distraction versus relaxation versus reinterpretation) to determine the generality of these findings.

These results may also have important practical implications. As applied to the medical context, the treatment of acute health problems—as well as the treatment of chronic disorders such as hypertension—should perhaps include a routine assessment of the individual's preferred coping style. Preparatory information pertinent to the nature of the patient's disorder and upcoming diagnostic and intervention procedure could then be varied accordingly, with monitors receiving maximal information and blunters receiving minimal information.

Attention to Internal "Bodily" Cues

Recently, we have been interested in further exploring and delineating differential health-seeking behaviors and health status between the different coping style groups. There is evidence that patients vary enormously in their sensitivity to bodily symptoms and in their preferences for information and psychosocial interventions in a number of health-care settings (Mechanic, 1980, 1983). Yet, in contrast to more extensive evidence on the process of coping with short-term medical procedures, little is known about the dispositional factors that determine how patients construe and attend to their general medical problems or what they expect and desire in terms of treatment.

To explore these issues, Miller et al. (1988a) studied 118 patients visiting a primary care setting for acute medical problems (e.g., gastrointestinal problems, flus), who had experienced new or increased levels of discomfort and dysfunction during the week preceding their medical visit. The results were strongest using the monitoring subscale and suggest three tentative conclusions.

First, high and low monitors differed in the level of seriousness of their actual medical problem. Evaluations by the physicians showed that high monitors actually had less severe medical problems than low monitors did. Only 9% of the low monitors had problems rated "not at all" serious, whereas twice as many high monitors fell into this category. The two groups had an equal number of problems rated as "slightly" serious, but one-third of the low monitors had moderately serious or quite serious problems, compared with only 10% of the high monitors. Indeed, about three times as many low monitors fell into these upper categories as high monitors. Consistent with this finding, physicians also indicated that high monitors had experienced less dysfunction and discomfort prior to the visit and that their medical problem had contributed less to the way they had been feeling than was the case for low monitors.

Thus, the first conclusion is that where an individual falls on the monitoring dimension appears, in part, to account for differential sensitivity to bodily symptoms. High monitors (and low blunters) have been shown to be more likely to scan for external threat-relevant cues than low monitors (and high blunters). The present results suggest that they may also have a lower threshold for scanning for "internal" bodily cues. This would make them more inclined to detect or over-interpret new or changing physical symptoms—from which they would find it difficult to distract. This, in turn, may increase arousal and prompt individuals to respond by soliciting medical attention as the most likely means of reducing their distress. In ongoing work, we are exploring whether high monitors fare better than low monitors in medical situations in which early detection of physical symptoms is life saving, such as in cancer and heart diseases.

The second conclusion concerns the way in which high and low monitors respond to and evaluate their symptoms. Despite the fact that their medical problems were less severe, high monitors' self-rated levels of discomfort, dysfunction, and perceived problem seriousness were identical to those of low monitors. Further, high monitors showed slower and less complete recovery than low monitors did. At a 1-week follow-up after the visit, low monitors manifested significantly more improvement than high monitors in specific medical symptoms and more improvement in their stress-related problems. For example, 1 week after the visit, low monitors rated themselves as showing twice as much improvement in their stress-related problems as high monitors did.

Third, high and low monitors differed in terms of the number of interventions desired as well as the level of information desired. In general high monitors in our study wanted both more interventions and more information. For example, high monitors were more likely to want tests done, and were more concerned about being treated with kindness and respect than were low monitors. Half of the high monitors expressed this concern, whereas 85% of the low monitors did not express any such concerns. One reason why high monitors might be so concerned about how the doctor treats them is that a physician who demonstrates the appropriate respect may be perceived as a more reliable source of reassurance and information than one who seems aloof or condescending. High monitors were also more likely to desire help and advice on how to deal with their stress-related problems and were significantly more likely to request reassurance about the effects of their stress on their health. For example, about one-third of the high monitors wanted to discuss their stress-related problems. In contrast, almost 90% of the low monitors did not want such discussion (see also Steptoe & O'Sullivan, 1986).

In addition, high monitors desired more voluminous information, especially pertaining to the cause of their medical problems, how healthy they were in general, how they could prevent future health problems, and possible medication side effects (see also Watkins et al., 1986). Finally, high and low monitors differed in the type of role they preferred to play in the care of their medical problem. Almost no patients desired to have the final say in their medical care. However, almost three-fourths of the low monitors preferred that treatment decisions be made jointly by them and their physicians, whereas under half of the high monitors desired such an active role. Indeed, twice as many high as low monitors desired to play a completely passive role in their own care.

So, high monitors have a greater need for medical and stress-related information than low monitors do. Yet, they do not appear to seek this information for its direct, instrumental value. This is consistent with other research, which shows that high monitors/low blunters scan for information even in the face of uncontrollable threats (Miller, 1987). Further, they appear to cope with threat by seeking out instrumental sources of social support (Carver et al., 1989). The present results provide additional evidence that high monitors may be, at times, more concerned with reducing uncertainty-or gaining access to expertise-than they are with exercising control themselves (see Miller & Birnbaum, 1988; 1989). [Editorial note-I would assume that this is mostly true for high monitors who are low resourceful. High monitors who are also high resourceful may be more likely to use the gained information for more effective coping (see Chapter 1)].

Developmental Considerations: Expanding the Construct Network

The results presented above raise several questions. Where do these informational styles come from? How do they hold over time and situations? What influences them? In contrast to the extensive evidence on coping patterns in adults, relatively little is known about the analogous process of coping in children. The evidence to date indicates that various cognitive factors do indeed alter the nature of the stress response in children. Yet, it is difficult to untangle conceptually the components that contribute to successful stress reduction (Miller & Green, 1985). Moreover, almost no evidence exists on dispositional or developmental factors that might play a moderating role. Indeed, more of the cognitively oriented work with children has concentrated on managing the so-called externalizing problems such as impulsivity, rather than on the so-called internalizing problems such as anxiety.

To begin to determine the breadth, consistency, and coherences of such phenomena necessitates a fine-grained and developmentally focused analysis of the coping process. Recently, then, we have begun to trace the nature and course of these self-regulatory patterns in young children (Miller, Savage, & Mischel, 1988b). Within this developmental perspective, we have continued to pursue a strategy that emphasizes the dynamic interplay between individual differences and situational factors, and the implications of this interaction for the acquisition, maintenance, and modification of informational preferences.

We also broadened the domain of affect under study, assessing not only informational preferences of children in response to threat, but also important, their informational preferences when waiting for preferred but delayed rewards. We became intrigued by the possibility of some important but as yet unexamined, conceptual links between the process of coping with threatening stimuli and information-seeking or information-avoidance during delay of gratification. Mischel and his colleagues (Mischel, 1974, 1979, 1984) have been finding that, just as distraction and affective blunting often help adults cope with impending stressful events, distraction from the expected outcome and avoidance of consummatory ideation prove to be important strategies for effective delay of gratification in children. That is, when children distract themselves, it is easier for them to wait for a delayed but better outcome (e.g., two marshmallows in ten minutes) rather than opting for an immediate but less good outcome (e.g., one marshmallow right away) (Mischel, 1974; Miller et al., 1988b). We have just begun to explore these cross-situational links (Miller et al., 1988b). Our results show that young children who effectively use distraction to cope with the frustration of waiting for deferred rewards appear to be similarly efficient in their use of distraction in the face of threat (see Miller, 1989).

We also are exploring how children (and adults) develop knowledge about what constitutes effective arousal-reduction and how this knowledge moderates their own behavior. Although much is known about children's knowledge of effective strategies for attention and memory, relatively little is known about the child's developing use and understanding of effective strategies for self-regulation (e.g., Mischel &

Mischel, 1983). There is considerable evidence concerning the situational factors that impede or facilitate adaptive coping. Yet, there is almost no evidence on children's (or adults') ability to identify critical situational factors or their ability to tailor their coping strategy to the situation. There is at least some evidence suggesting that children have a relatively sophisticated understanding of general psychological principles for social behavior, which increases with the progression of their cognitive development (Mischel, 1979). This implies that there is a somewhat spontaneous (and as yet unclear) process by which youngsters acquire rather sophisticated knowledge of psychological principles (Mischel & Mischel, 1983). This understanding, in turn, may be an important ingredient in developing personal and cognitive competencies.

In one recent study (Gallagher, Miller, & Mischel, 1988), we found that impulsive 6-year-old children ("externalizers") showed poor comprehension of adaptive strategies for successful delay, when faced with a hypothetical delay of gratification situation. Specifically, they did not appear to understand the reward consequences of waiting versus not waiting, and believed that it would be easier for them to wait if they thought about and looked at the rewards (strategies known to inhibit delay). Consistent with this, impulsive children also tolerated delay for a significantly shorter period of time, when faced with an actual delay of gratification task. Thus, the ability to successfully delay gratification (or cope with threat) may be dependent on the child's acquisition of the rule that distraction and blunting are appropriate strategies. We are currently exploring these patterns.

Implications for Maladaptive Coping

The evidence cited previously, from both the stress and delay literatures, suggests that low monitoring/high blunting are effective modes of coping both with uncontrollable threat and the aversive frustration of deferring gratification. Effective self-regulation, therefore, may involve the ability to discriminate variations in situational factors and to adjust one's coping strategies accordingly. Table 4.2 specifies the relationship between the individual's ability to alter an outcome and the corresponding cognitive strategy of choice.

Consider an individual dealing with a threatening, yet uncontrollable event, such as the parent who gives the family car to a child who does not plan to return home until early next morning. Once the child has driven away, this parent cannot change the outcome in any way. The parent who constantly thinks about the potential dangers and

TABLE 4.2. Adaptiveness of Coping Styles in Controllable and Uncontrollable Situations

	Low monitoring/ high blunting	High monitoring/ low blunting
Uncontrollable situations	A: Reduces anxiety and frustration	C: Increases anxiety and frustration
Controllable situations	B: Interferes with execution of instrumental actions	D: Allows for execution of instrumental actions

complications that could harm the child will become anxious (most likely needlessly so), without being able to do anything to prevent such an outcome (Cell C). Rather than ruminating about the possible hazards of night driving (e.g., "Will she drive slowly if fatigued?"), this parent would do better to distract from thoughts about the child's activities and continue with his or her own evening plans (Cell A).

Further, since anxiety appears, in part, to be a function of being in the continual psychological presence of arousing danger signals (especially when these are objectively absent), those who excessively monitor for threatening cues may be prone to chronic anxiety. Even in nonaversive situations, such individuals may be unable to engage in the strategies outlined in Cell A of Table 4.2, and, therefore, may misinterpret neutral cues as danger signals or fail to detect signals of safety. Some research with snake phobics has suggested that, unlike nonphobics, these individuals cannot tune out psychologically from danger signals even in the absence of actual danger. That is, they worry about being bitten or poisoned by harmless snakes, and they scan for snakes in unlikely places such as a crowded city sidewalk (May, 1977).

Recent research further indicates that individuals with anxiety disorders selectively focus on cues about potential dangers (Mathews & MacLeod, 1985). This suggests that stress inoculation techniques that teach the art of minimal monitoring and maximal distraction (such as deep muscle relaxation, thought stopping, reinterpretation) should help accomplish psychological withdrawal from threat and thereby reduce anxiety (see, for example, Goldfried, Decenteceo, & Weinberg, 1974; Meichenbaum & Cameron, 1983; Ross, 1981). In ongoing research, we are investigating which strategies are optimal for different types of patients (e.g., hypertensives) and how they can best be instructed in the use of distraction and related psychological techniques (see also Steketee, Bransfield, Miller, & Foa, 1989).

Similarly, consider an individual facing a potentially frustrating situation such as ordering the house specialty while at a fine restaurant and, therefore, having to wait the additional time for the meal to be prepared (rather than opting for an immediately available standard dish). An individual who monitors the situation or fails to distract (by scanning the entrees at adjacent tables and watching for the waiter to return) will only become frustrated and will probably fill up on bread in the interim (Cell C). In contrast, an individual who distracts from reward-relevant cues will be less frustrated and more likely to have room left to enjoy the meal when it does arrive (Cell A).

Taken to excess, monitoring of reward-relevant cues and the inability to tune out from such information may produce chronic frustration and be implicated in disorders of self-control. For example, impulsive children tend to respond too quickly and without deliberation to cognitive and other tasks that require patience and forethought. They seem unable to process, cognitively, forthcoming outcomes in a way that will blunt or attenuate their reward-value, possibly because they engage in "hotter" pictorial mental representations about it rather than in more symbolic representations (Finch & Montgomery, 1973). We have found that it is possible to teach impulsive children to divert attention away from arousing or frustrating stimuli and that this, in turn, improves their delay tolerance (see Gallagher et al., 1988).

Conversely, when the threat is controllable (such as reducing one's risk for cancer by giving up cigarettes), monitoring for information enables the individual to regulate appropriately his or her behavior (Cell D). People who ignore information and distract from the health hazards of continuing to smoke will be unmotivated to take adaptive action and, therefore, put their lives in danger (Cell B). Individuals who fail to process extremely traumatic and earth-shattering experiences may also suffer ill effects and show greater and more prolonged disturbance (Solomon, Mikulincer, & Arad, 1988). In positively valenced situations, when opting for an immediate reward is a safer course than waiting for a deferred (but unlikely) gratification, monitoring for reward-relevant cues may prompt the individual into adaptive action ("A bird in the hand is worth two in the bush"). For example, an individual in need of a job who attends to cues about the job market will weigh all the possibilities and be in a position to make the best career choice (Cell D). In contrast, an individual who ignores information which suggests that the probability of finding ideal employment is low will miss out on available jobs while waiting for a better (but highly unlikely) future opportunity (Cell B). Consistent with this, research with disruptive children suggests that excessive blunting of reward-relevant cues may lead to behavior problems. Simply reminding kindergarten-age children with behavior-problems to perform required tasks is sometimes enough to improve their behavior (Tucker & O'Leary, 1982).

Within this framework, then, the ability to cope effectively with threat and frustration appears to depend not only on the ability to avoid cognitively and/or seek information, but also is determined by the individual's ability first to discriminate the relevant situational factors, and then to execute the cognitive strategy appropriate to the particular situational contingencies. Thus, individuals who are flexible in their choice of cognitive strategies generally should fare better than those who are inflexible. Indeed, inflexibility in self-regulatory patterns may be the hallmark of maladaptive coping (Mischel, 1984). For children and adults, individuals who inflexibly adopt a high monitoring/low blunting style may be prone to impulse control disorders in the context of deferred rewards and to anxiety disorders, even in the absence of dangerous or aversive events. In contrast, those who inflexibly adopt a low monitoring/high blunting style may fail to maximize positive outcomes (in the face of frustration) or to minimize negative outcomes (in the face of threat).

Conclusions

In conclusion, an adequate analysis of the coping process has to take account of the interaction of different cognitive preferences with contextual features. The studies reviewed here attempt to do both simultaneously, by concentrating on two fundamental strategies for dealing with stress-related situations. The main mode for coping with uncontrollable events involves cognitive avoidance, high blunting, turning off and tuning down threat-relevant information as a means of reducing arousal. When situational or individual considerations make this inappropriate or difficult, individuals switch to a coping mode which involves cognitive sensitization, high monitoring, turning on and tuning in to threat-relevant information. Further, the fit between individual differences in coping style and the specific properties of the situation appears to determine how well people cope: with low monitors/high blunters benefiting more from distraction and high monitors/low blunters benefiting more from information. This approach reanimates the concept of vigilance and avoidance. The reason it appears to work well is that it does not indirectly tap some global measure, but specifically taps the kinds of information people want.

Acknowledgment

I thank Denise Durbin, Linda Kraus, Margot Savage, Bill Shadel, and Kim Sproat for their assistance. This research was partially supported by the Robert Wood Johnson Foundation and Temple University Grant-In-Aid of Research.

References

Averill, J. R., & Rosenn, M. (1972). Vigilant and nonvigilant coping strategies and psychophysiological stress reactions during the anticipation of an electric shock. *Journal of Personality and Social Psychology, 23,* 128–141.

Bandura, A. (April 1979). Self-efficacy: An integrative construct. Invited address presented at *The Western Psychological Association,* San Diego.

Bandura, A. (1981). Self-referent thought: A development analysis of self-efficacy. In J. H. Flavell and L. D. Ross (Eds.), *Social cognitive development: Frontiers and possible futures* (pp. 200–239). London: Cambridge University Press.

Byrne, D. (1961). The repression-sensitization scale: Rationale, reliability and validity. *Journal of Personality and Social Psychology, 29,* 334–349.

Byrne, D. (1964). Repression-sensitization as a dimension of personality. In B. A. Maher (Ed.), *Progress in experimental personality research: Volume 1* (pp. 169–220). New York: Academic Press.

Carver, C. S., Scheier, M. F., & Weintraub, J. K. (1989). Assessing coping strategies: A theoretically based approach. *Journal of Personality and Social Psychology, 56,* 267–283.

Caspi, T. (1987). Reaction and perception of pain by women during childbirth. Unpublished manuscript, Bar-Ilan University.

Cohen, F., & Lazarus, R. S. (1973). Active coping processes, coping dispositions, and recovery from surgery. *Psychosomatic Medicine, 35,* 375–389.

Efran, J., Chorney, R. L., Ascher, L. M., & Lukens, M. D. (1989). Coping style, paradox, and the cold pressor task. *Journal of Behavioral Medicine, 12,* 91–103.

Egbert, L. D., Battit, G. E., Welsh, C. E., & Bartlett, M. K. (1964). Reduction of postoperative pain by encouragement and instruction of patients: A study of doctor-patient rapport. *The New England Journal of Medicine, 270,* 825–827.

Finch, A. J., & Montgomery, L. E. (1973). Reflection-impulsivity and information seeking in emotionally disturbed children. *Journal of Abnormal Child Psychology, 3,* 47–51.

Folkman, S., & Lazarus, R. S. (1985). If it changes it must be a process: Study of emotion and coping during three stages of a college examination. *Journal of Personality and Social Psychology, 48,* 150–170.

Gallagher, R., Miller, S. M., & Mischel, W. (1988). Self-regulatory strategies with delayed rewards: Implications for behavioral adjustment. Unpublished manuscript, Temple University.

Gard, D., Edwards, P. W., Harris, J., & McCormack, G. (1988). Sensitizing effects of pretreatment measures on cancer chemotherapy nausea and vomiting. *Journal of Consulting and Clinical Psychology, 56,* 80–84.

Goldfried, M., Decenteceo, E., & Weinberg, L. (1974). Systematic rational restructuring as a self-control technique. *Behavior Therapy, 5,* 247–257.

Goldstein, M. J. (1959). The relationship between coping and avoidance behavior and response to fear arousing propaganda. *Journal of Abnormal and Social Psychology, 58,* 247–252.

Goldstein, M. J., Jones, R. B., Clemens, T. L., Flagg, G. W., & Alexander, F. G. (1965). Coping style as a factor in psychophysiological response to a tension-arousing film. *Journal of Personality and Social Psychology, 1,* 290–302.

Lamping, D. L., & Catechis, C. G. (1989). Consistency of coping style between providers and recipients of social support during a stressful laboratory analogue. Presented at the meeting of the *Society of Behavioral Medicine,* San Francisco.

Langer, E. S., Janis, I. L., & Wolfer, J. A. (1975). Reduction in psychological stress in surgical patients. *Journal of Experimental Social Psychology, 11,* 155–165.

Lerman, C., Rimer, B., Blumberg, B., & Cristinzio, M. S. (1989). Effects of coping style and relaxation on conditioned side-effects of anticancer chemotherapy. Presented at the meeting of the *Association for the Advancement of Behavior Therapy,* Washington D.C.

Leventhal, H. (1989). Emotional and behavioral processes in the study of stress during medical procedures. In M. Johnston & L. Wallace (Eds.), *Stress and medical procedures* (pp. 3–35). Oxford: Oxford Science Medical Publications.

Mathews, A., & MacLeod, C. (1985). Selective processing of threat cues in anxiety states. *Behavior Research and Therapy, 23,* 563–569.

May, J. R. (1977). Psychophysiology of self-regulated phobic thoughts. *Behavior Therapy, 8,* 150–159.

Mechanic, D. (1980). The experience and reporting of common physical complaints. *Journal of Health and Social Behavior, 21,* 146–155.

Mechanic, D. (1983). Adolescent health and illness behavior: Review of the literature and a new hypothesis for the study of stress. *Journal of Human Stress, 9,* 4–13.

Meichenbaum, D., & Cameron, R. (1983). Stress inoculation training: Toward a general paradigm for training coping skills. In D. Meichenbaum & M. E. Jaremko (Eds.), *Stress reduction and prevention* (pp. 115–154). New York: Plenum Press.

Miller, S. M. (1979a). Controllability and human stress: Method, evidence and theory. *Behavior Research and Therapy, 17,* 287–304.

Miller, S. M. (1979b). Coping with impending stress: Psychophysiological and cognitive correlates of choice. *Psychophysiology, 16,* 572–581.

Miller, S. M. (1980a). When is a little information a dangerous thing? Coping with stressful life-events by monitoring vs. blunting. In S. Levine and H. Ursin (Eds.), *Coping and Health* (pp. 145–169). New York: Plenum Press.

Miller, S. M. (1980b). Why having control reduces stress: If I can stop the roller
    coaster I don't want to get off. In J. Garber and M. E. P. Seligman (Eds.),
    Human helplessness: Theory and applications (pp. 71–95). New York:
    Academic Press.
Miller, S. M. (1981). Predictability and human stress; Towards a clarification
    of evidence and theory. In L. Berkowitz (Ed.), *Advances in experimental
    social psychology: Vol. 14* (pp. 203–256). New York: Academic Press.
Miller, S. M. (1987). Monitoring and blunting: Validation of a questionnaire to
    assess styles of information-seeking under threat. *Journal of Personality
    and Social Psychology, 52,* 345–353.
Miller, S. M. (1989). Cognitive informational styles in the process of coping
    with threat and frustration. *Advances in Behavioral Research and Ther-
    apy, 11,* 223–234.
Miller, S. M. (in press). Individual differences in the coping process: What to
    know and when to know it. In B. Carpenter (Ed.), *Personal coping: Theory,
    research, and application.* New York: Praeger.
Miller, S. M., & Birnbaum, A. (1988). Putting the life back into life events:
    Toward a cognitive social learning analysis of the coping process. In S.
    Fisher & J. Reason (Eds.), *Life stress, cognition, and health,* (pp. 497–509).
    Chichester, England: Wiley.
Miller, S. M., & Birnbaum, A. (1989). When to whistle while you work: A
    cognitive social learning approach to coping and health. In J. J. Hurrell, S.
    L. Sauter, & C. Cooper (Eds.), *Job control and worker health* (pp. 237–251).
    Chichester, England: Wiley.
Miller, S. M., Brody, D. S., & Summerton, J. S. (1988a). Styles of coping with
    threat: Implications for health. *Journal of Personality and Social Psychol-
    ogy, 54,* 345–353.
Miller, S. M., Combs, C., & Stoddard, E. (1989a). Information, coping and
    control in patients undergoing surgery and stressful medical procedures.
    In A. Steptoe & A. Appels (Eds.), *Stress, personal control and health* (pp.
    107–130). Chichester, England: Wiley.
Miller, S. M., & Grant, R. (1979). The blunting hypothesis: A view of pre-
    dictability and human stress. In P. O. Sjoden, S. Bates, & W. S. Dockens
    (Eds.), *Trends in behavior therapy* (pp. 135–151). New York: Academic
    Press.
Miller, S. M., & Green, M. (1985). Coping with threat and frustration: Origins,
    nature and development. In M. Lewis & C. Saarni (Eds.), *Socialization of
    emotion: Vol. 5* (pp. 263–314). New York: Plenum Press.
Miller, S. M., Lack, E. R., & Asroff, S. (November 1981). Preference for control
    and the Type A coronary-prone behavior pattern. Presented at the
    Association for the Advancement of Behavior Therapy, Toronto.
Miller, S. M., Leinbach, A., & Brody, D. S. (1989b). Coping style in hyperten-
    sives: Nature and consequences. *Journal of Consulting and Clinical Psy-
    chology, 57,* 333–337.
Miller, S. M., & Mangan, C. E. (1983). The interacting effects of information
    and coping style in adapting to gynecologic stress: Should the doctor tell
    all? *Journal of Personality and Social Psychology, 45,* 223–236.

Miller, S. M., & Mischel, W. (in preparation). A social learning approach to information-seeking styles in the coping process.

Miller, S. M., Savage, M. L., & Mischel, W. (1988b). Children's patterns of coping with threat and deferred rewards. Unpublished manuscript, Temple University.

Mischel, W. (1973). Toward a cognitive social learning reconceptualization of personality. *Psychological Review, 80,* 252–283.

Mischel, W. (1974). Processes in delay of gratification. In L. Berkowitz (Ed.), *Advanced in experimental social psychology: Vol. 7* (pp. 249–292). New York: Academic Press.

Mischel, W. (1979). On the interface of cognition and personality. *American Psychologist, 34,* 740–754.

Mischel, W. (1984). Convergences and challenges in the search for consistency. *American Psychologist, 39,* 351–364.

Mischel, W., & Mischel, H. N. (1983). The development of children's knowledge of self-control strategies. *Child Development, 54,* 603–619.

Monat, A. (1976). Temporal uncertainty, anticipation time, and cognitive coping under threat. *Journal of Human Stress, 2,* 32–43.

Monat, A., Averill, J. R., & Lazarus, R. S. (1972). Anticipatory stress and coping reactions under various conditions of uncertainty. *Journal of Personality and Social Psychology, 24,* 237–253.

Phipps, S., & Zinn, A. B. (1986). Psychological response to amniocentosis: II. Effects of coping style. *American Journal of Medical Genetics, 25,* 143–148.

Rosenbaum, M. (1983). Learned resourcefulness as a behavioral repertoire for the self-regulation of internal events: Issues and speculations. In M. Rosenbaum, C. M. Franks, and Y. Jaffe (Eds.), *Perspectives on behavior therapy in the eighties* (pp. 54–73). New York: Springer Press.

Ross, A. O. (1981). *Child behavior therapy: Principles, procedures and empirical basis.* New york: Wiley and Sons.

Sime, A. M. (1976). Relationship of preoperative fear, type of coping, and information received about surgery to recover from surgery. *Journal of Personality and Social Psychology, 34,* 716–724.

Solomon, Z., Mikulincer, M., & Arad, R. (1988). Styles of information seeking under threats: Implications for combat-related post traumatic stress disorder. Unpublished manuscript, Israel Defense Forces Medical Corps, Department of Mental Health.

Sparks, G. G. (1989). Understanding emotional reactions to a suspenseful movie: The interaction between forewarning and preferred coping style. *Communication Monographs, 56,* 325–340.

Sparks, G. G., & Spirek, M. M. (1988). Individual differences in coping with stressful mass media: An activation-arousal view. *Human Communication Research, 15,* 195–216.

Steketee, G., Bransfield, S., & Miller, S. M., & Foa, E. B. (1989). The effect of information and coping style on the reduction of phobic anxiety. *Journal of Anxiety Disorders, 3,* 69–85.

Steptoe, A. (1986). Avoidant coping strategies: The relationship between repressive coping and preference for distraction. Unpublished manuscript, St. George's Hospital Medical School, University of London.

Steptoe, A., & O'Sullivan, J. (1986). Monitoring and blunting coping styles in women prior to surgery. *British Journal of Clinical Psychology, 25,* 143–144.

Tucker, C. M., & O'Leary, S. G. (1982). Reasons and reminder instructions: Their effects on problematic behavior of kindergarten children. *Cognitive Therapy and Research, 6,* 231–234.

Vernon, D. T. A., & Bigelow, D. A. (1974). Effect of information about a potentially stressful situation of responses to stress impact. *Journal of Personality and Social Psychology, 29,* 50–59.

Watkins, L. O., Weaver, L., & Odegaard, V. (1986). Preparation for cardiac catheterization: Tailoring the content of instruction to coping style. *Heart and Lung, 15,* 382–389.

Weiss, J. M. (1970). Somatic effects on predictable and unpredictable shock. *Psychosomatic Medicine, 32,* 397–409.

5

Help-Seeking Behavior as a Coping Resource

Arie Nadler

This chapter differs from many others in this volume in its conceptual orientation and range of topics. By focusing on help-seeking behavior, it is concerned with inter- rather than intrapersonal aspects of coping. It seeks to elucidate the processes involved when individuals cope with distress by seeking help from others.

In spite of this dissimilarity, this chapter has several common areas of overlap with other chapters in this volume. One dimension of similarity is the problem that is being dealt with. The issue at center of all the discussions is coping. When faced with a problem, an individual may do nothing and succumb passively to his or her grim situation. Or, people may take their fate into their own hands and act. If they decide to do so, they can rely on themselves, persist, and attempt to surmount the predicament on their own. Alternatively, the individual may choose to seek others' assistance. From this perspective, help-seeking and self-control/self-regulation are two sides of the same coin.

Beyond a common general problem, there is also a theoretical affinity between the present discussion and the other chapters in this volume. As will become evident through the following sections, this chapter draws on concepts such as perceived control, helplessness, and self-evaluation processes, which are also discussed in other pages of the present volume. One purpose of this chapter is be to note the conceptual links between the body of theory and research in the "behavioral-clinical tradition" that deals with effective coping (i.e., learned helplessness, learned resourcefulness, and self-regulation) and that included in the theory and research on the social psychology of help seeking.

Much of the chapter will be devoted to a review of conceptual and empirical developments in the area of help-seeking behavior. This review will be organized around two perspectives on the help-seeking phenomenon. In the first part, data and theory that relate to the psychological costs inherent in the seeking of help will be discussed. Here, studies and conceptions that have centered on the self-threatening aspects associated with the seeking of help, (i.e., public admission of one's inability) and inhibit one's willingness to seek help will be reviewed. The second part of the review will present efforts that view the seeking of help more positively. Here, data and theory that regard help-seeking as an instrumental behavior that can greatly facilitate problem solving will be considered. From this perspective, the seeking of help is viewed as a strategy no different from other strategies (e.g., persistence, self-help) that a person may adopt in overcoming a difficulty. Thus, the second part of the review will center on processes that facilitate an individual's readiness to rely on others for help. This review will set the stage for a final part, in which conceptual connections between theory and research on help-seeking, and the processes suggested in the coping literature will be considered.

Help-Seeking in Perspective: Its Place in the Social Psychology of Prosocial Action

Over the past 20 years, social psychologists have been increasingly concerned with the study of helping behavior. Any cursory look through the table of contents of major textbooks in social psychology would reveal that each devotes at least one chapter to this issue. This together with the fact that recent years have seen the publication of several volumes on this issue (e.g., Rushton & Sorrentino, 1981; Staub, Bar-Tal, Karylowski & Reykowski, 1984) attests to its central role in social psychology.

Although the titles of these works may vary (i.e., helping behavior, prosocial behavior), their contents are similar. All reflect interest in questions of: who helps whom, why, and when. Thus, for example, numerous studies explore the conditions that facilitate bystander intervention (Latane' & Nida, 1981), and a body of knowledge now exists on processes that govern the development of the helpful person (Eisenberg, 1982). In fact, much of past research has been interested in help-giving behavior and has neglected the full range of helping relations (cf., Nadler, 1983, for a fuller discussion of this issue).

In recent years, this one-sided emphasis has changed. A number of investigators have extended their outlook to explore helping relations as a dynamic process that unfolds over time: process which begins with a persons' awareness of a state of need, their decision to seek or not seek help (De Paulo, Nadler & Fisher, 1983), and their reactions to the receipt of help (Fisher, Nadler & De Paulo, 1983). Such an outlook on the phenomenon of helping raises new questions that have not been attended to before. Thus, for example, questions regarding the stigmatizing effects associated with help-seeking and help-receiving now occupy a more central place.

This new perspective on the social psychology of helping relations has been at least partly spurred by discussions on helping relations in a variety of applied settings. Discussions in the areas of clinical and rehabilitational psychology (Fischer, Winer, & Abramowitz, 1983; Ladieu, Hanfman, & Dembo, 1947; Nadler, Sheinberg, & Jaffe, 1981), analyses of the consequences of foreign aid programs (Gergen & Gergen, 1983), reports in the gerontology literature (e.g., Kalish, 1967; Lipman & Sterne, 1962), and writings on social welfare programs (Pettigrew, 1983) have all noted that the experience of being helped can be best construed as a mixed blessing. On the one hand, being helped contains many positive aspects. Help is often instrumental in alleviating a current state of need, and it often conveys signs of caring and concern from the helper to the recipient. On the other hand, however, being helped can be a self-threatening experience because of the implied inferiority, dependency, and inadequacy that are inherent in this culture in the role of being a recipient. The fact that dependency stands in sharp contrast to the deeply ingrained norm of self-reliance in this culture (Bellah, Madsen, Sullivan, Swidler, & Tipton, 1985; Merton, 1968) amplifies this self-threat. Because of this self-threatening aspect of receiving help, people often refrain from seeking needed help and react negatively to its receipt (e.g., Nadler, Fisher, & De-Paulo, 1983).

This mixed blessing aspect of helping relations has received a conceptual treatment in the recent work of several investigators (e.g., Ames, 1983; Rosen, 1983). Fisher, Nadler, & Whitcher-Alagna (1982) have given this concern a systematic expression by proposing that a parsimonious account of help-seeking and help-receiving can be best achieved by identifying the degree of relative self-threat and self-support in aid, which is determined by conceptually relevant situational and personal variables.

A full description of this model is beyond the scope of the present chapter, and the reader is referred elsewhere for such a detailed account (i.e., Fisher et al., 1982; Nadler & Fisher, 1986). However, since its principles have guided much of the research that will be presented in later sections, its essentials will be reviewed. The model assumes that when aid-related conditions render the receipt of help a supporting experience a cluster of positive recipient reactions occur (e.g., positive affect, favorable evaluations, etc). This cluster of positive responses includes an enhanced willingness to seek help. If however, the receipt of help includes a high degree of self-threat, a cluster of negative responses (e.g., lower self-evaluations, unfavorable evaluations of the helper) occurs. This cluster of negative responses includes a relative reluctance to seek help. Of importance to the present discussion is the assertion that individuals will not seek help if aid-related conditions render the receipt of help a self-threatening experience (Nadler, 1987).

Help-Seeking Dilemma: Psychological Costs Versus Instrumental Benefits

Taken from this perspective, the person who needs assistance is seen as caught up in a "help-seeking dilemma" (Nadler, 1983). On the one hand, seeking help is likely to expedite solutions of current problems. From this perspective, seeking help is an instrumental-task-oriented behavior qualitatively similar to other modes of active and adaptive coping efforts such as persistence (cf. Rosen, 1983). On the other hand, help-seeking is associated with psychological costs (i.e., admitting failure and inadequacy to self and others). Until the person seeks help, he or she may still hope to overcome the problem alone and retain a sense of independence. By actively seeking help the person is making a behavioral commitment to a self-definition of dependency and relative inferiority vis-à-vis the helper. What are the variables that "tip" the scales towards either side of this dilemma?

As noted earlier, one line of research and theory has centered on the psychological costs in help-seeking, whereas a second has explored variables that increase the salience of the instrumental aspects in help-seeking. The next sections will be devoted to a review of these two lines of study. A final section will consider the integration of these two lines of research with concepts suggested by the self-control literature discussed in other parts of this volume. Before continuing, it should be noted that the following review is not intended to be an exhaustive review of research done in the area. Rather, it intends to provide the reader with a view on the kind of research done and the explanations used. The interested reader is referred elsewhere for more comprehensive accounts (i.e., DePaulo et al., 1983; Fisher et al., 1982; Nadler, 1986; Nadler, DePaulo & Fisher,1983; Nadler & Fisher, 1986).

Cost of Seeking Help

Research in this line has tried to identify situational and personality conditions that moderate the relative weight of threat and support in aid. Regarding situational conditions, two distinct classes of variables have been explored: context-related and helper-related variables. In the first category, one finds studies that have looked at variables which define the context of the helping transaction (e.g., whether or not one remains anonymous when seeking help; the nature of the problem on which help is sought, etc.). The second group of studies has looked at the effects of the characteristics of the helper (e.g., his or her attractiveness) on willingness to seek help.

Situational Variables

Context Related: Normativeness, Centrality, and Anonymity

Normativeness and Ego-centrality

In a pioneering study in the help-seeking literature, Tessler and Schwartz (1972) have examined the effects of situational and personality variables on help-seeking behavior. The effects of the situational variables of "normativeness" and centrality of need, and the personality variables of self-esteem and achievement orientation on help seeking-were examined. Because the "personality" findings will be discussed at some length in a later section, the rationale and data relevant to the situational variables will be discussed here.

Tessler and Schwartz reasoned that if a person knows that the failure that brought about the need for assistance is normative (i.e., many other people failed at the same task), he or she is less likely to attribute the need to internal reasons (e.g., lack of ability) than in a case in which the failure is not normative (i.e., most of the other people do not need help on a similar task). Thus, a normative state of need should facilitate external attributions for failure and render the seeking of help relatively nonthreatening.

Another context variable that is likely to moderate the self-threat/ support in aid is the ego-centrality of the task on which help is needed. When a task on which a person needs help is ego-central (e.g., one believes that his or her need, reflects on qualities such as intelligence), admitting inferiority by seeking help is potentially self-threatening. When the need for help reflects on personal qualities that are not central to one's feelings of esteem (e.g., inferiority on manual dexterity) admitting inferiority by seeking help is relatively nonthreatening.

Thus, one should be more likely to seek help when the state of need is seen as non-ego-central than when it is perceived as ego-central.

To test these predictions, first-year women college students were asked to rate the degree of a neuroticism in a taped discussion (i.e., an ambiguous and difficult task) and were told they could consult "guidelines" that were conspicuously placed on the experimenter's desk. Latency of help-seeking (i.e., how much time elapsed until a subject decided to seek help) served as a dependent measure. Normativeness of need for help was manipulated by informing half the subjects that in previous runs of the experiment many or few students have found themselves in need for such consultation (i.e., high or low normativeness, respectively). Regarding the ego-centrality variable, subjects in the ego-central need state were told that performance on the task reflects on I.Q. and mental hygiene, whereas subjects in the non-ego-central need state condition were told that performance is not related to such personal qualities.

The data indicate that in line with expectations subjects sought more help when the state of need was defined as normative and more help under non-ego-central than ego-central conditions (i.e., normativeness and centrality main effects). Of interest is that a self-esteem by centrality interaction indicates that high self-esteem individuals were more intensely affected by the centrality manipulation than were low self-esteem individuals. Yet, this finding and its implications will be discussed in a later section.

These and other findings (e.g., Nadler, 1987; Nadler et al., 1983) and theoretical discussions (e.g., Nadler, 1986; Nadler & Fisher, 1984; 1986; Rosen, 1983) indicate that the context characteristics of normativeness and centrality affect help-seeking in a conceptually consistent manner. A need for help that is seen by the person in need as non-normative (i.e., most of other people do not need help in a similar context) and/or ego-central (i.e., reflects inadequacy on ego relevant dimensions) induces a greater degree of potential threat to self-esteem than do states of need that are seen as normative and/or non-ego-central, respectively. Under these conditions, the costs involved in seeking help seem greater than the costs incurred by not seeking it, and the person solves the help-seeking dilemma by avoiding help seeking.

Public-Anonymous Nature of the Helping Interaction

Another context variable that has been explored in this context is the anonymity or identifiability of the person seeking help. A person who seeks help and is identifiable is making a public admission of need.

Such an admission of need has been shown to be more damaging than a private admission of failure (Wallston, 1976). Thus, a person should be more likely to seek help when anonymous than when identifiable.

Research has supported this proposition. Nadler and Porat (1978) found that the afore described effects of normativeness on help-seeking occur only under conditions of anonymity. When subjects were given the safety of anonymity, they sought more help if they had believed the state of need to be normative than nonnormative. This finding replicated the findings of Tessler and Schwartz (1972). When identifiable, however, subjects refrained from seeking help regardless of normativeness of state of need. These data indicate that an important context variable that affects degree of self-threat in aid is the public or private nature of the help-seeking event. In the study described above, anonymity could be conceptualized as a necessary condition for help-seeking to have occurred. Only when anonymity was secured were the effects of other variables (e.g., normativeness) evident.

In a related manner, Shapiro (1983) emphasized the facilitating role of anonymity on help-seeking by using Modigliani's conception of embarrassment (Modigliani 1968; 1971). Adapting this conception to the context of help-seeking, Shapiro (1978) reasoned that since embarrassment occurs only when others view one's behavior as violating expectations, individuals should be more embarrassed and seek less help when their request is to be made in front of an audience. In support of this prediction, Shapiro (1978) reports that those in the private help-seeking conditions sought more help than those in the public help seeking conditions. This effect was especially pronounced when performance was made to be important for subjects (mean percentages of help-seeking were 88% and 33%, respectively).

An interesting question at this juncture relates to the nature of the audience that observes the seeking of help. In the study reported by Shapiro (1978), the audience was passive. Yet, in many real life situations, the audience is active. In fact, at times, an audience of varying sizes may itself be the provider of help. For example, a person in need may be faced with one, two, or more helpers (e.g., one professional helper versus a committee of professional helpers). Would the same audience effects hold when the audience is not passive but is made up of the helpers themselves? Williams and Williams (1983) have given this question an affirmative answer. In their study, they found that subjects sought significantly less help when there were three helpers who would hear the request for help as compared to only one.

It seems that the costs incurred by making a public admission of need by seeking help are magnified in proportion to the audience size. Using Latane's (1981) social impact theory as an explanatory framework, Williams and Williams conclude by stating: "Not only are individuals less likely to offer help as the number of bystanders increases . . . people are also less likely to ask for help as the number of others present increases . . . From anyone's perspective, large number of potential helpers are simply not useful" (p. 199).

In all, public seeking of help has a greater self-threat potential than a private request for help. People in need are less willing to use others' assistance when they feel that they are publicly exposed when making such a request. Conceptually, various constructs have been employed to deal with this phenomenon (i.e., embarrassability, Shapiro, 1983; social impact theory, Williams & Williams, 1983; perceived inadequacy, Rosen, 1983). But underneath all these explanations runs the statement that public help-seeking increases the threat to feelings of esteem, and, therefore, it inhibits help-seeking.

On the applied level, the conclusion above has been amply demonstrated in various community services. In fact, one of the underlying reasons for the success of various hot line helping programs (e.g., Hill & Harmon, 1976) seems to reside in the fact that the caller does not identify him or herself when requesting assistance. Using this logic to comment on the adequacy of various social welfare programs, Shapiro (1983) analyzes the effectiveness of food stamps programs. Since programs based on the idea of food stamps for the poor increase the visibility of help-seeking, they may inhibit the needy's willingness to seek help.

In sum, when context variables (a) facilitate internal attributions for the need in help (i.e., low normativeness), on (b) a psychologically relevant personal quality (i.e., central help), and (c) the help-seeking encounter is public, the resultant degree of self-threat is high and individuals choose not to seek help.

Helper's Characteristics

As many help-seeking situations are interpersonal encounters (i.e., a person in need solicits another person's assistance), a number of studies have been concerned with the effects of helper's characteristics on help-seeking. The basic question here is as follows: Does the helper's identity affect willingness to seek help? Exploring this question, one line of research has studied the effects of the overall similarity and social proximity between the helper and the recipient on help seeking. Another line of research has examined the effects of helper's attractiveness on help-seeking behavior.

Helper's Similarity and Social Proximity

Regarding the effects of helper similarity and social proximity, two conflicting lines of theory and research present themselves. On the one hand, several investigators note the more intense level of social support inherent in help from a close other. These investigators suggest that individuals will be more likely to disclose inadequacy by seeking help if the helper is a socially close other. The other line of research discusses the adverse consequences of negative comparison inherent in being dependent on someone similar to oneself, who serves as a frame of reference for self-judgments.

Regarding the first line of study, the social support literature indicates that individuals prefer to seek help from socially close others. Gourash (1978) reports that people turn to professional helpers only after they have sought help from a close relation. On the basis of this literature, Wills (1983) notes that "the evidence from community studies consistently shows that people tend to seek help first from friends and family members" (p. 133). In support of this conclusion, several controlled studies indicate that offers of help are more easily accepted from friends and family members than from strangers (e.g., Bar-Tal, Bar-Zohar, Greenberg & Hermon, 1978; Weinstein et al., 1969 ; Shapiro, 1975).

In analyzing this phenomenon, Clark (1983) makes the distinction between communal and exchange relations (cf., Clark & Mills, 1979). In communal relations (i.e., relations between friends, family members), people expect assistance to be based on need considerations. Thus, one expects a person with whom he or she is in communal relations to help him or her because they need help and not because one had helped the other person in the past. Reciprocity considerations are paramount when the relations are defined as exchange relations (i.e., between strangers). Because of the expectation that close others should be more sensitive to one's need, individuals seek more help from close others than from strangers.

Considering the concept of social proximity from the vantage point of social comparison theory portrays an opposite picture. Social comparison theory (Festinger, 1954) suggests that only individuals similar to oneself serve for purposes of self-evaluation. Accordingly, the self-threatening elements inherent in the seeking of help (i.e., admitting inadequacy) would be more intense when the helper is a psychologically close other who serves as a frame of reference for self-judgments than when the helper is a stranger. Consequently, individuals would avoid seeking help from someone whom they regard as similar or otherwise socially close.

In support of this prediction, Clark, Gotay, and Mills (1974) found that individuals sought less help from attitudinal similar others than from attitudinal dissimilar others when they saw no opportunity to reciprocate the help. In the context of recipient reactions to aid, it has been repeatedly found that individuals react more negatively to the receipt of help from a similar than from a dissimilar other (e.g., Fisher & Nadler, 1974; Nadler, Fisher & Streufert, 1976;) and from a friend than from a stranger (Nadler, Fisher & Ben Itzhak, 1983). In the organizational literature, Blau (1964) has discussed the reluctance in seeking advice from peers in terms of the needy person's fear to lose status by exposing need ("weakness") to someone similar to him or herself (cf., also Glidewell, Tucker, Todt & Cox, 1983).

To recapitulate, regarding the effects of social proximity on help-seeking, the data portray a complex picture. The "social support" line of thinking asserts that the positive elements inherent in close relations facilitate seeking help from socially close others. The "comparison stress" line of thinking notes that close relationships include a more intense level of "comparison stress," and, therefore, social proximity inhibits help-seeking. How can these two lines of research be reconciled?

A closer inspection of the concepts employed suggests that this empirical inconsistency is more apparent than real. The logic of threat to self-esteem model of reactions to help (i.e., Fisher et al., 1982; Nadler & Fisher, 1986) and help-seeking (Nadler, 1986) suggests that self-threatening elements in aid would be present only when the task on which help is given is relevant for self-evaluation (e.g., the person in need perceives the task as reflecting on his or her intelligence). When the task on which help is needed is not relevant for self-evaluation, the information of dependency and relative "inferiority" implied in help should not produce any comparison stress. The effects of social proximity on help-seeking should be moderated by the ego-relevance of the task on which help is needed.

To test this possibility, Nadler (1987) had subjects perform an anagram task. Half the subjects were told that performance on the task reflected one's creative abilities (i.e., an ego-central condition) and the other half were told that performance was related to chance factors (i.e., non-ego-central conditions). Also, half the subjects were under the impression that their partner was someone similar to themselves (i.e., social proximity), whereas the other half were under the impression that their partner was dissimilar to themselves. Since some of the anagrams were made to be extremely difficult, subjects were given the opportunity to seek help from their partner. In line with predictions, seeking of help from a socially close other was self-threatening only when the need for help reflected on ego-central qualities. The results indicate that subjects in the similar other-ego-central task condition sought least help, whereas subjects in the similar other-non-ego relevant task sought most help.

Further support for these findings is available from a recent study (Nadler et al., 1983) of recipient's reactions to being helped. This study found that compared to individuals who were helped by a stranger to accomplish an ego-central task, subjects who had received such help from a friend had worse reactions (e.g., less positive affect, less favorable evaluations of the helper) to the receipt of help. On the other hand, subjects who had been helped by a friend on a non-ego-central task had better reactions to the receipt of such help than subjects who received non-ego-relevant help from a stranger.

These data reconcile the afore described empirical controversy. In the context of helping relations, social proximity is a two-edged sword. Under certain conditions, it leads to more help-seeking and better reactions to the receipt of help, whereas under different conditions it inhibits help-seeking and is associated with negative reactions to the receipt of help. When the task on which help is needed is ego-central, the comparison stress inherent in seeking and receiving help outweighs the self-supporting elements, which are otherwise inherent in receiving help from a socially close other. These data and their conceptualization are also congruent with Tesser's (1988) recent self-esteem maintenance model.

Helper's Attractiveness

Another helper-related variable which has received systematic attention in this context is helper's attractiveness. The rationale here was that since attractive others are also perceived as a more potent source of self-evaluation (Zanna & Pack, 1975) individuals may feel more reluctant to expose their weakness by seeking help from an attractive as opposed to an unattractive helper.

In the first study to test this hypothesis (Stokes & Bickman 1974), women subjects were to work on a technically complex task on which they could seek help from a physically attractive or unattractive woman helper. The data indicate that in line with prediction, subjects chose to seek more help from a physically unattractive than a physically attractive woman helper. In further support for the greater evaluation apprehension potential of an attractive helper, Nadler (1980) has found that women subjects chose to seek less help from a physically attractive than unattractive other woman only when they expected a future interaction with their helper. When the experimental procedures made it clear that a meeting between oneself and the helper will not take place, helper's attractiveness did not affect subjects' willingness to seek help from her.

The effects of helper's attractiveness on help-seeking are more complex when the gender combination of the helper-recipient pair is considered. Nadler et al. (1982) have explored how the physical attractiveness of a man or woman helper affects men's and women's willingness to seek help. The results of this study replicate the findings of the earlier investigations in that in same gender combinations (i.e., man helper-man subject; woman helper-woman subject), subjects sought less help from a physically attractive than unattractive helper. Yet, in opposite-gender combinations, the highest level of help-seeking occurred when a woman subject encountered a physically attractive man helper, and the least help-seeking occurred when a man subject encountered a physically attractive woman helper.

On the basis of these data, Nadler et al. (1982) suggested that the decision as to whether or not to seek help involves self-presentation considerations. Such a behavioral decision may be motivated by "face-saving" or "ingratiation" concerns. If the norms surrounding the context of the helping interaction imply that the person presents him or herself as independent and self-reliant then help-seeking is inhibited because of the person's motivation to "save face." If however, the situation is such that the person would benefit by presenting him or herself as weak and dependent, ingratiation through help-seeking occurs. The afore described data suggest that gender-role norms is one determinant of either of these two situational demands. The male gender role focuses on elements of independence, whereas the female gender role focuses on dependency (Gross & McMullen, 1983; Nadler, Maler, & Friedman, 1984). As noted by the self-presentation literature, the impact of self-presentation concerns is greater with attractive others who are a more potent source of self-evaluation (Zanna & Pack, 1975). Thus, the presence of a physically attractive woman served to intensify this process: Male subjects sought least help from a physically attractive woman. Conversely, the same norms allow a woman in need to be dependent on a man helper. The physically attractive man aroused motivation for ingratiation: Women sought most help from a physically attractive man.

On a more general level, it has been suggested that when one considers physical attractiveness as a special case of social status (cf., Berger, Rosenholtz & Zelditch 1980), then the data may be phrased in the language of "status-organizing processes." When interacting with a "higher-status" other, motivation for ingratiation is high. One may, therefore, seek help as a way of accepting the status discrepancy.

On the whole, this section indicates that the identity of the helper is a major determinant of the self-threat inherent in receiving aid. It seems that helper-related variables that render him or her as a more potent source of self-evaluation for the recipient (i.e., a socially close other who induces more "comparison stress"; a physically attractive other who induces a higher level of evaluation apprehension) inhibit the seeking of help. In line with the logic of the threat to self-esteem model of help-seeking (Nadler, 1986) and help-receiving (Nadler & Fisher, 1986) this self-threat is present only in ego-relevant tasks.

Personality Variables: Self-Esteem and Help-Seeking

The preceding sections have focused on the effects of situational variables that define the helping interaction on psychological costs in help-seeking. Yet, since threat to feelings of esteem is conceptualized as a major determinant of help-seeking behavior (e.g., Ames, 1983; Rosen, 1983; Shapiro, 1983), it is logical to assume that a key variable that predicts and explains willingness to seek help is the person's level of self-esteem. High and low self-esteem persons are likely to be differentially sensitive to the self-threat and self-support inherent in seeking help and display differential degrees of willingness to partake in such behavior.

Vulnerability Versus Consistency Predictions

The task of making specific predictions as to whether the high or low self-esteem person will be more sensitive to the potential self-threat in aid is not an easy one. Two opposite predictions present themselves in this context. These predictions were labeled by Tessler and Schwartz (1972) as "vulnerability" and "consistency" hypotheses.

The vulnerability position suggests that since the low self-esteem person has very few positive self-cognitions, they are more vulnerable to incoming negative self-information than are high self-esteem individuals. This leads to the prediction that if receiving help is potentially self-threatening, low self-esteem individuals would be more sensitive than the high self-esteem persons to this self-threat. Phrased in operational terms, this approach suggests that low self-esteem individuals would be less likely than high self-esteem individuals to disclose need by seeking help.

An opposite prediction stems from a consistency approach. This conception relies on the assumption that negative information about the self is disturbing only when it is inconsistent with existing self-cognitions. Since the elements of relative inferiority and dependency inherent in receiving help are more inconsistent with the existing positive self-cognitions of the high self-esteem individual, being helped should be more disturbing for the high than for the low self-esteem recipient. For the low self-esteem recipient, the information of relative inferiority and dependency is relatively consistent with existing self-cognitions and is, therefore, less threatening. Phrased in operational terms, the consistency approach suggests that, other things being equal, high self-esteem people would be less likely to seek needed help than would low self-esteem individuals.

What is the empirical evidence regarding these two conflicting predictions? In the following sections, data bearing on the validity of each position will be reviewed.

Base Relationships: Empirical Evidence

In the study by Tessler and Schwartz (1972), described earlier, subjects were divided on the basis of their scores on a self-esteem scale into high and low self-esteem groups. As noted previously, this investigation explored the effects of the normativeness and ego-centrality of the need for help on help-seeking behavior. Regarding effects of subjects' self-esteem, an ego-centrality by self-esteem interaction indicates that high self-esteem individuals were more sensitive than low self-esteem people to the self-threat associated with help on an ego-central task. When the task was described as ego-relevant, high self-esteem individuals sought significantly less help than did low self-esteem individuals. Such differences were not found when the task was described as non-ego-relevant.

The above findings support a consistency hypothesis in this context. Further support for the consistency formulation has been provided by Nadler (1987). In this study, described in a preceding section, subjects could seek help from a socially close or a socially distant other on an ego-central or noncentral task. Here also, subjects were divided on the basis of their scores on the Coopersmith (1967) self-esteem scale into high and low self-esteem groups. As noted earlier, highest self-threat existed in the central task-socially close other condition. In line with a consistency prediction, the least amount of help-seeking was evident for high self-esteem subjects in this cell (means for high and low self-esteem groups were 1.31 and 2.11, respectively, $p < 0.05$).

Self-Esteem, Reciprocity, and Help-Seeking

Taken together, the above two studies indicate that under conditions that render the request for help a self-threatening event for the needy person (e.g., when there is a high level of "comparison stress" in aid), high self-esteem individuals are more sensitive to this self-threat and seek it less. Further support for this conclusion is available from a recent study that has examined the way in which help-seeking behavior of high and low self-esteem individuals is affected by the perceived opportunity for future reciprocity (Nadler, Mayseless, Peri, & Chemerinski, 1985).

Several theoretical discussions have noted that a central norm that governs many forms of interpersonal exchange is the norm of equity in social exchange (Hatfield & Sprecher, 1983). Applying this notion to the context of helping relations, Greenberg and Westcott (1983) have proposed that individuals who enter nonreciprocal helping relations suffer a psychological distress that he termed "feeling of indebtedness." This affective distress is aroused by the deviation from the internalized values associated with the norm of equity in personal relations. As such, this affective state is similar to what has been previously termed "threat to feelings of esteem."

Applying the finding that high and low self-esteem people are differentially sensitive to the self-threat in aid suggests that they would also be similarly affected by whether or not they expect to be able to reciprocate the help that they need. More specifically, in line with the afore mentioned findings that supported a consistency approach in this context, high self-esteem people should be more concerned about their equity with others. They should therefore (a) assign greater importance to reciprocity in interpersonal relations and (b) seek less help if future reciprocity is not expected than when it is.

To test these predictions, two studies were conducted. The first consisted of correlating subjects' scores on the Rosenberg self-esteem scale (Rosenberg, 1965) with a specially constructed Sensitivity to Reciprocity Questionnaire. The results of this study indicated a significant positive relationship between the two measures: The higher the person's self-esteem score, the more was reciprocity in interpersonal relations important to him or her. A second study showed that these differential levels of commitment to the norm of reciprocity affected actual help-seeking behavior. When reciprocity had not been foreseeable, high self-esteem individuals sought less help than when it was. Help-seeking behavior of low self-esteem individuals was not affected by whether or not reciprocity had been expected.

Finally, Nadler and Fux (1985) have studied the role of "self-defensive" and "self-consistency" needs in this context. In this study, subjects' help-seeking behavior was negatively related to their scores on self-esteem and ego defensiveness scales. Subsequent analyses indicate that although defensiveness scores explain part of the help-seeking variance, the amount of variance explained by self-esteem is significantly larger. These findings lend further support to the role of self-consistency explanations as the most parsimonious in this context.

Beyond the above studies, which provide direct support for the consistency hypothesis in the help-seeking context, research on recipient reactions to aid provides further, albeit somewhat indirect, support. Nadler et al. (1976, 1979) report that when the helping interaction contained a high level of self-threat potential (i.e., high level of donor-recipient similarity), high self-esteem individuals were more self-threatened than low self-esteem persons by the receipt of help. This greater self-threat led to unfavorable recipient's reactions (i.e., worse self-evaluations and affective distress). It is important to note that these effects of self-esteem on recipient reactions to aid were evident when self-esteem was defined on the basis of subjects' scores on a self-esteem scale (Nadler et al., 1976) and also when self-esteem was experimentally induced (Nadler et al., 1979).

Empirical Support in Applied Settings

Before concluding, it should be noted that a number of studies concerned with help-seeking in applied settings report findings that concur with the above results. In the organizational literature, Burke and Weir (1976) report that low self-esteem employees are more likely to seek needed advice than are high self-esteem employees. Weiss and Knight (1980) took this finding one step further and showed that low self-esteem workers succeeded more than high self-esteem people on tasks that required cooperation and consultation. This success was attributed to the greater willingness of low self-esteem individuals to rely on existing sources of assistance. Weiss and Knight labeled this phenomenon as "the utility of humility." Having a high self-esteem is not always beneficial. In situations that demand that one foregoes his or her independence and be dependent on others' assistance to accomplish a given task, high self-esteem individuals may suffer because of their unwillingness to enter dependency roles.

In a recent study, Hobfoll and London (1985) interviewed Israeli women whose husbands were in active military duty during the 1982 war in Lebanon. The results indicate that for women characterized as possessing high coping traits (i.e., high on self-esteem and self-efficacy scales), receiving support and intimacy from significant others was associated with higher levels of emotional strain (correlations between "intimacy with friends," "amount of social support," and measures of emotional strain were 0.54 and 0.38, respectively). For women characterized as low in coping traits (i.e., low on self-esteem and self-efficacy scales), there was no significant relationship between indices of social support received from other intimates and emotional strain. If anything, an opposite trend suggests that the more the intimacy received from friends, the less the emotional strain felt by these women ($r = -0.17$).

From an overall perspective, the following conclusions emerge: (a) When situational conditions highlight the salience of the self-threat potential in aid, high self-esteem individuals are more affected by this self-threat and choose not to seek needed help. (b) This phenomenon occurs regardless of the specific nature of the self-threat involved (i.e., donor–recipient social proximity; inability to reciprocate; task centrality). (c) The findings seem most parsimoniously explained by self-consistency processes.

Instrumental Benefits in Help-Seeking

The discussion thus far has centered on the affective ego threatening aspects of seeking help. This discussion considered the costs associated with the seeking of help. Yet, as noted by several authors, help-seeking is not always governed by ego threat considerations. At times, seeking assistance from others is an instrumental response to current difficulty. The person may seek assistance in order to bypass a difficulty on the road to future success and task completion. In the following sections, research concerned with these instrumental aspects will be discussed.

The review of this research will be organized around three major concepts that have been used in the analysis of the instrumental aspects of help seeking: (a) attributional analysis, (b) focus of attention, and (c) perceived control. As is the case with many overviews of this kind, these three concepts have a high degree of theoretical overlap, and the distinction is made for sake of clarity of presentation.

Attributional Analysis

Attribution theorists and researchers tell us that performance attributions for past failures often serve an ego defensive function. Thus, a student who failed may use a number of excuses to avoid the attribution that lack of ability was the reason for the unsuccessful performance (Covington & Omelich, 1979). In a similar manner, Ames (1983) suggests that attributional processes may serve to disarm the ego-threatening elements in seeking help and highlight the instrumental benefits of seeking it. When this is the case, the person is likely to show an enhanced willingness to utilize existing sources of assistance.

This occurs when (a) the need for help is attributed to lack in specific skill while the person maintains an overall positive view of global ability; (b) the person believes that he or she controls future success (i.e., attributions for the state of need involve lack of effort explanations, and discard external excuses). Viewing these attributional elements in one statement may sound like "I am basically O.K., but I did not try hard enough and there are no external forces that bar future improvement if I put my mind to it." Such a statement reflects the maintenance of a positive view of self and a sense of control over future performance. Such an attributional pattern is labeled by Ames "help-relevant attributions."

In a study designed to test the proposition that such an attributional pattern is linked to greater willingness to seek help, Ames and Lau (1982) offered students to attend review sessions. As might have been expected, students who had failed the first test were more willing to attend the review sessions than those who had succeeded in this first test. Of greater importance in this context is the finding that low performers were more likely to attend the helping session when their attributions for performance in the first test matched the afore discussed help-relevant attributional pattern.

Focus of Attention and Help-Seeking

Of relevance here is Nichols' reanalysis of achievement motivation (Nichols, 1980). Nichols argues for two kinds of ability evaluations in achievement settings. In the first, the person's evaluations are based on mastering a new task or bettering past performance. In this case the individual is assumed to be focused on the task and to process task-relevant information. Nichols has termed a person whose achievement behavior is characterized by the above features as displaying "task-involved achievement." In contrast, a person's achievement behavior may be "ego-involved achievement." In this case, the person judges his or her own worth on the basis of comparison with others. He or she is more self-aware and concerned with whether or not he or she is able, rather than whether or not, his or her's task performance has gotten better. It is further argued that the ego-involved personal orientation is more likely to be associated with affective and evaluative reactions. Under such an ego-involved achievement orientation, help-seeking is likely to be associated with ego-threat.

This conception has many implications for the issue at hand. As noted by Ames, the help-relevant attributional pattern closely resembles Nichols' description of the task-involved orientation: The person's attention is focused on task-relevant properties, and the role of self-evaluation is minimized. Such an attentional focus should facilitate help-seeking. On the other hand, ego-involved achievement orientation closely parallels the conditions described as conducive for ego-threat. Such attentional focus should inhibit help-seeking.

Similar positions regarding the links between attention (i.e., on task versus self) and help-seeking have been made by several investigators. Research spurred by Duval and Wicklunds's self-awareness theory (1972) and more recent restatements of the theory (Carver, 1979) indicate that individuals who are made self-aware or possess such a dispositional tendency are more self-critical than those who are not self-aware. Based on this research, Rosen (1983) has suggested that under conditions of heightened self-awareness people in need of help would be relatively unwilling to seek it because of the salience of the self-threatening implications. Rosen (1983) notes the lack of research to test this proposition and cites only one study that bears on this prediction (La Morto-Corse & Carver, 1980). In this study, the authors attribute the differences in help-seeking between people characterized as high and low in private self-consciousness (i.e., the personality analog of self-awareness) (Scheier, Fenigstein, & Buss, 1975) to the greater sensitivity of the highs to the self-threatening potential in aid.

In a similar vein, De Paulo, Brown, and Greenberg (1983) have recently suggested that the existence of instrumental versus evalua-tive-threatening aspects in help-seeking may be moderated by the person's focus of attention. When attention is focused on the task (i.e., one's own level of success and failure on the task), the instrumental aspects of help-seeking are likely to become paramount. When atten-tion is focused on the self, (i.e., on one's performance relative to others), the ego-evaluative aspects of help-seeking are likely to be dominant. In the first case, help-seeking is likely to be pursued as an instru-mental task-completion activity. In the second case, the self-threaten-ing elements in aid are likely to inhibit one's willingness to use as-sistance because of the negative self-implications that such a behavior entails.

Similar predictions would be made if one borrowed from other theoretical models which deal with the self-environment attentional focus. Thus, research in the area of self- differentiation (e.g., Nadler, Goldberg, & Jaffe, 1982; Witkin, Goodenough, & Oltman, 1979) sug-gests that relative to the non self-differentiated individual (i.e., field dependent) self-differentiated (i.e., field independent) people will be more task oriented and view the seeking of help from an instrumental perspective.

In all, looking at the common theoretical variance between the aforementioned concepts suggests that individuals who attend to self-evaluative elements in achievement situations (e.g., ego-oriented; high in self-consciousness; and relatively nondifferentiated) are less likely to seek help than their opposite counterparts (i.e., task-oriented; low in self-consciousness; self-differentiated) who adopt a task rather than an ego orientation. This difference is likely to be maximized when the task on which help is needed reflects on ego-central qualities. At this stage there is not much evidence which bears directly on this hypothesis. Yet, the fact that independent sources of theoretical speculation suggest the same direction, points to the importance of considering attentional mechanisms in the study of help seeking.

Perceived Control

A third element which facilitates an instrumental perspective on help seeking is the individual's perceived control over future outcomes. Several writers have noted that one likely and unfortunate consequence of being helped, is the potential loss of control. The recipient of help may conclude from his or her dependency that their future fate is beyond their control and is dependent on others' good will. This position has received conceptual expression in the application of reactance theory (Brehm, 1966) to the area of help seeking and receiving (cf., Fisher et al., 1982). The importance of perceived control in this context has been amply demonstrated in several discussions of seeking and receiving help in applied settings. Whitcher-Alagna (1983) notes that a major consequence of receiving medical help is the transfer of control from the patient to the medical team. Merton, Merton, and Barber (1983) in their discussion of professional help seeking have noted the fact that this transfer of control is characteristic of many professional helping relations. They state that "the less helpless the client, the less helpful the professional can be" (p. 22). Pettigrew (1983) discusses the angry reactions of recipients of public assistance in terms of their perceived lack of control over the helping arrangements. Finally, the victimization literature (e.g., Greenberg, Ruback, & Westcott, 1983; Janoff-Bulman, 1983) suggests that only a person who retains perceptions of personal control will view the seeking of help in an instrumental manner. Such perceptions are said to facilitate future coping.

A similar emphasis on the role of perceived control is echoed in Ames' (1983) formulation described earlier. If the person is to seek instrumental help that will better his or her chances for future coping, they must believe that their current difficulty was not caused by uncontrollable factors (e.g., luck and other external excuses). They need to believe that the need for help is related to the controllable personal element of effort expenditure. Further, in a restatement of the threat to the self-esteem model of recipient reactions to aid, Nadler and Fisher (1986) have distinguished between a state of "controllable" and "uncontrollable" self-threat. In both states, the person receiving help is threatened by its receipt, and motivated to terminate the uneasy dependency. In the controllable threat condition, the person believes that he or she can control their future performance, and this motivation is translated into instrumental behaviors. The person may help him or herself by investing more efforts, or seek instrumental help to better their position and achieve future independence. In the uncontrollable threat situation, the person's self-esteem is threatened by the receipt of help, but he or she does not see him or herself as able to control their future fate. The uncontrollable threat situation is said to result in a helplessness-like state. Here the person passively accepts help from a posture of weakness and dependency and help leads to helplessness.

Indirect support for the role of perceived control in shaping an instrumental view towards helping exists in the literature on recipient's reactions to receiving help. In one study, Nadler and Ben Itzhak (1985) have found that for subjects who received self-threatening help (i.e., help from a close friend which induced a high level of comparison stress) and were made to believe that they can control their future performance (i.e., a state of controllable self-threat) help was most effective in stimulating a high level of self-help efforts. The interpretation for these findings was that the self-threat (i.e., comparison stress) motivated the individual to terminate the uneasy dependency by investing efforts, and perceptions of control channelled this motivation into an instrumental course of action. This study measured self-help behavior and did not offer subjects the possibility to seek assistance as a way of coping with their difficulties. Yet, in light of the reasoning developed above it is likely that if such a behavioral avenue was open to subjects, they would also utilize sources of external assistance.

Styles of Help-Seeking and Instrumental Perspective

What kind of help is likely to be sought by individuals who believe that they can control their future performance? Asser (1978) makes an interesting distinction which bears on this question. Studying help seeking in a community setting, Asser found that some of his respondents tended to seek full solutions to their problems, whereas others tended to seek partial solutions. Thus, for example, if a person was unemployed, he or she could approach a societal agency and ask for money to enable them to provide for their families (i.e., full solution) or ask to be sent to a course in which they could learn a trade with which they would later provide for their families on their own. The first mode of help-seeking (i.e., seeking complete solutions) was termed "didactic style," and the second mode "negotiating style" of seeking help. Of interest is the finding that members of the lower social classes adopt a didactic style, whereas members of the middle and upper classes adopt a negotiating style (Asser, 1978).

Viewed through the prism of "perceived control," it is quite clear that by opting for a negotiating style of seeking help the person seeks help, but retains control over his or her fate. In fact, the individual defines a task-relevant deficiency (e.g., not having a marketable job) and seeks help to amend this specific deficiency (i.e., asking to be sent to a professional course). While doing so, the individual retains a sense of independence and a high level of control over his or her future fate (e.g., "when I have the skill I can better my position").

Ego Relevant and Instrumental Aspects: Concluding Remarks

The data and theory discussed in the preceding sections indicate that the act of seeking help is a complex psychological phenomenon. This behavior contains costs associated with the seeking of help and costs associated with not seeking it. The costs of seeking help are ego related and center around the concept of threat to self-esteem. In the first part of the review it has been shown that both situational and personality dimensions moderate the intensity of these psychological costs, thereby affecting the individual's willingness to seek needed help.

Help-seeking can also be viewed from an instrumental-task-achievement perspective. For this to occur, the self-threat implications in help seeking should first be minimized. Such is the case when the individual views the need for help as reflecting a lack in specific ability, while retaining an overall positive view of self (Ames, 1983). There is a conceptual parallel between Ames' distinction between global and specific self-esteem and the concept of ego-centrality of need for help discussed earlier. In fact, if a person sees the need for help as related to specific self-esteem, then the need for help can be said to reflect on non-ego-central dimensions. Thus, for example, the greater reluctance of the high self-esteem individual to seek help may be attributed to the fact that for them any admission of deficiency is viewed as a threat to global esteem. Thus, if one was to try and encourage high self-esteem person's help seeking, a viable strategy may involve (a) a clear distinction between specific and global self-esteem and (b) associating the need for help with the former.

The person's instrumental perspective on the seeking of help may also depend on the individual's focus of attention when seeking help. If the person's attention is focused on task related rather than ego related elements, the individual is more likely to seek help to overcome current difficulty than if attention is focused on ego related elements. Finally, the role of perceived control as facilitating an instrumental orientation towards help seeking has been discussed. If the individual needing help sees him or herself as in control of their future, help-seeking is likely to be seen as an instrumental strategy designed to solve a transient difficulty. It has also been observed that when seeking help in a negotiating style, the person is likely to see him or herself as trying to amend a specific deficiency while avoiding the damaging label of dependency.

If we turn to the previous example of the person who is unemployed and has to provide for his or her family, the above principles will take the following behavioral form: the person focuses attention on the task facing him or her (e.g., getting a job), retaining a high degree of global ability and attributing the current distress to lack of specific ability (e.g.,"I am basically O.K. and can get a job, all I need are the specific skills that will get me a job"), believes that he or she can affect the successful coping (e.g.,"If I tried and invested I would get the job") and seeks help in a negotiating style (e.g.,asks to be enlisted in a course which will earn him or her a skill).

Help-Seeking as Coping: Links with the Self-Control Literature

In this final section, the phenomenon of help-seeking will be discussed in light of research and theory on self-control discussed in other parts of this volume. This integration will highlight the links between the contents of the present chapter and issues discussed throughout the book.

Helplessness and Helping

One of the ironies associated with helping relations is that help may often breed its passive cousin: helplessness. Although Seligman and his associates regard helplessness as influenced by an organism's unique history of noncontingent reinforcements, recent research indicates that helplessness can also be affected by social factors. Feelings of helplessness are intensified when the individual believes that he or she can not control events, while others can (Garber & Hollon, 1980). Also, placing individuals in a dependent position may cause them to act helpless even though they did not have a direct experience with noncontingent outcomes (Langer & Benevento, 1978; Langer & Imber, 1979). Voicing a similar view about the links between help and loss of control, Skinner (1978) argues that when one rushes to help another person, one may deprive the recipient from exerting own efforts to remedy the problem.

These links between help and helplessness are implied in the preceding sections of this chapter. People often refrain from seeking help because they do not wish to relinquish personal control. Phrased somewhat differently, individuals in need avoid the seeking of help because of the implications about personal helplessness that such a behavior may entail. By not seeking help, the person tells us that he or she prefers independence even if it is to be associated with the costs of continued difficulties.

Yet, relying on self and avoiding the seeking of help from others is not a uniform response to emerging difficulties. Some individuals are more likely than others to seek help, and certain situational conditions discourage, while others encourage the seeking of help. How are these data integrated within the broader body of knowledge on self-control and self-regulation?

Help-Seeking as "Mindless" or "Thoughtful": Habitual Versus Deliberate Help-Seeking

An important aid in drawing such an integrative outlook is the distinction regarding the degree to which the behavior displayed by a person who encounters a difficulty reflects or does not reflect self-regulatory mechanisms. Several authors have recently noted the difference between behaviors that do not involve much thinking and are performed almost automatically and behaviors that involve active thinking processes. The more automatic behaviors are said to reflect well-learned and well-established habits, whereas the less automatic behaviors involve cognitive processes such as evaluating between alternatives and decision making. Self-regulation occurs only when these cognitive processes are activated. The identifying mark of self-regulation is a conscious appraisal of alternatives and decision making before an action is initiated or stopped (Rosenbaum, 1990, Chapter 1).

The distinction between the more and less automatic modes of behavior has been labeled by Langer and her associates (Langer, Blank, & Chanowitz, 1978) "mindless" versus "thoughtful" forms of behavior, and by Rosenbaum and colleagues as behaviors that do or do not involve Process Regulatory Cognitions (PRC). Rosenbaum (1990) suggests that "when the smooth execution of "mindless" behavior is disrupted or interfered with, the PRC repertoires are activated for the purposes of self-regulation."

When is the "mindless" or "thoughtful" behavior likely to occur? Self-control theorists tell us that a shift from a "mindless" to a "thoughtful" mode of action occurs when the execution of the automatic behavior is disrupted by the introduction of informational elements which are inconsistent with well held beliefs. This inconsistency triggers a process of self-evaluation that is followed by cognitive processes of appraisal of alternative behaviors and decision making (e.g., Beck, 1976; Ellis & Harper, 1975; Rosenbaum, 1990; Chapter 1).

Applied to the context of help-seeking, when a person faces a difficulty and an external source of assistance is available he can engage in help seeking in a "mindless" fashion. Such behavior will be engaged in without much consideration for the costs involved in the seeking or not seeking of help. The person seeks help because this behavior is habitual and well learned and does not involve the activation of self-examination processes. On the other hand, the person may initiate a cognitive appraisal of the various costs involved and decide either (a) to refrain from the seeking of help because of its associated costs, or (b) seek it in spite of these costs. In the "habitual" mode of help-seeking, no self-appraisal or cognitive processes operate. In the deliberate mode of help-seeking behavior, the decision whether or not to seek help is a consequence of self-appraisal.

How is this distinction between habitual and deliberate help-seeking relevant for findings described in previous sections? The data suggest that one is more likely to engage in habitual help-seeking in situations that do not trigger self-evaluation processes. Such is the case when situational conditions render the receipt of help a normative behavior (i.e., almost anyone seeks help) or when the need for help does not reflect inadequacy on an ego-central task. In both cases, a person's tendency to seek help to solve current difficulty is not interfered with by the arousal of self-evaluative processes. Also, habitual help-seeking is more likely when the helper is a relatively nonpsychologically relevant other (e.g., a stranger) whose presence does not activate self-appraisal processes associated with social comparison.

When, however, aid-related and helper-related variables trigger a process of self-evaluation, the habitual seeking of help is less likely.

An ego-central task or an intense level of evaluation apprehension associated with a particular helper (e.g., an attractive helper, a friend) interferes with the habitual mode of seeking help. This interference causes the activation of cognitive mechanisms. The person assesses the costs associated with the seeking and not seeking of help, and makes a decision whether or not to seek it. Under these conditions, help-seeking is deliberate.

In addition to situational variables, personality characteristics may also determine the habitual versus deliberate nature of help-seeking. The findings that high self-esteem individuals are more sensitive to the self-threat in aid than people with low self-esteem may now be reconceptualized. Since dependency is more habitual for the low than for the high self-esteem person, help-seeking for these individuals should have a more habitual nature than it would for the high self-esteem individual. As noted in previous sections, the prospect of dependency constitutes a departure from beliefs about the self for the high, but not for the low self-esteem person who needs help. For this individual, the prospects of dependency is likely to interfere with ongoing behavior, and activate self-appraisal processes, which may or may not result in the seeking of help. If it results in a decision to seek help, this is a deliberate rather than habitual help-seeking.

In a way of summing up, when degree of self-threat in seeking help is minimal, the seeking of help tends to be habitual. When however, self-threat interferes with the execution of this habitual request for help, self-regulation processes are aroused. These processes are associated with greater attention to the relative costs and rewards in help-seeking, which result in a deliberate decision to seek or not seek help. Finally, due to the lack of self-threat in habitual help-seeking, such requests for help are likely to be didactic. The relatively higher subjective cost of dependency in deliberate help-seeking will tend to render the style of such help seeking to be a negotiating style.

Consequences of Process Regulatory Cognitions: "Going it Alone" or Instrumental Help-Seeking

What are the consequences of the arousal of self-regulation processes in the help-seeking context? One such consequence is that after assessing the costs associated with seeking or not seeking help, the individual makes a decision not to seek it. Such would be the case when the self-threatening elements in aid are so intense (e.g., it is to be made in a public fashion) as to overshadow the negative consequences of not seeking it (e.g., continued hardships; increased likelihood of failure). At times, the outcomes of the self-regulation process are markedly different. The person in need may assess the situation and decide that help seeking is a viable alternative to be utilized on the road towards solving a problem. In this situation, after weighing the various alternatives the person is likely to decide to go ahead and utilize available sources of assistance. Seeking help which occurs in the wake of self-regulation mechanisms is not habitual or automatic. It is deliberate and reflects an assessment of situational alternatives and subsequent active decision making. This form of help-seeking is what was termed earlier "instrumental help-seeking."

Instrumental Help-Seeking and Effective Coping: Two Sides of the Same Coin

As noted earlier, instrumental help-seeking is likely when the person (a) enjoys perceptions of control over the situation, (b) attributes the difficulty to specific factors, (c) retains a favorable image of the "global" self, and (d) has a task- rather than an ego-oriented attention. There exists a remarkable overlap between these conditions and the factors which in the self-control literature are said to facilitate effective coping. Regarding the first element of personal control, almost every conceptual framework that discusses effective coping notes this element as a key factor in sustaining coping efforts in the face of emerging difficulties. This is the implication of Seligman's concept of learned helplessness (Seligman, 1981), Rosenbaum's theorizing on learned resourcefulness (Chapter 1), and Bandura's conception of self-efficacy (Bandura, 1977, 1982). Regarding the second element of attributions to specific and not global deficiencies, the attributional analysis of learned helplessness (Miller & Seligman, 1982) suggests that individuals who attribute difficulties to global lack of ability (i.e., global, stable, and internal attributions of failure) are likely to become helpless and depressed. The attribution of difficulty to specific factors facilitates persistence and active coping efforts.

Finally, some data in the self-regulation and self-awareness literature support the link between task orientation, as contrasted with ego orientation, and effective coping. Rosenbaum and Ben Ari (1985) found that individuals who possessed relatively lower coping skills (i.e., low in resourcefulness) tended to be more preoccupied with their inadequacies (i.e., ego orientation) than with the task at hand. In the self-awareness literature, Brockner and Hulton (1978) assumed that the lower performance of low self-esteem individuals may be attributable to their tendency to focus attention on themselves rather than on the task in question. This tendency results in a continuous process of self-evaluation that interferes with performance. It was reasoned that if one redirected the low self-esteem person's attention to the task-related properties, their performance would be significantly improved. The data supported this proposition: Redirecting attention to the task at hand resulted in an improved performance of the low self-esteem individuals. This finding provides further, albeit somewhat indirect, support to the proposition that effective coping may be facilitated by a shift from an ego to task orientation.

In sum, the above indicates that three major factors are associated with effective coping and instrumental help-seeking. These three factors are (a) beliefs in personal control, (b) specific rather than global attributions, and (c) a task rather than an ego orientation. Under these conditions, if an external source of help does not exist, the person is likely to persist more and try to help him or herself. If an external source of help exists the person is likely to adopt an instrumental perspective on the seeking of help, and seek it to further future success. This will constitute a deliberate rather than habitual seeking of help.

From an overall perspective, the present discussion can be summarized in the following manner (see also Figure 5.1): (a) When the seeking of help does not involve self-evaluative processes, help-seeking is likely to be a mindless form of behavior. This will constitute habitual help-seeking, which is likely to be pursued in a didactic style. (b) The arousal of self-evaluative processes is dependent on both situational (e.g., public nature of help-seeking) and personality variables (e.g., self-esteem). (c) Once such self-evaluative processes are aroused, the person may decide not to seek help or seek it from an instrumental perspective. This will constitute deliberate help-seeking, which is likely to be pursued in a negotiating style. (d) Whether or not instrumental help-seeking will occur depends on a number of variables. Three such major variables have been identified: belief in personal control, attributions of specific lack of ability, and task rather than ego orientation.

Final Word

The present chapter has sought to accomplish two related goals. First, we attempted to provide the reader with a brief overview of the kind of research that social psychologists do when they are concerned with help-seeking behavior. As already noted earlier, this has not been meant to be an exhaustive review of the literature, but a presentation

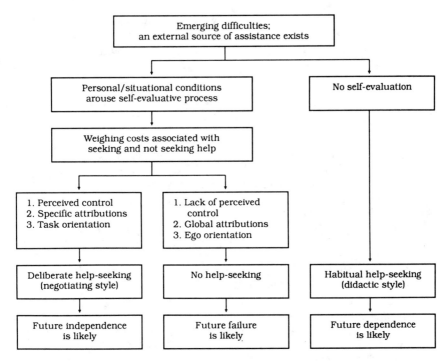

FIGURE 5.1. A process description of the antecedents of habitual and instrumental help-seeking.

of some major research issues and concerns in this context. The overall picture denotes that the phenomenon of help-seeking is a complex one that is associated with various costs, benefits, and values. A second and related purpose of this chapter was to show that the social-psychological findings are in close affinity with research and theorizing in the general coping literature. This integrative outlook puts the phenomenon of help-seeking in a broad perspective and serves a heuristic function in pointing out areas for future research.

Finally, throughout the chapter we have not made a distinction between different kinds of need states. We have not differentiated between such diverse situations as one involving a need to solve an emotional problem and another involving a need to solve a financial problem. The fact that different states of need were not discussed separately implies that the processes described here apply to both of the above described states of need. For example, regardless of whether one needs monetary advice or has difficulty talking to strangers, the labeling of the problem in terms of specific skill deficiency is likely to be associated with more help-seeking. Also, in either of the above examples such help-seeking is likely to be deliberate and made in a negotiating style. In sum, the concepts discussed in the present chapter reflect on content-free general processes that are relevant to a diversity of help-seeking situations.

References

Ames, R. (1983). Help seeking and achievement orientation: Perspectives from attribution theory. In B. M. DePaulo, A. Nadler, & J. D. Fisher (Eds.), *New directions in helping (Vol. 2): Help seeking* (pp. 165–187). New York: Academic Press.

Ames, R. & Lau, S. (1982). An attributional analysis of help seeking in academic settings. *Journal of Educational Psychology, 74,* 414–423.

Asser, E. S. (1978). Social class and help seeking behavior. *American Journal of Community Psychology, 6,* 465–474.

Bandura, A. (1977). Self-efficacy: Toward a unifying theory of behavior change. *Psychological Review, 84,* 191–215.

Bandura, A. (1982). Self-efficacy mechanism in human agency. *American Psychologist, 37,* 122–147.

Bar-Tal, D., Zohar, Y. B., Greenberg, M. S., & Hermon, M. (1977). Reciprocity in the relationship between donor and recipient and between harm doer and victim. *Sociometry, 40,* 293–298.

Beck, A. T. (1976). *Cognitive therapy and the emotional disorders.* New York: International Universities Press.

Bellah, R. N., Madsen, R., Sullivan, W. M., Swidler, A., & Tipton, S. M. (1985). *Habits of the heart: Individualism and commitment in American life.* New York: Harper & Row.

Berger, J., Rosenholtz, S. J. & Zelditch, M. (1980). Status organizing processes. *Annual Review of Sociology, 6,* 479–508.

Blau, P. M. (1964). *Exchange and power in social life.* New York: Wiley.

Brehm, J. W. (1966). *A theory of psychological reactance.* New York: Academic Press.

Brockner, J., & Hulton, B. (1978). How to reverse the vicious cycle of low self-esteem: The importance of attentional focus. *Journal of Experimental Social Psychology, 14,* 564–578.

Burke, R. J., & Weir, T. (1976). Personality characteristics associated with giving and receiving help. *Psychological Reports, 38,* 343–353.

Carver, C. S. (1979). A cybernetic model of self-attention processes. *Journal of Personality and Social Psychology, 37,* 1251–1281.

Clark, M. S. (1983). Some implications of close social bonds for help seeking. In B. M. DePaulo, A. Nadler, & J. D. Fisher (Eds.), *New directions in helping (Vol. 2): Help seeking* (pp. 205–203). New York: Academic Press.

Clark, M. S., Gotay, C. C., & Mills, J. (1974). Acceptance of help as a function of similarity of the potential helper and opportunity to repay. *Journal of Applied Social Psychology, 4,* 224–229.

Clark, M. S., & Mills, J. (1979). Interpersonal attraction in exchange and communal relationships. *Journal of Personality and Social Psychology, 37,* 12–24.

Coopersmith, S. (1967). *The antecedents of self-esteem,* San Francisco: Freeman.

Covington, M. V., & Omelich, C. L. (1979). Effort: The double edge sword in school achievement. *Journal of Educational Psychology, 71,* 169–182.

De Paulo, B. M., Brown, P. J., & Greenberg, J. M. (1983). The effects of help on task performance in achievement contexts. In J. D. Fisher, A. Nadler, & B. M. DePaulo (Eds.), *New directions in helping (Vol. 1): Recipient reactions to aid* (pp. 1224–1253). New York: Academic Press.

DePaulo, B. M., Nadler, A., & Fisher, J. D. (Eds.). (1983). *New directions in helping (Vol. 2): Help seeking.* New York: Academic Press.

Duval, S., & Wicklund, R. A., (1972). *A theory of objective self-awareness.* New York: Academic Press.

Eisenberg, N. (1982). *The development of pro-social behavior.* New York: Academic Press.

Ellis, A., & Harper, R. A. (1975). *A new guide to rational living.* New York: Wilshire.

Fenigstein, A., Sheier, M. F., & Buss, A. H. (1975). Public and private self-consciousness: Assessment and theory. *Journal of Consulting and Clinical Psychology, 43,* 522–527.

Festinger, L. (1954). A theory of social comparison processes. *Human Relations, 1,* 117–140.

Fischer, E. H., Winer, D., & Abramowitz, S. I. (1983). Seeking professional help for psychological problems. In B. M. DePaulo, A. Nadler & J. D. Fisher (Eds.), *New directions in help seeking (Vol. 2)* (pp. 163–189). New York: Academic Press.

Fisher, J. D., & Nadler, A. (1974). The effect of similarity between donor and recipient on recipient reactions to aid. *Journal of Applied Social Psychology, 4,* 230–243.

Fisher, J. D., Nadler, A., & DePaulo, B. M. (Eds.) (1983). *New directions in helping (Vol. 1): Recipient reactions to aid.* New York: Academic Press.

Fisher, J. D., Nadler, A., & Whitcher-Alagna, S. (1982). Recipient reactions to aid : A conceptual review. *Psychological Bulletin, 91,* 27–54.

Garber, J.,& Hollon, S. D., (1980). Universal vs. personal helplessness in depression: Belief in uncontrollability or incompetence?. *Journal of Abnormal Psychology, 89,* 56–66.

Gergen, M., & Gergen, K. J. (1983) Interpretive dimensions of International aid. In A. Nadler, J. D. Fisher, & B. M. DePaulo (Eds.). *New directions in helping (Vol. 3): Applied perspectives on help seeking and receiving* (pp. 329–349). New York: Academic Press.

Glidewell, J. C., Tucker, S., Todt, M., & Cox, S. (1983). Professional support systems: The teaching profession. In B. M. De Paulo, A. Nadler, & J. D. Fisher (Eds.). *New directions in helping (Vol. 2): Help seeking* (pp. 189–214). New York: Academic Press.

Gourash, N. (1978). Help seeking: A review of the literature. *American Journal of Community Psychology, 6,* 413–423.

Greenberg, M. S., & Westcott, D. R. (1983). Indebtedness as a mediator of reactions to aid. In J. D. Fisher, A. Nadler, & B. M. De Paulo (Eds.). *New directions in helping (Vol. 1): Recipient reactions to aid* (pp. 86–114). New York: Academic Press.

Greenberg, M. S, Ruback, B. R., & Westcott, D. R. (1983). Seeking help from the police: The victim's perspective. In A. Nadler, J. D. Fisher, & B. M. DePaulo (Eds.), *New directions in helping (Vol. 3): Applied perspectives on help seeking and receiving* (pp. 71–107). New York: Academic Press.

Gross, A. E., & McMullen, P. A. (1983). Models of help seeking. In B. M. DePaulo, A. Nadler, & J. D. Fisher (Eds.), *New directions in helping (Vol. 2): Help seeking* (pp 47–73). New York: Academic Press.

Hatfield, E., & Sprecher, S. (1983). Equity theory and recipient reactions to aid. In J. D. Fisher, A. Nadler, & B. M. De Paulo (Eds.). *New directions in helping (Vol. 1): Recipient reactions to aid* (pp. 113–144). New York: Academic Press.

Hill, F. E., & Harmon, M. (1976). The use of telephone tapes in a telephone counseling telephone counseling program. *Crisis Intervention, 7,* 88–96.

Hobfoll, S. E., & London, P. (1986). The relationship of self-concept and social support to emotional distress among women during war. *Journal of Social and Clinical Psychology, 12,* 87–100.

Janoff-Bulman, R., Madden, M. E., & Timko, C. (1983). Victim's reactions to aid: The role of perceived volnurability. In A. Nadler, J. D. Fisher, & B. M. DePaulo (Eds.), *New directions in helping (Vol. 3): Applied perspectives on help seeking and receiving* (pp. 21–46). New York: Academic Press.

Kalish, R. A., (1967). Of children and grandfathers: A speculative essay on dependency. *The Gerontologist, 7,* 43–56.

Ladieu, G., Hanfman, E., & Dembo, T. (1947). Studies in adjustment to visible injuries: Evaluation of help by the injured. *Journal of Abnormal and Social Psychology, 42,* 169–192.

La Morto-Corse, A. M., & Carver, C. S. (1980). Recipient reactions to aid: Effects of locus of initiation, attributions and individual differences. *Bulletin of the Psychonomic Society, 16,* 265–268.

Langer, E. J., & Benevento, A. (1978). Self-induced dependence. *Journal of Personality and Social Psychology, 36,* 866–893.

Langer, E., Blank, A., & Chanowitz, R. (1978). The mindlessness of ostensibly thoughtful action: The role of placebic information in interpersonal interaction. *Journal of Personality and Social Psychology, 36,* 635–642.

Langer, E. J., & Imber, L. (1979). When practice makes imperfect: Debilitating effects of overlearning. *Journal of Personality and Social Psychology, 37,* 2014–2024.

Latane, B. (1981). The psychology of social impact. *American Psychologist, 36,* 343–356.

Latane, B., & Nida, S. (1981). Ten years of research on group size and helping. *Psychological Bulletin, 89,* 308–324.

Lipman, A., & Sterne, R. (1962). Aging in the United States: Ascription of a terminal sick role. *Sociology and Social Research, 53,* 194–203.

Merton, R. K.,(Ed.) (1968). *Social theory and group structure.* New York: Free Press.

Merton, V., Merton, R. K., & Barber, E. (1983). Client ambivalence in professional relationships: The problem of seeking help from strangers. In B. M. DePaulo, A. Nadler, & J. D. Fisher (Eds.), *New directions in helping (Vol.2): Help seeking* (pp. 14–47). New York: Academic Press.

Miller, S. M., & Seligman, M. E. P. (1982). The reformulated model of helplessness and depression: Evidence and theory. In R. W. J. Neufeld (Ed.), *Psychological stress and psychopathology* (pp. 149–179). New York: Mc-Graw Hill.

Modigliani, A. (1968). Embarrassment and embarassability, *Sociometry, 31,* 313–326.

Modiliagni, A. (1971). Embarrassment, face work and eye contact: Testing a theory of embarrassment. *Journal of Personality and Social Psychology, 17,* 15–24.

Nadler, A. (1980). Good looks do not help: Effects of physical attractiveness and expectations for future interaction on help seeking. *Personality and Social Psychology Bulletin, 6,* 378–383.

Nadler, A. (1983). Personal characteristics and help seeking. In B. M. DePaulo, A. Nadler, & J. D. Fisher (Eds.), *New directions in helping (Vol. 2): Help seeking* (pp. 303–341). New York: Academic Press.

Nadler, A. (1983). Social psychology and social issues: Research on help seeking and receiving in applied settings. In A. Nadler, J. D. Fisher, & B. M. DePaulo (Eds.), *New directions in helping (Vol. 3): Applied perspectives on help seeking and receiving* (pp 3–19). New York: Academic Press.

Nadler, A. (1986). Self-esteem and the seeking and receiving of help: Empirical and conceptual perspectives. In B. Maher & W. Maher (Eds.), *Progress in experimental personality research* (pp. 115–164). New York: Academic Press.

Nadler, A. (1987). Personality and situational variables as determinants of help seeking. *European Journal of Social Psychology, 17,* 57–67.

Nadler, A., Altman, A., & Fisher, J. D.(1979). Helping is not enough: Recipient's reactions to aid as a function of positive and negative self-regard. *Journal of Personality, 47,* 615–628.

Nadler, A., & Fisher, J. D. (1984). Effects of donor recipient relationships on recipient's reactions to being helped. In E. Staub, D. Bar-Tal, J. Karylowski & J. Reykowski (Eds.), *Development and maintenance of pro-social behavior: International perspectives* (pp. 317–421). New York: Plenum Press.

Nadler, A., & Fisher, J. D. (1986). The role of threat to self-esteem and perceived control in recipient reactions to aid: Theory development and empirical validation. In L. Berkowitz (Ed.), *Advances in experimental social psychology (Vol. 19)* (pp. 81–123). New York: Academic Press.

Nadler, A., Fisher, J. D., & DePaulo, B. M. (Eds.). (1983). *New directions in helping (Vol. 3): Applied perspectives on help seeking and receiving.* New York: Academic Press.

Nadler, A., Fisher, J. D., & Ben-Itzhak, S. (1983). With a little help from my friend: Effects of single or multiple act aid as a function of donor and task characteristics. *Journal of Personality and Social Psychology, 44,* 310–321.

Nadler, A., Fisher, J. D., & Streufert, S. (1976). When helping hurts: The effects of donor-recipient similarity and recipient self-esteem on recipient reactions to aid. *Journal of Personality, 44,* 392–409.

Nadler, A., & Fux, B. (1985). Self-esteem and ego defensiveness as determinants of help seeking behavior. Unpublished manuscript, Tel Aviv University.

Nadler, A., Goldberg, D. R., & Jaffe, Y. (1982). Effects of self- differentiation and anonymity in group on deindividuation. *Journal of Personality and Social Psychology, 42,* 1127–1136.

Nadler, A., Mayseless, O., Peri, N., & Tchemerinski, A. (1985). Effects of self-esteem and ability to reciprocate on help seeking behavior. *Journal of Personality, 53,* 23–36.

Nadler, A., & Porat, I. (1978). When names do not help: Effects of anonymity and locus of need attributions on help seeking behavior. *Personality and Social Psychology Bulletin, 4,* 624–628.

Nadler, A., Shapira, R., & Ben-Itzhak, S. (1982). Good looks may help: Effects of helper's physical attractiveness and sex of helper on males' and females' help seeking behavior. *Journal of Personality and Social Psychology, 42,* 90–99.

Nadler, A., Sheinberg, L., & Jaffe, Y. (1981). Coping with stress by help seeking: Help seeking and receiving behavior in male paraplegics. In C. Spielberger, I. Sarason, & N. Milgram (Eds.), *Stress and anxiety (Vol. 8)* (pp. 375–386). Washington, DC: Hemisphere.

Nichols, J. G. (1979). Quality and equality in intellectual development: The role of motivation in education. *American Psychologist, 34,* 1071–1084.

Pettigrew, T. F. (1983). Seeking public assistance: A stigma analysis. In A. Nadler, J. D. Fisher, & B. M. DePaulo (Eds.), *New directions in helping (Vol. 3): Applied perspectives on help seeking and receiving* (pp. 273–294). New York: Academic Press.

Rosen, S.(1983). Perceived inadequacy and help seeking. In B. M. DePaulo, A. Nadler, & J. D. Fisher (Eds.) *New directions in helping (Vol. 2): Help seeking* (pp. 73–109). New York: Academic Press

Rosenbaum, M. (1983). Learned resourcefulness as a behavioral repertoire for the self-regulation of internal events: Issues and speculations. In M. Rosenbaum, C. M. Franks, & Y. Jaffe (Eds.), *Perspectives on behavior therapy in the eighties* (pp. 54–73). New York: Springer.

Rosenbaum, M. (1990). A model for research on self-regulation: Reducing the schism between behaviorism and general psychology. In G. H. Eifert & I. M. Evans (Ed.), *Unifying behavior therapy: Contribution of paradigmatic behaviorism.* New York: Springer Publishing Co.

Rosenbaum, M., & Ben-Ari, K. (1985). Learned helplessness and learned resourcefulness: Effects of noncontingent success and failure on individual differing in self-control skills. *Journal of Personality and Social Psychology, 48,* 198–215.

Rosenberg, M. (1965). *Society and the adolescent self-image.* Princeton, NJ: Princeton University Press.

Rushton, J. P., & Sorrentino, R. M. (Eds.) (1981). *Altruism and helping behavior: Social, personality and developmental perspectives.* Hillsdale, NJ: Erlbaum.

Scheier, M. F., Fenigstein, A., & Buss, A. H. (1974). Self-awarness and physical aggression. *Jouranl of Experimental Social Psychology, 10,* 264–273.

Seligman, M. E. P. (1981). A learned helplessness point of view. In L. P. Rehm (Ed.), *Behavior therapy for depression: Present status and future directions* (pp. 123–141). New York: Academic Press.

Shapiro, G. E., (1978). Help seeking: Effects of visibility of task performance and seeking help. *Journal of Applied Social Psychology, 8,* 163–173.

Shapiro, G. E. (1983). Embarrassment and help seeking. In B. M. DePaulo, A. Nadler, & J. D. Fisher (Eds.), *New directions in helping (Vol. 2): Help seeking* (pp. 143–165). New York: Academic Press.

Skinner, B. F. (1978). The ethics of helping people. In L. Wispe' (Ed.), *Sympathy, altruism and helping behavior* (pp. 249–262). New York: Academic Press.

Staub, E., Bar-Tal, D., Karylowski, J., & Reykowski, J. (Eds.) (1984). *Development and maintenance of pro-social behavior: International perspectives.* New York: Plenum.

Stokes, S. J., & Bickman, L. (1974). The effects of the physical attractiveness and the role of the helper on help seeking. *Journal of Applied Social Psychology, 4,* 286–294.

Tesser, A. (1988). Toward a self-evaluation maintenance model of social behavior. In L. Berkowitz (Ed.), *Advances in experimental social psychology, Vol. 21* (pp. 181–227). New York: Academic Press.

Tessler, R. C., & Schwartz, S. H., (1972). Help seeking, self-esteem, and achievement motivation: An attributional analysis, *Journal of Personality and Social Psychology, 21,* 318–326.

Wallston, B. S. (1976). The effects of sex role ideology, self-esteem, and expected future interaction with and audience on male help seeking. *Sex Roles, 2,* 353–365.

Weinstein, E. A., De Vaughn, W. L., & Wiley, M. G. (1969). Obligation and the flow of deference in exchange. *Sociometry, 32,* 1–12.

Weiss, H. M., & Knight, P. A. (1980). The utility of humility: Self-esteem, information search and problem solving efficiency. *Organizational Behavior and Human Performance, 25,* 216–223.

Whitcher-Alagna, S. (1983). Receiving medical help: A psychosocial perspective on patient reactions. In A. Nadler, J. D. Fisher, & B. M. DePaulo (Eds.), *New directions in helping (Vol. 3): Applied perspectives on help seeking and receiving* (pp. 131–163). New York: Academic Press.

Williams, K. B., & Williams, K. D. (1983). A social impact perspective on the social inhibition of help seeking. In B. M. DePaulo, A. Nadler, & J. D.

Fisher (Eds.), *New directions in helping (Vol. 2): Help seeking* (pp. 109–143). New York: Academic Press.

Wills, T. A.(1983). Social comparison in coping and help seeking. In B. M. DePaulo, A. Nadler, & J. D. Fisher (Eds.), *New directions in helping (Vol. 2): Help seeking* (pp. 109–143). New York: Academic Press.

Witkin, H. A., Goodenough, D. R., & Oltman, D. K. (1979). Psychological differentiation: Current status. *Journal of Personality Personality and Social Psychology, 37,* 1127–1145.

Zanna, M. P., & Pack, S. J. (1975). On self-fulfilling nature of apparent sex differences in behavior. *Journal of Experimental Social Psychology, 11,* 583–591.

Resourcefulness in Specific Areas

6

Learned Resourcefulness in the Performance of Hazardous Tasks

Stanley Rachman

As part of the movement away from "pathological" models of psychological problems, psychologists began to redefine so-called neurotic and other difficulties in behavioral terms. Neurotic behavior displayed in the presence of other people, for example, can be redefined in terms of social skills deficits. These redefinitions, in terms of behavioral deficits, led inevitably to an examination of behavioral and other assets. Increasingly, psychologists turned their attention to skills, coping abilities, problem solving, preparatory training, self-efficacy—and most recently, to learned resourcefulness.

This trend is productive and optimistic and, therefore, welcome. It may also help to overcome the widespread tendency, within and without psychology, to underestimate human capabilities and resilience. A visitor from Mars who formed his or her view of human qualities entirely from our textbooks and journals (a fate not to be wished upon any self-respecting Martian visitor) would expect to encounter an extremely timid species that very readily acquires new fears to add to an existing cauldron of anxieties. As we have recognized, however belatedly, it takes considerably more than a single or repeated association between a stimulus and a nasty event to produce significant fear (Rachman, 1978, 1984). People are resilient, and they display a remarkable capacity to cope and to adapt, even to repeated horrors and dangers such as blitz bombing during World War II (Rachman, 1978). Instead of confining our attention to failures of adaptation and to the emergence of psychological difficulties, we stand to learn and benefit a great deal from fuller consideration of how people adapt and cope, especially under stress.

The concept of "learned resourcefulness" is one such attempt and has already met with some success (Rosenbaum, 1983; Rosenbaum & Palmon, 1984; Rosenbaum & Rolnick, 1983; Rosenbaum & Jaffe, 1983). The questions that can be addressed in this manner include the following: Can resourcefulness (coping) be acquired? If so, how? Is resourcefulness a general and generalizable attribute? If so, can it generalize across situations and across time? These are worthy questions and there is a reasonable expectation that the concept of resourcefulness will help to answer some of them. In my view however, progress will be facilitated by careful review and re-statement of the concept, and by an equally careful analysis of its relation to concepts such as self-efficacy, self-regulation, coping skills, and so on. At present, the concept is not unambiguous and is open to inconsistent use. It is also too narrow, and unnecessarily so. There is no particular reason to limit the concept, as Rosenbaum (1983) proposes, to the self-regulation of internal responses, such as pain and emotions. Such a limitation is an unnecessary restriction.

The term "learned resourcefulness" was introduced by Meichenbaum (1977) to denote a change from a state of learned helplessness; after a person develops the skill necessary to cope with an unwanted, uncontrollable outcome that is the source of helplessness, it is said that he or she displays "learned resourcefulness." In a fuller analysis, learned resourcefulness was defined by Rosenbaum and Jaffe (1983) as "an acquired repertoire of behaviors and skills (mostly cognitive) by which a person self-regulates internal responses (such as emotions, pain, and cognitions) that interfere with the smooth execution of a target behavior" (p. 216)(See also Rosenbaum, 1983).

It is not clear that resourcefulness, as so defined, can be anything but acquired. If skills necessarily are acquired, then we can simply delete the adjective. Rosenbaum and Jaffe (1983) were particular to exclude from their list of "enabling skills," those referring to intellectual resourcefulness. It is said (Rosenbaum & Jaffe, 1983) that learned resourcefulness "may involve a number of enabling skills . . . but does not refer to intellectual, motoric, or social resourcefulness" (p. 216). Their definition also limits resourcefulness to the self-regulating "of internal responses."

Rosenbaum regards learned resourcefulness as a quantifiable attribute. People differ in the degree of their resourcefulness: they can be low in resourcefulness or highly resourceful, and Rosenbaum has developed a self-control schedule for assessing this general and measurable attribute (Rosenbaum, 1980). The conception of learned resourcefulness as an enduring attribute, and one that is confined to the regulation of internal responses, has some value, but it no longer is the mirror image of learned helplessness. *That* concept refers to a psychological state and not to an enduring, general attribute. Moreover, it is not confined to the regulation of internal responses.

The refined definition put forward by Rosenbaum encounters difficulty in reconciling his specific exclusion of intellectual resourcefulness with his emphasis on learned resourcefulness as a repertoire of behaviors and skills that are "mostly *cognitive*" (Rosenbaum & Jaffe, 1983, p. 216, emphasis added). Furthermore, Rosenbaum's Self-Control Schedule, which he appears to be justified in describing as a useful instrument for measuring resourcefulness, includes several specific intellectual abilities, such as "the application of problem solving strategies, the use of cognitions" (p. 216). The scale includes four categories: cognitions to cope with emotional responses, problem solving strategies, ability to delay gratification, and a general belief in one's ability to self-regulate internal events (Chapter 1, this volume). The narrowness of the conception is at variance with the breadth of the scale. In all, it seems preferable to use a broader definition of resourcefulness, one that includes intellectual qualities as well as the other skills of which Rosenbaum speaks. The case for excluding intellectual qualities is not made, and the exclusion creates problems of inconsistency. Notwithstanding the potential usefulness of a self-report scale of resourcefulness, the development of behavioral assessments of resourcefulness is a necessary step that has yet to be taken.

The success of Rosenbaum's experiment on individual differences in learned resourcefulness is encouraging (Rosenbaum & Jaffe, 1983), and the results, which emphasize the importance of such differences, raise interesting questions that will be discussed below.

For the present, it is safe to say that if one agrees to a broadening of the definition and the deletion of the adjective "learned," a number of connections with other psychological concepts become obvious. First, resourcefulness in the sense in which Rosenbaum is using the term, comes very close to the concept of coping behavior put forward by Lazarus and his colleagues (Roskies & Lazarus, 1980). Second, there is a connection between resourcefulness and Bandura's (1977) concept of self-efficacy. This connection is made explicit in the conclusion of Rosenbaum and Jaffe's paper (1983): "As has been shown in the present study, self-efficacy expectancies, and most probably self control skills, determine the extent to which the effects of helplessness are transferred from an uncontrollable failure situation to a subsequent learning task" (p. 224).

In Bandura's theory, self-efficacy refers to the person's estimation of his probable success in dealing with an anticipated problem or difficulty. Rosenbaum's concept of resourcefulness, on the other hand, refers to a repertoire of skills, not an expectation estimate. A connection between the two can be forged by saying that the person's repertoire of skills helps to determine his self-efficacy estimates. This introduces a different emphasis to that set out in Bandura's theory, in which he traces the development of self-efficacy estimates to four different sources of information, not solely to the establishment of repertoires of skill. It is correct however that the acquisition of appropriate skills could, within Bandura's theory, contribute to an estimate of self-efficacy (see the important role of performance accomplishments in Bandura's theory). There is another similarity between the two approaches: both theorists ascribe dispositional properties to self-efficacy and/or resourcefulness. As mentioned earlier, Rosenbaum regards resourcefulness as a general attribute, and Bandura has been moving away from his earlier emphasis on situation-specific estimations of self-efficacy, with the accompanying need for micro-analytic measurements, to generalized expectations. Recently, he stated that: "People who regard themselves as highly efficacious act, think and feel differently from those who perceive themselves as inefficacious" (Bandura, 1984, p. 231).

There is another, less obvious, connection between Rosenbaum's concept and self-efficacy. Resourcefulness as measured by Rosenbaum's Scale consists of estimates of self-perceived resource skills (Rosenbaum, 1983, Chapter 1), and one of the four content areas of the scale is the general belief in one's ability to self-regulate internal events (p. 63), which bears a resemblance to Bandura's self efficacy concept.

Despite these similarities and the possibility of forging the connection mentioned above, it can be argued that there is a closer schematic affinity between Rosenbaum's concept of resourcefulness and Lazarus's theory of coping. To begin with, some of the questions posed by Lazarus and Rosenbaum have a similar ring. Roskies and Lazarus (1980) state that there is a need for further understanding of the rules that govern the emergence and manifestation of coping, and equally interesting, "how and why people differ in coping patterns" (p. 41). These writers specifically disclaim the value of trait theories of coping, and introduced a classificatory scheme for coping processes in which the strategies are divided according to the mode used and the function which they serve.

They go on to list six categories of resources for coping. Four of these categories are to be found within the person (health/energy, morale, problem-solving skills, and system of beliefs). The other two resources are drawn from the environment (social support and material resources). Roskies and Lazarus correctly point out that the social support resources have been mostly explored so far, and that remark underlines the need for the type of investigation recommended by Rosenbaum—the kind that concentrates on the development of the person's own resources.

Given Lazarus's approach to the question of coping, it comes as no surprise that he devotes so much consideration to the training of coping skills. It is this aspect of the development of resourcefulness that is best illustrated by research into the psychology of military bomb-disposal operators and parachutists, which forms the core of this chapter. After considering the nature and effect of this military training on resourcefulness, it is necessary to return to the problem of generalized dispositions and general attributes of resourcefulness—despite Lazarus's dismissal of the trait approach. Having argued in favor of a broad definition of resourcefulness, we can now turn to our research work that has the greatest bearing on the concept. It will not pass unnoticed that despite my views about the desirability of a broad definition, some of the research that I have carried out on this subject fits comfortably into the narrow definition put forward by Rosenbaum.

Performance of Hazardous Duties

My research, which was carried out in collaboration with Cox, Hallam, and O'Connor, addresses the procedures that are used for preparing military bomb-disposal operators to carry out their duties, and the training of military parachute-jumpers. The majority of these soldiers reported experiencing fear at some stage during the execution of their duties or in anticipation of them. Nevertheless, the overwhelming majority performed their duties competently, despite the considerable danger involved. In recalling Rosenbaum's definition of resourcefulness as acquired skills "by which a person self-regulates internal responses that interfere with the smooth execution of a target behavior" (p. 216), these studies are apposite.

In the course of a protracted series of studies of the bomb-disposal operators, the purpose of which was to obtain information that might help us illuminate the nature of fear and courage, attention was paid to the question of how people are trained to carry out these hazardous acts (Rachman, 1983). How is it possible to prepare someone to carry out this highly skilled, but very dangerous work?

The research was concentrated on bomb-disposal operators who are regularly required to deal with dangerous, improvised explosive devices. The tasks often involve highly technical work, requiring careful judgments and calm execution. All of the bomb-disposal operators who participated in the studies had completed a tour of duty in Northern Ireland. Since the bombing campaign gained momentum over ten years ago, the annual rate of incidents reached nearly 4,000, or approximately 10 per day. In the period from 1969 to 1981, over 31,000 incidents were dealt with. The hazardous nature of the work can be gauged from the fact that 17 operators were killed during this period, and roughly one in four operators received decorations for gallantry.

All suitably qualified officers and soldiers in the Royal Army Ordinance Corps with the rank of sergeant and above are considered eligible for these duties, and when selected they are given specialized training to enable them to carry out their hazardous work. The operators are organized into small cohesive units and typically spend four months on a tour of duty.

The training is highly specialized and intensive, and it should be mentioned here that over 50% of the trainees were unaware on joining the RAOC that bomb-disposal work would be part of their duties. Before starting the training course, the soldiers had little confidence in their bomb-disposal skills, rated the danger as high, and expressed little willingness to serve as operators under combat conditions. The soldiers were asked to rate themselves with respect to their skills and willingness to perform seven types of dangerous tasks, using a scale ranging from 0 to 100. The tasks included dealing with a land mine in a culvert, a car bomb in an urban area, a bomb placed in a petrol tanker, and so on. Their self-estimation of their ability to carry out these tasks increased from 49% prior to the training, to 83% after completion of the training. This level of 83% comes very close to the self-rated skill reported by experienced operators in the field. The specialized training brought the self-efficacy estimates of the trainees close to those of field operators. Similarly, their self-rated willingness to carry out the tasks increased from a precourse level of 44% to 78% on completion of the training. A comparison between experienced and inexperienced operators showed that prior to training there were large and significant differences between the experienced and inexperienced operators, in respect to self-rated skill and in willingness. At the end of the training, there were no longer any statistical differences between the experienced and inexperienced operators. The training course successfully bridged the gap between the experienced and inexperienced operator. It is of interest that previous military experience in Northern Ireland appears to have exerted no influence on the operators' self-estimate skill and willingness, unless they had specific experience of bomb-disposal work in the territory. Military experience of other kinds had no detectable influence on their skill or willingness to carry out bomb-disposal duties. No evidence here for generalized resourcefulness. Not surprisingly, we found that there was a highly significant relationship between self-estimated skill and willingness to carry out the tasks ($r = 0.87$). The self-estimates of skill before and after training, in the middle of a tour, and after the tour, are shown in Figure 6.1 below.

As can be seen from Figure 6.1, the high levels of self-estimated skill and willingness were sustained during the tour of duty. The powerful effects of the training become more evident when one examines the estimates given by the novices. Among these operators, their self-rated skills prior to the training course were put at a lowly 28%. After

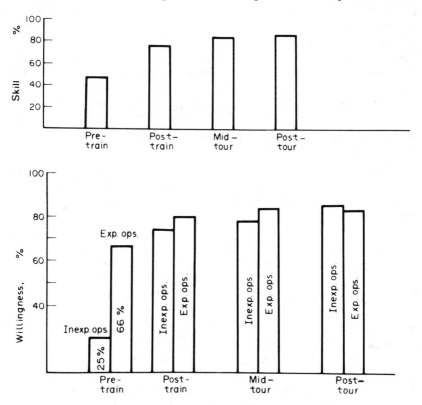

FIGURE 6.1. Bomb-disposal duties. Self-rated estimates of skill and of willingness, provided before and after training, then at mid-tour and posttour. The estimates were increased markedly after training and remained high. The pretraining differences between novices and experimental operators in willingness to carry out bomb-disposal were washed out after training.

completing the training course however, their self-rated skill increased to 80%. To the extent that these ratings of skill bear on resourcefulness, we can use this result as evidence of the trainability of resourcefulness.

These findings of the substantial boost in self-estimated skill and willingness to perform are the more remarkable when one considers the soldiers' ratings of the dangerousness of the tasks which they were required to carry out. Prior to receiving the specialized training, the soldiers rated the most difficult task as being highly dangerous (60 on a 100-point scale). Remarkably, the estimates of danger had diminished only slightly on completion of the course (51%). Despite these high and relatively stable estimates of the dangerousness of bomb-disposal duties, the trained soldiers reported—and showed—considerable willingness to carry out the tasks after they received the training. The connection appears to be simple and direct, and one that is compatible with Bandura's (1977) theory of self-efficacy. Once they feel confident of their ability to deal with dangerous tasks, their willingness to perform rises despite their recognition of the danger involved.

The critical question was whether these self-reported estimates predicted performance under operational conditions, and so our next investigation dealt with the adjustment of the operators during a tour of duty in Northern Ireland. The most important fact is that almost all of them performed their duties successfully and without problems. Moreover they quickly adapted to the danger of their work despite the fact that most of them had to live and work under constricted and rather difficult, improvised conditions. The process of adaptation was accelerated once the operator successfully carried out his first operation on a genuine device. Experience of dealing with hoaxes or false alarms made no contribution to their confidence or competence. However, once the inexperienced operators successfully completed one bomb-disposal task, their confidence and feelings of competence rose close to the level of the experienced operator. During the tour of duty, most of the operators reported feeling calm for much of the 4 months. Seven of the 20 operators reported no fear at any time—the fearless ones; but four of the 20 had a great deal of fear, and can be described as the courageous performers. In general, there was a close correspondence between weekly ratings of self-efficacy and reported fear, but clear exceptions were encountered. A few operators maintained high self-efficacy ratings throughout the 4-month tour but nevertheless reported very large fluctuations in their fear scores.

The fact that 13 of the operators performed well despite their fear leaves us with a choice of either expanding Rosenbaum's definition to include smooth performance even when "internal responses" such as fear are present (but perhaps dampened) or to reject these acts as not representing resourcefulness. The first choice seems preferable. It can be said that the operators had learned to "regulate" their internal responses in a way that did not interfere with the performance of their duties.

Does the successful performance of the operators tell us anything new about learned resourcefulness? Certainly, their response to training and their operational performance provide good examples of resourcefulness, but do little to expand our knowledge of the processes involved—unless one couches the data in terms of Bandura's theory (1977). The training led to increases in self-efficacy estimates and these in turn were associated with (perhaps, promoted?) persevering and competent performance. These effects were inclined to be situation-specific and do little to strengthen the view of resourcefulness or self-efficacy as generalized competencies.

The successful operational performance of the so-called fearless operators fits more easily into Bandura's scheme. It cannot be said that they had learned to be resourceful, in the narrow sense of "regulating internal responses"; at least not those same "internal responses" reported by the fearful operators.

Evidence of competent performance of a hazardous task was also obtained in a study of 21 members of the Parachute Regiment. These soldiers had a mean age of 19.6 years, and all but one of them completed the parachute training course successfully, including the required jumps from an aircraft. The only failure was a soldier who injured his ankle during one of the jumps. None of them failed to complete the course for reason of psychological inadequacy or fear. That is not to say that fear was not reported.

Among this group of paratroop trainees, the mean self-rated fear prior to undergoing the training was 48%, and their fear after completion of the training had declined significantly, but only to the level of 40%. There was a wide range in these reports of fear: three parachutists reported fear levels above 75%, and five were in the lower range of 20% or lower. As in the studies of bomb-disposal operators before and after training, the parachute troops showed a steep increase in estimates of self-efficacy. Before starting the training, their mean self-efficacy score was 29%. This rose very significantly to 73% on completion of training. The dissociation between self-efficacy and estimates of dangerousness that was observed among the bomb-disposal operators was seen in the parachute trainees as well. The mean estimate of the dangerousness of jumping was 40% prior to training, and 42% after completing the training. Over the same period, however, self-efficacy estimates rose steeply. There was a slight but significant reduction in fear after training.

The main findings on the effects of parachute training, which parallel those in the bomb-disposal research, can be summarized in this way. Ratings of dangerousness remain relatively constant; there is a slight reduction in self-rated fear and a steep increase in estimates of self-efficacy. Equally interesting was the significant negative correlation between perceived self-efficacy and self-reported fear ($r = -0.58$). Somewhat surprisingly, there was no correlation between the trainees' posttraining estimates of the dangerousness of the task and the amount of their self-reported fear.

The effects of training soldiers to render safe explosive devices or jump from aeroplane are consistent, and much of it can be accommodated within a narrow definition of resourcefulness. Whether they achieved their goals by regulating "internal processes" or not, the data are clear evidence of acquired resourcefulness, of a kind that enables one to perform hazardous duties competently.

As far as Bandura's (1977) theory of self-efficacy is concerned, the correlations between precourse self-rating and experienced fear were all substantial and negative, as predicted. That is to say, trainees who expressed high self-efficacy ratings experienced little fear even during the most dangerous jumps. Less favorable for the theory, however, were the correlations between self-efficacy ratings and jumping performance. They were positive, but low and nonsignificant.

Given the validity of Bandura's theory, the substantial self-efficacy rating observed after training for bomb-disposal duties or for parachute jumping indicate that the training programs are highly successful in achieving their aims. Moreover, the bomb-disposal operators and the paratroop soldiers performed well, the former under operational conditions as in training.

Generality?

In the course of the investigations, we became interested in the question of whether or not this fearless/courageous performance (see Rachman, 1978, 1984) was indicative of a general attribute or whether such performance was situation-specific. The early information, some of it mentioned above, supported the idea that at least the self-estimates were situation-specific. Then, we discovered a psychometric distinction between those bomb-disposal operators who had been given awards for gallantry and their equally experienced and competent, but nondecorated colleagues (Hallam, 1983). The decorated soldiers had earlier reported themselves to be slightly, but significantly, healthier and even more satisfied with their mental and physical condition. Prompted by this finding, we set out to discover whether there might not be some more general differences between the decorated and nondecorated operator. Seven soldiers from each category were asked to complete a laboratory stress test, and it turned out that the two groups of subjects did not differ in subjective reactivity or in self-reports of fear before or during the stress test. However, during the most difficult and stressful period of the test, the decorated subjects showed a physiological difference in the form of a significantly lower heart than did the comparison subjects (Cox et al., 1983). In a recently completed replication of this study, this highly specific difference was confirmed (O'Connor, Hallam, & Rachman, 1985).

These results raised the intriguing possibility that there might exist a small group of people who are particularly resistant to the stresses encountered in the extremely hazardous work. The possibility is strengthened by the finding that among the paratroop trainees, the five soldiers who showed a similar psychometric pattern to that of the decorated bomb-disposal operators did, in fact, report less fear during the execution of the jumps, reported fewer bodily reactions before and during the jumps, and rated the dangerousness of the situation as lower than did the 5 paratroop soldiers whose psychometric patterns were most different from the "decorated pattern." The 20% of the paratroopers who had the highest scores on bodily complaints and lower levels of alertness pretraining, reported greater fear before and during the jumps and a significantly larger number of bodily reactions during the jump.

In our laboratory investigation of the bomb-disposal operators, we also compared their performances to those of a small group of civilians and young soldiers. The civilians reported greater fear and showed larger cardiac responses than did the experienced operators, both decorated and nondecorated. This may point to the contribution of (military) training for coping with stress. As in our psychometric study of the distinction between courageous actors and courageous acts, we seem to require a bifactorial explanation. The decorated and nondecorated operators have a great deal in common (stability of mood, professional competence, etc.), but some slight differences can be found. The differences between the soldiers and the civilians, if confirmed in a full replication, would point to the influence of military training and/or military selection. Without denying the value of selection, it should be said that in the various related, but unpublished, projects carried out on these bomb-disposal operators, we have repeatedly come across evidence of the substantial contribution made by training as such. It remains to be shown, however, that such training contributes to a generalized resistance to stress. As far as the question of courageous actors is concerned, we now have some evidence, drawn from the different investigations, to support the identification of a group of people who have carried at least one act of gallantry, appear to react differently when placed in an experimental stress situation and who obtain some different scores on self-report psychometric tests in which they indicate an optimal level of functioning. These people may be unusually resilient.

The possibility that military training contributes to some general changes in stress resistance is compatible with Gray's (1982) emphasis on the process of "toughening up" that appears to be promoted by repeated exposure to small amounts of stress. Whether processes of "toughening up" can promote increased resourcefulness or whether it is too passive, remains to be seen. With a little imagination, "toughening up" exercise can be shaped to incorporate training in active resourcefulness. In this case, the effects of "toughening up" would improve the person's resources, rather than his resourcefulness (see below).

The results from these studies suggest that it is indeed possible to train people to acquire the skills and perceived self-efficacy that put them in a position to carry out hazardous work, the dangerousness of which is recognized. Moreover, it may be that there is a smallish group of people who are particularly capable of benefitting from such training and are especially able to carry out these hazardous tasks. It would not be surprising if these people produced distinctive scores on Rosenbaum's (1980) test of self-control.

It is not stretching matters too far to draw comparisons between these findings on military training and the effects of certain kinds of behavior therapy on neurotic patients whose primary difficulty is that they suffer from excessive fear (Rachman, 1978, 1984, 1990). In both cases, one is attempting to provide the person with the requisite skills and sense of self-efficacy that will enable him/her to deal with a disturbing or distressing task. In Rosenbaum's terms, they are being taught to self-regulate their internal processes in a way that enables them to perform normal actions in a smooth fashion. It is no accident that the source for much of Bandura's theorizing on the subject of self-efficacy is that willing pool of subjects who display intense but circumscribed fears. Observations on populations of this kind have provided for him the most important evidence of the development of self-efficacy and its function.

Determinants

The three major determinants of the performance of hazardous duties are adequate training, group cohesion, and situational demand (Rachman, 1983). The second of these determinants, group cohesion, important though it is, falls outside the scope of this discussion on resourcefulness. Situational determinants, however, are of considerable importance in calling out the resources that lie within the person's repertoire [see, for example, Gal's (1987) report on courageous acts performed by Israeli soldiers].

It has also been proposed that when people are required to carry out dangerous and difficult tasks that are socially desirable, they often manage to do so effectively (Rachman, 1978, 1979). Under the incentive of high social demands, helpers can act more effectively and more persistently than at other times. The execution of successful acts of required helpfulness may, in turn, lead to enduring changes in the helper himself—a case of virtue being rewarded.

Our information on the effects of required helpfulness comes from observations of people exposed to stress, including wartime conditions, and observations on psychiatric patients who are able to overcome their own disabilities, however temporarily, in the course of assisting someone else whose need is greater. We have in addition some information drawn from laboratory studies (e.g., Rakos & Schroeder, 1976; Beckham & Adams, 1983).

During the Second World War, Vernon (1941) observed that defense workers mostly recovered their poise readily and set about rescuing casualties, firefighting, etc., immediately. On similar lines, Wilson (1942) observed that there were very few psychological casualties after aerial bombardment and emphasized that hardly any of the people employed in essential services ever required help in overcoming adverse psychological reactions. Lewis (1942) also remarked on the comparative invulnerability of firefighters and other people engaged in essential services. He went on to propose that engaging in a socially useful occupation might have provided a form of inoculation against stress. Janis (1951) stated that people who face danger tend to feel less fearful if they are able to engage in some form of useful overt activity.

In the laboratory, Rakos and Schroeder (1976) showed that fearful people experienced a reduction in their own fear after having helped other subjects overcome fears. Beckham and Adams (1983) reported that the second most helpful form of behavior reported by depressed outpatients was that of helping other people. No less than 49% of their sample reported that they felt better after helping someone else. In brief, it seems that acts of required helpfulness can produce short-term or long-term increases in competence. Conceivably these changes are partly the result of having to be resourceful, having to develop new coping skills in order to be helpful.

Discussion

The broad definition of resourcefulness, perhaps more satisfactorily than the narrow definition, seems to describe well certain kinds of coping behavior. It remains to be shown that the concept is different from or more than Lazarus's notion of coping skills. At present, there seems to be a case for subsuming resourcefulness under Lazarus's concept of coping, but instead a slightly simplified definition is proposed. Resourcefulness is the ability to use one's personal and social resources for successfully dealing with problems, especially those that are novel.

Pursuing that line, one can ask whether the types of military training described here can usefully be construed in terms of resourcefulness. Certainly there is no difficulty in identifying all six of Lazarus's categories of resources in our data. The soldiers gave indications of possessing and using all six categories-energy, morale, problem solving skills, beliefs, material resources, and social support. Evidently, the task of recasting our data presents no difficulty, but the categories are so general and so inclusive that their merits are apt to drown in a pool of comprehensiveness. Hence, the simplification into personal and social resources is proposed.

The prominent alternative, of recasting our data in terms of Bandura's theory of self-efficacy, seems to be promising and has already proven its value as an organizing force for the data and as a basis for drawing fresh predictions (Rachman, 1983). For this reason, researchers interested in resourcefulness might wish to place the concept firmly in the general framework of Bandura's theory. The results might well be productive.

Concluding Analysis

The concept of learned resourcefulness as applied to our findings on training people to perform hazardous duties, leads to the following analysis. Resourcefulness can now be defined as the ability to apply one's personal and social resources successfully to deal with novel problems and particularly to those which are taxing and/or hazardous. These personal and social resources, defined as available skills, knowledge, and power-are mostly acquired, but not entirely so (e.g., physical power, stress resistance). The resourcefulness lies in the ability to call upon and successfully use one's existing skill and powers. Although there is no intrinsic reason for recommending the course, other than common usage, the term "resourcefulness" is best applied to the ability to use these resources in order to deal with problems that contain novelty. Using one's resources to deal, however successfully, with the same problems day after day is not to be taken as a mark of resourcefulness. The element of novelty is missing.

Calling out the necessary skills, knowledge, and power, and executing the necessary acts, requires ability. This ability to employ one's powers successfully, especially to novel problems, should share some features with other types of ability—and hence, show stability and some generality. If the revised concept of resourcefulness proposed here is to warrant attention, it will be necessary to demonstrate these properties of ability and generality. Furthermore, resourcefulness as ability, should be open to improvement by practice as are other types of ability.

Resources, referring to existing powers and skills, are distinguished from resourcefulness, which is the ability to garner one's resources and use them successfully in dealing with problems. The two terms refer to different qualities and can be measured and investigated separately, if necessary.

The proposed revision is of course, largely the product of our work on bomb-disposal operators and should, therefore, fit well with the performances and abilities of these people. Certainly bomb-disposal work requires the ability to apply one's resources to hazardous problems in which novelty is encountered. The required resources, personal and social, can be identified. Defined in terms of skills, knowledge, and powers, these are mainly acquired, but as we have seen, some of the "powers" of resistance may be constitutional. Seen as an ability, the resourcefulness of a bomb-disposal operator should be open to improvement by training (it certainly is), and it should show stability and generality-which it does to some degree.

To conclude, resourcefulness can be construed as the ability to engage one's resources—personal and social, in order to overcome problems, especially those with elements of novelty.

References

Bandura, A. (1977). Self-efficacy: Toward a unifying theory of behavioral change. *Psychological Review, 84,* 191–215.

Bandura, A. (1984). Recycling misconceptions of perceived self-efficacy. *Cognitive Therapy and Research, 8,* 231–255.

Beckham, E., & Adams, R. (1984). Coping behavior in depression. *Behaviour Research and Therapy, 22,* 71–76.

Cox, D., Hallam, R. S., O'Connor, K., & Rachman, S. (1983). An experimental analysis of fearlessness and courage. *British Journal of Psychology, 74,* 107–117.

Gal, R. (1987). Combat stress as an opportunity: The case of heroism. In G. Belenky (Ed.), *Contemporary studies in combat psychiatry* (pp. 31–46). Westport, CT: Greenwood Press.

Gray, J. (1982). *The neuropsychology of anxiety.* Oxford University Press.

Hallam, R. S. (1983). Psychometric analyses. *Advances in Behavior Research & Therapy, 4,* 105–120.

Janis, I. L. (1951). *Air, war, and emotional stress.* New York: McGraw Hill.

Lazarus, R. S. (1975). The self-regulation of emotion. In L. Levi (Ed.), *Emotions: Their parameters and measurement* (pp. 47–67). New York: Raven Press.

Lewis, A. (1942). Incidence of neurosis in England under war conditions. *Lancet, 2,* 175–183.

Meichenbaum, D. (1977). *Cognitive behavior modification.* New York: Plenum Press.

O'Connor, K. R., Hallam, R. S., & Rachman, S. (1985). Fearlessness and courage: An experimental replication. *British Journal of Psychology, 76,* 187–197.

Rachman, S. (1978). *Fear and courage.* San Francisco: Freeman.

Rachman, S. (1979). The concept of required helpfulness. *Behaviour Research and Therapy, 17,* 1–6.

Rachman, S. (Ed.). (1983). Fear and courage among military bomb-disposal operators. *Advances in Behaviour Research and Therapy, 4.*

Rachman, S. (1984). Fear and courage. *Behavior Therapy, 15,* 109–120.

Rachman, S. (1990). *Fear and courage* (Revised Second Ed.). New York: W.M. Freeman.

Rakos, R., & Schroeder, H. (1976). Fear reduction in help-givers as a function of helping. *Journal of Counseling Psychology, 23,* 428–435.

Roskies, E., & Lazarus, R. (1978). Coping theory and the teaching of coping skills. In P. O. Davidson & S. M. Davidson (Eds.), *Behavioral medicine: Changing health lifestyles* (pp. 38–69). New York: Brunner/Mazel.

Rosenbaum, M. (1980). A schedule for assessing self-control behaviors: Preliminary findings. *Behavior Therapy, 11,* 109–121.

Rosenbaum, M. (1983). Learned resourcefulness as a behavioral repertoire for the self-regulation of internal events. In M. Rosenbaum, C. M. Franks, Y. Jaffe (Eds.), *Perspectives on behavior therapy in the eighties* (pp. 54–73). New York: Springer Publishing Co.

Rosenbaum, M., & Jaffe, Y. (1983). Learned helplessness: The role of individual difference in learned resourcefulness. *British Journal of Social Psychology, 22,* 215–225.

Rosenbaum, M., & Palmon, N. (1984). Helplessness and resourcefulness in coping with epilepsy. *Journal of Consulting and Clinical Psychology, 52,* 244–253.

Rosenbaum, M., & Rolnick, A. (1983). Self-control behavior and coping with sea-sickness. *Cognitive Therapy and Research, 7,* 93–98.

Vernon, P. (1941). Psychological effects of air raids. *Journal of Abnormal and Social Psychology, 36,* 457–476.

Wilson, H. (1942). Mental reactions to air raids. *Lancet, 2,* 284–287.

7

Resourcefulness and Successful Treatment of Agoraphobia

Mia W. Biran

Not a long time ago, agoraphobia was regarded by most clinicians as a poor-prognosis syndrome. Today, agoraphobia is considered treatable, mainly by behavioral interventions. However, many questions still remain regarding the understanding of the agoraphobic syndrome and its etiology and the comprehensiveness and adequacy of existing treatment methods. The complexity of the agoraphobic syndrome, conflicting research findings about etiological and precipitating factors, and the limitations of behavioral and cognitive-behavioral treatments for this disorder, all point to the need to continue the search for missing links in our understanding and treatment of agoraphobia. In this chapter, I will review the accumulated knowledge about the agoraphobic syndrome and its treatment, emphasizing aspects of the existing data that support the possibility of utilizing the concept of resourcefulness as an important mediating factor in both the development and the modification of agoraphobia.

Agoraphobic Syndrome

Primary agoraphobia is defined as a marked fear of and avoidance of being alone in public places from which escape might be difficult or help is not available (American Psychiatric Association, 1980). Burns (1982) ascribes the presenting symptoms in the three-response system:

(a) In the cognitive system, the patient experiences apprehension and fear. Patterns of thought are frequently unproductive, irrational, and anxiety-producing; they often relate to an inability to cope with the feared situation and the psychophysiological arousal evoked by it. Thoughts about escape from the situation become prominent; if such escape is possible, the person will engage in ruminative self-defeating thinking involving a sense of failure and demoralization.

(b) In the psychophysiological system, a high level of arousal, which might involve increased muscular tension, rapid heart rate, sweating, hyperventilation, feeling of fainting, etc. occurs.

(c) In the behavioral system, the distress may result in withdrawal from the feared situation altogether. On contact with the situation, impaired performance may occur. When avoidance behavior takes place, it is likely to be followed by a rapid decrease in the fear and the autonomic arousal.

Most agoraphobics also suffer from generalized anxiety, depression, and social anxieties (Chambless & Goldstein, 1981). Panic attacks are common.

Background and Precipitating Factors

Several researchers find problems in the family background of agoraphobic. Thus, Snaith (1968) and Buglass et al. (1977) found an excess of unstable family background for these patients.

In reviewing the literature, a tentative picture of the "typical" agoraphobic may be drawn: This person tends to be a woman housewife who is anxious, depressed, unassertive, and low in self-esteem. A rather extroverted person, she is fearful of many social situations due to overconcern about criticism and evaluation. A concern about physical health and somatic symptoms in quite common as well (Chambless & Goldstein, 1981). Agoraphobics show strong tendencies to avoid different activities. Most of them go to great length to avoid such feelings as anger and frustration.

According to the recent reviews, agoraphobia rarely begins with the kind of traumatic conditioning event that is often found to produce simple phobias. Rather, the onset of panic comes without warning and with no apparent traumatic event (Goldstein & Chambless, 1978). However, close investigation reveals that in many cases the condition may begin after important alteration in life or following a chronic and stressful conflict in interpersonal relationships. Roth (1959) indicated that as many as 85% of agoraphobics reported such precipitating events, and Burns and Thorpe (1977) reported that 70.3% of their sample agoraphobics experienced a precipitating event such as a major change in life, illness, bereavement, pregnancy, etc. Finally, Shafar (1976) noted the presence of precipitating factors in 83% of the phobic sample. Relationship problems were an important causative factor in 57% of the cases. Other factors were pregnancy/childbirth, separation from a key figure, illness or operation, psychiatric illness, financial stress and threat of or loss of employment, and accident/assault events.

Theories of Etiology

Early behavioral theories proposed that agoraphobia, like other anxieties, was acquired by classical or instrumental conditioning. More recently, cognitive mediators were introduced to explain the acquisition and maintenance of phobic behavior (e.g., Bandura, 1977). The basic assumption here is that phobias develop as a result of a combination of specific environmental events in concert with cognitions employed by the individual to interpret these events, as well as expectations for the future. Still, due to the complexity of the agoraphobic syndrome and the prevalence of panic attacks and social anxieties as part of the clinical picture, several theorists go beyond the cognitive–behavioral explanations to indicate more sociological and underlying emotional issues as causative factors in agoraphobia.

Most studies indicate that at least two-thirds of agoraphobics are women (e.g., Chambless, 1978). Fodor (1974, 1978) suggests that sex-role stereotyping by society leads women to assume passive, fearful social postures. And since traditionally women have been tied to the home and developed less experience in dealing with the world, this could more easily contribute to their developing agoraphobia. Fishman (1980) relates to the preponderance of women patients by emphasizing the conflict women experience in feeling the need to succeed in independent tasks while lacking in basic self-assurance that men have acquired during their upbringing in traditional society.

The concept of conflict is strongly suggested by Goldstein and Chambless (1978). They see the agoraphobic as presenting with a general tendency to depend on others for support (due to low self-sufficiency skills) and, therefore, feeling trapped in relationships that provide her with such support. According to Goldstein and Chambless (1978), most agoraphobics belong to the complex type of agoraphobia (as opposed to the simple type), which is characterized by the following: (a) low level of self-sufficiency due either to high levels of anxiety or lack of appropriate skills; these people are seen as highly dependent, unassertive with acute social anxieties; (b) onset under conditions of conflict, generally of an interpersonal nature, usually in a relationship with a spouse or a parent; the person feels trapped in the conflict, unable to move; (c) a tendency to misunderstand the causal antecedent to emotional distress and an inability to label accurately such feelings as anger and frustration; these people experience such feelings as diffuse autonomic arousal which is then labeled as inexplicable anxiety; (d) fear of fear and anticipatory anxiety, which can elicit an attack of panic; this increases the dependency, and the person cannot afford to alienate those on whom she or he relies.

Some other recent views have a different bearing on the dependency issue. Hallam (1978) argues that agoraphobia is a misnomer and that individuals diagnosed as agoraphobic are better classified as cases of anxiety neurosis. Agoraphobics have to cope with a diffuse tendency to be anxious. Some cope by depending on alcohol or other measures of soothing, some cope by avoidance of a variety of potentially challenging situations. Mullaney and Trippett (1979) provide some support for this line of argument by showing that there is considerable overlap between agoraphobia and alcohol dependence.

Still other theorists (e.g., Klein, 1981) base their understanding of agoraphobia on Bowlby's (1973) notion of "anxious attachment" and see the agoraphobic symptom as resulting from an ongoing underlying depression and panic about abandonment.

Finally, Guidano and Liotti (1983) present a structural cognitive orientation to agoraphobia, combining some of the previous conceptualizations with a cognitive one. In their account of agoraphobia, the sufferer has been sensitized to possible separations and confinements in early childhood. The ideational hard core contains the tacit knowledge of the world as hostile and constrictive and the self as weak. Included are conflictual needs for freedom (autonomy) and for protection (dependence). Consequently, the agoraphobic-prone person develops a "protective belt" of rigid identity around themes of control over personal weakness and denial of conflicting emotions and cognitions abut self and others. In life, this person feels an inner need to be perfect, strong, and functional, thereby securing the dependency of family on her and preventing separations and desertions. A change in life, such as illness or the birth of a child, presents a threat to the rigidity of the "protective belt" and produces the anxiety-related symptoms of agoraphobia.

Outcome of Treatment for Agoraphobia

Recent evidence has established the effectiveness of cognitive-behavioral treatments for phobic disorders (Wilson, 1982). In vivo exposure, in particular, is considered a highly effective procedure for combating avoidance behavior, producing increases in approach behavior and reducing the persistent "fear of fear." The enhancement in the sense of self-efficacy makes this procedure an appealing one in dealing with agoraphobics (Williams & Rappoport, 1983). Jansson and Ost (1982) estimate that in vivo exposure treatment for agoraphobia has a success rate of approximately 63%. Barlow and Wolfe (1981) have estimated that 65% to 75% of clinical phobics who complete behavioral treatment show substantial improvement. These figures, although clearly encouraging, call our attention also to the 25% to 35% that constitute treatment failure. Accounting for the additional number of patients who drop out from treatment might put the success/failure ratio at approximately 50%. Unfortunately, there is a paucity of research addressing the factors which might facilitate or hinder the success of behavioral treatments.

In addition to the question of treatment failure, there are some important conceptual issues inherent in the treatment research literature on agoraphobia. We will review the specific findings and discuss these issues.

In Vivo Exposure Versus Cognitive Treatments

The outcome research with agoraphobics point so far to the following two assertions: (a) In vivo exposure is superior to cognitive treatment in increasing agoraphobics' approach behavior toward their respective "main phobia" and decreasing phobic anxiety (Emmelkamp, Brilman, Kuiper, & Mersch, 1986; Emmelkamp, Kuipers, & Eggeraat, 1978; Emmelkamp & Mersch, 1982). (b) In vivo exposure alone is as effective as the combination of in vivo exposure and a form of cognitive treatment in treating agoraphobia (Emmelkamp & Mersch, 1982; Williams & Rappoport, 1983). In addition, the cognitive strategies are not found to enhance the effects of exposure in vivo.

Emmelkamp et al. (1978) reported that in vivo exposure was superior to three methods of cognitive modification in increasing agoraphobics' approach behavior and in producing cognitive change. Agoraphobic subjects "spontaneously" reported that their thoughts had undergone a greater change during in vivo exposure than during cognitive modification. The authors suggested that "it is possible that a more effective cognitive modification takes place through prolonged exposure in vivo than through a procedure which is focused directly on such a change" (p. 40).

Williams and Rappoport (1983) directly assessed their subjects' fearful ideation and found that exposure alone decreased fearful thoughts as much as a combined cognitive and exposure treatment. The authors concluded: "It thus appears unnecessary to address people's thoughts explicitly in order to reduce their fearful ideation" (p. 308). Although the combined group in this study evidenced an increase in the use of coping self-statements, it showed no better results on the behavioral approach tests than the exposure alone group, indicating that the use of coping self-statements was not a significant agent of change.

Mavissakalian, Michelson, Greenwald, Kronblith, and Greenwald (1983) investigated the impact of two different cognitive strategies (self-instructional training and paradoxical intention) on exposure in vivo. They found that paradoxical intention plus exposure evidenced greater gains than did self-instructional training plus exposure. The paradoxical intention plus exposure treatment decreased agoraphobics' "self-defeating thoughts" as much over time as the self-instructional plus exposure treatment. And although the later group maintained the level of coping self-statements, the paradoxical intention plus exposure group actually decreased their use of coping self-statements. Again, the use of coping self-statements did not appear to be related to behavioral improvement. Since an exposure-only group was not included in this study, it is unclear whether the cognitive strategies enhanced the effects of exposure in vivo.

In the above studies, the remission of agoraphobic symptomatology was associated with a decrease in self-defeating, fearful, or unproductive self-statements. The use of positive or coping self-statements appeared to have little association with improvement. A possible interpretation is that in vivo exposure is a powerful method of behaviorally disputing specific unrealistic beliefs that constitute the dysfunctional internal dialogue of agoraphobics. What better disputation of beliefs such as "I can't stand my anxiety" or "I am unable to approach a supermarket" is there than to observe oneself "standing it" or "approaching it?" Behavioral disputation of these beliefs decreases the perceived danger of the feared situation and increases the perceived ability to cope. We will return to this interpretation later on, when we discuss resourcefulness and the treatment of agoraphobia.

Although research results have shown purely cognitive interventions to be inferior to exposure in vivo [see also a review of the literature on treatment of different phobias by Last (1984)], such findings do not necessarily indicate that cognitive modification is unimportant in the fear-reduction process. As previously mentioned, negative cognitions are clearly important in phobic disorders and agoraphobia and different researchers indicate changes in "self-defeating" thoughts following a behavioral intervention. Why is it, then, that cognitive interventions are clearly less effective than in vivo exposure?

The typical cognitive treatment applied in the phobic research consists of an attempt to directly modify internal dialogue. Typically, these treatments teach clients more positive, rational, or adaptive self-statements. Consequently, the phobic patients find it difficult to believe the adaptive self-statements and continue to emit irrational self-talk, which is consistent with their underlying negative beliefs.

Support for this explanation of the weakness of cognitive-behavioral modification comes from research in other areas. Kendall and Korgeski (1979) reviewed two studies which had examined the relationship of coping and negative cognitions and modification of behavioral problems (adjustment to a catheterization procedure and assertiveness). They concluded, "In both cases, the score on the negative scales were more highly related to the criteria of assertiveness or adjustment than were those of the positive self-statements. These findings suggest that negative or maladaptive cognitions, more than paucity of positive, are important contributions to behavioral problems" (pp. 13–14). Cash, Rimm, and MacKinnon (1979) studied the effect of irrational and rational belief systems on the impact of self-statement training. They found that unless the repeated self-statements were congruent with the subjects' belief system, they did not have their expected elative or depressive effects.

Follow-up Studies: The Limitation of Behavioral Treatment for Agoraphobia

Clinical experience and follow-up research (e.g., Emmelkamp & Kuipers, 1979; Mahoney, 1979) suggest that behavioral and cognitive-behavioral procedures are incomplete treatments for agoraphobia. Goldstein (1982) examined the follow-up literature and concluded that although symptom substitution is rare, the agoraphobic will often suffer recurrence of symptoms associated with agoraphobia: depression, chronic anxiety, panic, obsessiveness, as well as avoidance and fear of fear. Williams and Rappoport (1983) suggest that the long-term effectiveness of exposure may be "markedly exaggerated." In their study, the main phobia scale-the major outcome measure in the phobia research-did not correlate with the behavioral performance scale. Guidano and Liotti (1983) indicate that their agoraphobic clients successfully control their panic attacks by using behavioral and cognitive coping techniques, but worry over whether they will be able to control all future attacks. In our work with agoraphobics (Biran, Shreve,

Hill, Thebarge, Hamilton, & Jasbeck, 1987), we have noted the incredible amount of mental energy these patients use to maintain their gains and their subsequent desire to give up. In follow-ups, most agoraphobics treated with exposure and cognitive methods report marked improvement but their comments suggest that they feel they have a long way to go.

Noting that many agoraphobics treated with *in vivo* exposure "are left with residual problems of no small magnitude and significance" (Rachman, 1983, p. 1), Rachman considers safety signal, disconfirmation (of expectations of inability to tolerate panic), and self-efficacy theories as "fresh possibilities" for improving our understanding and treatment of agoraphobia. Although recognizing the superiority of exposure techniques as reported in the literature, Rachman advocates self-instructional training and other verbal nonexposure methods to increase self-efficacy, sense of safety, and control of fearful expectancies, as supplements to exposure. In short, Rachman is proposing to treat the residual problems remaining after treatment with exposure by using methods that have proven significantly less potent than exposure in changing these cognitive structures.

In sum, the outcome literature depicts exposure in vivo as an effective, yet incomplete treatment for agoraphobia. There is a felt need to continue the search for a better understanding of agoraphobia and the ingredients of its successful treatment. We will proceed to discuss Rosenbaum's (1983) concept of "resourcefulness" and its possible heuristic value for future research on agoraphobia.

Resourcefulness and the Treatment of Agoraphobia

We have reviewed some of the current knowledge about agoraphobia and its treatment. Both with regard to etiology and treatment, it seems clear that our understanding is not complete. Thus, for example, although several investigators found an excess of unstable family background (phobic, alcoholic, psychotic, or neurotic parents) for agoraphobics, some researchers find evidence that agoraphobics come from stable and close-knit (even overprotective) families (Marks & Gelder, 1965; Roth, 1959). The same problem exists with the question of personality style; agoraphobics have often been described as passive, dependent individuals. Although clinical observations lend credence to this, such a characterization would not be limited to agoraphobics. Hallam (1978) sees agoraphobics as basically cases of anxiety neurosis who have to cope with a diffuse tendency to be anxious.

Several researchers have suggested that interpersonal and inner dynamic factors are central in the etiology of agoraphobia and its maintenance. However, the high incidence of agoraphobia amongst females casts doubt on the specifity of this speculation. In fact, this finding support an alternative view, following Hallam's suggestion, that agoraphobics are highly anxious people, possibly lacking in the appropriate skills for coping with stressful situations or situations requiring independent functioning without immediate available support or help. This deficiency might originate from lack of appropriate modeling or preparation in early childhood, and/or lack of opportunities to exercise assertive, coping behaviors during normal development, as could be the case for many women in our society. The findings that high percentages of agoraphobics report some precipitating event occurring prior to the development of the illness point to the same direction.

In 1983, Rosenbaum presented a theory of learned resourcefulness (see also Chapter 1). He cites Marks (1983), who suggested that "maybe we should think not in terms of why phobias and rituals are acquired in the first place, but rather why once these are acquired, patients have failed to extinguish them" (pp. 115–116). The argument is that many individuals acquire at some point in their life trivial fears and rituals but are able to overcome them. Following this line of thought, learned resourcefulness theory suggests that most individuals have acquired throughout their life a basic behavioral repertoire that enables them to cope effectively with those factors which were often assumed to cause depressive or phobic disorders. This repertoire, labeled as "learned resourcefulness," constitutes a compendium of skills by which an individual controls the interfering effects of certain internal events (e.g., emotions, pain, undesired thoughts) on the performance of desired behaviors. Learned resourcefulness means the ability to self-regulate these internal events in order to minimize their undesirable effects on behavior. An example that is brought by Rosenbaum (1983) is the lack of one-to-one correspondence between test anxiety and test performance. Thus, some students may experience test anxiety but have a basic behavioral repertoire of resourcefulness that enable them to perform well on tests despite their anxiety.

Learned resourcefulness is defined as a skill, mainly a cognitive skill, for the self-regulation of emotions, pain, and cognitions. It may involve a number of "enabling skills" such as the ability to self-monitor internal events, verbal abilities to label feelings and self-evaluative skills (Rosenbaum, 1983). At the present, the concept is assessed in subjects using the Self-Control Schedule (SCS) (Rosenbaum, 1980). The construct validity of the concept was investigated in several studies using the SCS (see Chapter 1).

The concept of learned resourcefulness and its assessment provides a new and productive avenue for research on agoraphobia. The possibility of identifying agoraphobics as people low in resourcefulness may enhance our understanding of this disorder. Since resourcefulness is regarded as a nonspecific, basic, and generalized repertoire of behavior, it could explain the multiple-faceted symptomatology of agoraphobia. Moreover, the concept of resourcefulness could contribute to our ability to design more complete and successful treatment programs for agoraphobics. The behavior therapist could guide the clients to employ the resourceful skills that are already in their repertoire to confront their anxieties rather than attempting to teach them new skills. Or, treatment could focus on strengthening and reinforcing weak "enabling skills" thereby allowing the patients to leave therapy with more enduring and generalizable strength in facing life stresses and their anxious reactions to them.

We have reviewed the outcome literature with agoraphobic and pointed to the limitations of exposure in vivo and the relative weakness of cognitive intervention. It is possible that the success rate of behavioral techniques with agoraphobics can be increased and treatment failures and drop-out decreased if treatment programs are more individually tailored to fit the existing repertoire of resourceful skills for each patient. The relative success of exposure in vivo may stem from the fact that it provides an opportunity for patients to experiment with and improve their resourcefulness skills. This explains the cognitive change (reduction in fearful ideation) which has been reported to take place concomitantly with the exposure treatment. However, since treatment is focused on very specific behavioral situations, its success in enhancing resourcefulness is limited, as is demonstrated by follow-up research and by clinical evidence that patients continue to worry about future relapses. The repeated finding that cognitive interventions do not contribute to the success of exposure in vivo might be misleading. Most cognitive interventions focus on the training of patients to employ more coping and realistic self-statements. It is possible that this is a misguided orientation. Patients may feel that the coping self-statements are foreign to their inner experiences and do not match their existing repertoire of resourcefulness. A more productive cognitive intervention might focus on utilizing available "enabling" cognitive skills and train patients in strengthening them.

Finally, the concept of resourcefulness might provide the clinicians with an important source of prediction regarding treatment outcome. If treatment outcome is found to be related to patients' level of resourcefulness prior to their entering the treatment program, then therapists could identify those patients who are more likely to fail and who may require a more prolonged and intensive course of treatment.

In the following section we will describe a research treatment project for agoraphobics conducted at Miami University. We included measures of resourcefulness as part of the assessment battery and will briefly review the findings of the project.

Treatment Program for Agoraphobia and Findings

Subject Selection

Patients were selected from a total of 55 respondents to advertisements placed in local community newspapers announcing the availability of a treatment program for agoraphobia at the Psychology Clinic of Miami University. The program was established 4 years ago and has been conducted as an ongoing project since then. Respondents were invited for a 50-minute initial interview. On the basis of the information obtained in this interview, responders were excluded if (a) they did not report their fears severe enough to largely restrict their daily activities; (b) they presented with other major mental disturbance (e.g., major depression or psychotic illness); (c) they suffered from a major physical illness (e.g., heart disease); or/and (d) they exhibited insufficient motivations or were unable to comply with treatment requirements. Forty respondents so far had met the selection criteria and underwent treatment.

Subject Characteristics

There were 33 women and seven men patients in the final sample. The average age was 46 years (range: 32–62 years), and the average duration of phobic symptoms was 11 years (range: 2–28 years). Thirty-three of the patients were married. Fifteen were employed outside of the home. Thirty-four of the 40 patients made periodic use of minor tranquilizers, and 35 had some form of psychotherapy prior to entering the program. The reported frequency of panic attacks ranged from occasional, to three to four times per week. Example of difficulties in daily life associated with the illness included fear and avoidance of driving, shopping in a supermarket or in shopping malls, being alone at home, traveling on public transportation, and eating in public. Although all invited patients appeared at the first treatment session, five (8%) dropped out at different stages of treatment.

Assessment Procedures

Assessment was conducted before, during, and after treatment. In the initial interview, information about the history of the problem, level of current functioning, frequency of panic attacks, current symptoms, and history of previous treatment was obtained.

In the behavioral test, the patient was requested to walk alone a standardized course from the clinic. The course was divided into 20 steps, and the performance score was the number of the last step completed.

The following self-report measures were administered: Social Avoidance and Distress Scale (SAD)(Watson & Friend, 1969); Fear of Negative Evaluation (FNE) (Watson & Friend, 1969); Beck Depression Inventory (BDI) (Beck, 1972); Fear Survey Schedule (FSS; Wolpe & Lang, 1964); Rathus Assertiveness Scale (RAS) (Rathus, 1973); Marital Adjustment Scale (MAS) (Locke & Wallace, 1959); Symptom Checklist (SCL-90) (Derogatis, 1977); Fear Questionnaire (Marks & Mathews, 1979) of which the agoraphobic subscale was used for analysis; and the SCS as a measure of learned resourcefulness (Rosenbaum, 1980; Chapter 1; Appendix A) given only before treatment.

During treatment, therapists collected weekly self-reports from the patients on the performance of "homework assignments." These self-reports provided data about the tasks patients attempted to complete in between sessions, how well they met their stated goals, and how much anxiety they experienced in anticipating and performing these tasks. At the end of treatment the therapists rated these self-reports using a 5-point scale (1 = little or no compliance; 5 = maximum compliance). The ratings were based on (a) the number of self-reports turned in; (b) intensity of practice in between sessions (number of times per week tasks were attempted); and (c) task difficulty. These ratings of each self-report were averaged to give an index of compliance with therapy requirements.

Therapists also used a 5-point scale to evaluate patients' improvement based on the patients' verbal reports in the sessions and their actual performance during in vivo exposure sessions (1 = no improvement; 5 = great improvement).

Follow-up questionnaires were mailed to all patients six months after treatment, requesting them to rate their current phobic situation on a 5-point scale of improvement.

Treatment

The patients were assigned to groups according to the order of their application to the program. There were six to seven patients in each group. Treatment was conducted in 12 weekly group sessions of 2 hours each. Two graduate students (a female and a male) in clinical psychology served as cotherapists for each group.

Treatment consisted of a combination of cognitive and behavioral strategies. The first two sessions were devoted to providing information about the nature of agoraphobia and helping patients establish short-term goals for each week. Therapists helped the patients construct performance hierarchies for each of their main problem areas (e.g., shopping in a supermarket; taking a ride on a bus or in the car, etc.). In the first week of therapy, the spouses were invited for one session with the therapists, in which they received information about agoraphobia and the goals of the program, including how they could be of help to their partners' progress. The next sessions were devoted to cognitive restructuring and exposure in vivo. Following Goldfried and Davidson (1976) and Meichenbaum (1977), patients were first trained in imagery, and then were asked to actively imagine themselves in different fearful situations and to verbalize any ongoing internal dialogue at the time. Irrational and defeating self-statements were discussed and confronted and patients were trained to replace them with more rational and positive self-statements. Patients were instructed to continue this type of cognitive rehearsal on their own at home. In vivo behavioral practice sessions involved venturing as a group, accompanied by the therapists, to unfamiliar nearby locations where patients could practice approaching different frightening situations. Examples of such locations were downtown centers and shopping malls. Each patient chose a relevant task for herself or himself and attempted to accomplish different performance goals. The last phase of treatment was devoted to training. In the last week of treatment, the spouses were invited for an additional session with the therapists in which they reviewed their perceptions of their partners' progress. The treatment program was highly structured, with therapists serving mainly to provide information and guidelines and to encourage and reinforce mastery experience. Thirty to forty-five minutes of each in-office session were devoted to free discussion of difficulties and achievements, and to interaction among group members.

Results

Treatment led to a significant improvement on the behavioral measure with a change from pretreatment score of 5.3 to posttreatment score of 14.1 ($t = 3.1, p < 0.02$). Results of the self-report measures indicated an overall trend of improvement. Changes from pre- to posttest on the SAD, FNE, BDI, and SCL-90 were statistically significant (see Table 7.1).

The averaged rating of improvement, based on a 5-point scale, was 3.1 (improved). The averaged rating of compliance, based on the

TABLE 7.1 Pre-and post-term mean scores and *t*-test scores for self-report questionnaires[a]

Measure	Pretest	Posttest	t	p
Social Avoidance & Distress Scale (SAD)	18.0	4.5	3.24	0.02
Fear of Negative Evaluation (FNE)	23.0	10.0	4.86	0.01
Beck Depression Inventory (BDI)	10.0	2.0	2.50	0.05
Fear Survey Schedule (FSS)	197.0	157.0	0.82	NS
Rathus Assertivness Scale (RAS)	2.0	23.0	1.45	NS
Marital Adjustment Scale (MAS)	86.0	88.0	0.25	NS
Symptom Checklist (SCL-90)	138.0	91.0	2.40	0.05
Fear Questionnaire	76.0	46.0	1.40	NS

[a]$N = 35$.
NS, not significant.

amount and intensity of practice in between sessions, was 3.42 (on a 5-point scale).

The mean SCS score for our patients at present was 23.5, with a standard deviation (SD) of 20.2 which were similar to the means and the standard deviations reported by Rosenbaum (1980).

Correlational analyses were conducted between scores on the SCS and (a) change scores on the behavioral test from pre-to posttest, (b) ratings of improvement, (c) ratings of compliance, and (d) attendance (number of sessions attended by each patient). All four product-moment correlations were positive and significant [$r(33)= 0.56$, $p < 0.01$; $r(33)= 0.61$; $p < 0.001$; $r(33)= 0.55$, $p < 0.01$; and $r(33) = 0.54$, $p < 0.01$, respectively]. In addition, correlational analyses were conducted between (a) ratings of improvement and attendance (number of sessions attended by each patient), (b) ratings of improvement and compliance, and (c) attendance and compliance. All three product-moment correlations were statistically significant ($r = 0.75, p < 0.01$; $r = 0.88, p < 0.01$; and $r = 0.75, p < 0.01$, respectively). Thus compliance and attendance correlated positively with greater improvement as well as with each other.

All data analyses were based on N of 35, excluding patients who dropped out from treatment.

Follow-up reports were received from all 35 patients. The patients' ratings of their current state of improvement 6 months after treatment correlated positively with the therapists' ratings of improvement at posttreatment. However, in their notes, most patients indicated a continuous struggle to maintain their gains with recurrent relapses into anxiety and avoidance. Only those patients who had been rated as "greatly improved" at posttest indicated a relative freedom from symptoms.

Discussion

The findings of this project contribute to the accumulated evidence for the efficacy of cognitive-behavioral intervention for agoraphobia and the useful utilization of the group format for that purpose. While the analyses reported here do not include the dismantling of the relative contribution of the different elements of the treatment (i.e., exposure in vivo, self-statement training, etc.) to the success of treatment, it is clear that the program as a whole was effective. We should not overlook, though, the clear indications for the limitations of the program. On the self-report measure, we did not find significant changes on scales assessing phobic fears (FSS and Fear Questionnaire). And at follow-ups, patients clearly indicated their concern about possible relapses and the return of fear. These findings indicate the incompleteness of the behavioral program.

The findings most relevant to the content of this chapter are obviously the high correlations between outcome and compliance measures and the measure of resourcefulness. These correlations indicate that patients high in resourcefulness were more likely to benefit from the treatment program. Their performance on the behavioral test improved considerably from pre- to posttest, they were more likely to be rated as "greatly improved" by the therapists, and they complied more readily with treatment requirements, namely, they invested greater efforts in practicing approach behaviors on their own between sessions and they tended to attend more therapy sessions. These indications of therapy adherence and improvement were also correlated with each other. According to learned resourcefulness theory, the treatment program was more successful with these patients because it capitalized on a preexisting repertoire reflected in high SCS scores. The treatment helped these patients to develop and apply skills already in their behavioral repertoire. It is interesting to note in this regard that the three patients with the highest SCS scores were women holding full-time jobs out of their homes. Patients with low SCS scores, on the other hand, may require more prolonged and extensive training in these skills. A finding of a strong correlation between pretreatment SCS score and scores collected at short- and long-term follow-ups could provide further evidence for the predictive value of resourcefulness. It may help in supporting the speculation that for patients with medium to low resourcefulness, behavioral treatment is limited in its effectiveness because it builds on assumptions about existing skills which these patients may not possess in their behavioral repertoire to a sufficient extent. Furthermore, the behavioral treatments are specific in their focus, directed toward the specific phobic problems. This orientation may not be sufficient for the strengthening of the "enabling skills" which constitute the resourcefulness repertoire. This line of reasoning applies both to the behavioral (in vivo exposure) and the cognitive components of the treatment program.

Simons, Lustman, Wetzel, and Murphy (1985) discuss another important explanation of the connection between resourcefulness and treatment success. Two inherent elements in the cognitive-behavioral treatment programs for agoraphobia are already included in the measure of resourcefulness. First, the emphasis on self-mastery and self-help orientation must be considered. Agoraphobics low on SCS may find it difficult to accept this self-help quality of therapy. There is some evidence in the literature that agoraphobics tend to endorse an external locus of control (Emmelkamp & Cohen-Kettenis, 1975). It is, thus, important to consider this factor in tailoring treatment programs for agoraphobics. Second, the cognitive components of behavioral programs are based on the belief that thoughts, attitudes, and interpretations mediate feelings and behavior. Since several items on the SCS relate to this type of conceptualization of emotional problems, a patient must already endorse this explanatory model in order to achieve a high score on the SCS (e.g., item 3, "Often, by changing my way of thinking, I am able to change my feelings about almost everything"). Patients with low resourcefulness might experience a lack of congruence between their own and the therapist's conceptualization of the problem and how best to approach it. We have emphasized earlier in this chapter the importance of congruence between the patient's internal dialogue and the treatment focus on cognitive change.

The findings in our project regarding resourcefulness are preliminary and more research is needed on the utility of learned resourcefulness in predicting treatment outcome, so that its components could be productively integrated into the treatment program. It would also be important to explore the distribution of resourcefulness scores amongst agoraphobics in comparison to normative and other psychiatric samples, in order to further examine the place of resourcefulness in a theory of etiology for the agoraphobic syndrome.

Conclusions

Agoraphobia is a multifaceted phobic syndrome presenting a major obstacle to conducting a productive, functional life for the sufferers. Its course often involves a gradual retreat from independent interactions with the world and increased need for dependency and security. This phenomenology stimulated researchers and theorists to speculate about core conflicts, separation issues, and interpersonal problems at the core of the agoraphobic illness. The characteristics of agoraphobic patients and the life events that often precede the development of the illness lend some credence to these speculations. These explanations, however, have not bred effective therapeutic approaches for agoraphobia. At present, behavioral interventions are still considered the most effective and economic mode of therapy for this disorder. The focus on in vivo exposure to specific fearful situations and the restructuring of internal dialogues of agoraphobics seem to produce beneficial results for agoraphobics. However, for many patients, this success is attenuated by the return of fear and recurrent relapses.

Learned resourcefulness theory provides an alternative avenue for understanding and treating agoraphobia. It provides a bridge between etiological speculations and research-based data on treatment effects. With regard to etiology, the theory emphasizes differences between people in terms of their resourcefulness, due to different histories of development and life opportunities. This may include restricted development of autonomous functioning, separation difficulties, and deficient inner sense of secure attachment, as speculated by dynamic theories. At the same time, resourcefulness is defined as a measurable and quantified behavioral repertoire of enabling skills which can be modified through behavioral interventions.

Research on resourcefulness and the findings of our treatment project for agoraphobia indicate the predictive value of resourcefulness in identifying patients who cope better with distress and anxiety and who benefit to a greater extent from treatment programs. With additional supporting evidence about the predictive power of this construct and more data about the distribution of resourcefulness scores amongst agoraphobic patients (compared to control groups), this new alternative may prove extremely useful in designing effective treatments for agoraphobia with more enduring and generalized results.

References

American Psychiatric Association. (1980). *Diagnostic and statistical manual of mental disorders* (3rd ed.). Washington, DC: The American Psychiatric Association.
Bandura, A. (1977). Self-efficacy: Toward a unifying theory of behavior change. *Psychological Review, 84,* 191–215.

Barlow, D. H., & Wolfe, B. E. (1981). Behavioral approaches to anxiety disorders: A report of the NIMH-SUNY Albany Research Conference. *Journal of Consulting and Clinical Psychology, 49,* 448–454.

Beck, A. T. (1972). *Depression: Causes and treatment.* Philadelphia: University of Pennsylvania Press.

Biran, M., Shreve, E., Hill, A., Thebarge, R., Hamilton, A., & Jasbeck, S. (1987). *Cognitive-behavioral treatment of agoraphobia.* Unpublished manuscript, Miami University, Oxford, OH.

Bowlby, J. (1973). *Separation: Anxiety and anger.* New York: Basic Books.

Buglass, D., Clarke, J., Henderson, A. S., Kreitman, N., & Preley, A. S. (1977). A study of agoraphobic housewives. *Psychological Medicine, 7,* 73–86.

Burns, L. E. (1982). Fear and phobias—epidemiological and phenomenological aspects. *Psychiatry in Practice, 1,* 25–28.

Burns, L. E., & Thorpe, G. L. (1977). Fears and clinical phobias: Epidemiological aspects and the National Survey of Agoraphobics. *The Journal of International Medical Research, 5* (supplement 1), 132–139.

Cash, T. F., Rimm, D. C., & MacKinnon, R. (1979). Rational-irrational beliefs and the effects of Velten Mood induction procedure. *Cognitive Therapy and Research, 3,* 151–162.

Chambless, D. L. (1978). *The role of anxiety in flooding with agoraphobic client.* Unpublished doctoral dissertation, Temple University.

Chambless, D. L., & Goldstein, A. J. (1981). Clinical treatment of agoraphobia. In M. Mavissakalian & D. Barlow (Eds.), *Phobia: Psychological pharmacological treatment* (pp. 103–144). New York: Guilford.

Derogatis, L. R. (1977). *SCL-90, administration, scorning and procedures manual for the revised version.* Baltimore, MD: Johns Hopkins University School of Medicine.

Emmelkamp, P. M. G., Brilman, E., Kuiper, H., & Mersch, P. P. (1986). The treatment of agoraphobia; A comparison of self-instructional training, rational emotive therapy, and exposure in vivo. *Behavior Modification, 10,* 37–53.

Emmelkamp, P. M. G., & Cohen-Kettenis, P. (1975). Relationship of locus of control to phobic anxiety and depression. *Psychological Reports, 36,* 390.

Emmelkamp, P. M. G., & Kuipers, A. C. M. (1979). Agoraphobia: A follow-up study four years after treatment. *British Journal of Psychiatry, 134,* 352–355.

Emmelkamp, P. M. G., Kuipers, A. C. M., & Eggeraat, J. B. (1978). Cognitive modification versus prolonged exposure in vivo: A comparison with agoraphobics as subjects. *Behaviour Research and Therapy, 16,* 33–41.

Emmelkamp, P. M. G., & Mersch, P. P. (1982). Cognition and exposure in vivo in the treatment of agoraphobia: Short-term and delayed effects. *Cognitive Therapy and Research, 6,* 77–88.

Fishman, S. (1980). *Agoraphobia: Multiform behavioral treatment.* New York: BMA Audio-Cassette Publications.

Fodor, I. G. (1974). The phobic syndrome in women. In V. Franks & V. Burtle (Eds.) *Women in therapy* (pp. 132–168). New York: Brunner/Mazel.

Fodor, I. G. (1978). *Phobia in women: Therapeutic approaches.* New York: BMA Audio-Cassette Publications

Goldfried, M. R., & Davidson, G. C. (1976). *Clinical behavior therapy.* New York: Holt, Rinehart & Winston.

Goldstein, A. J. (1982). Agoraphobia: Treatment successes, treatment failures, and theoretical implications. In D. L. Chambless & A. J. Goldstein (Eds.), *Agoraphobia. Multiple perspectives on theory and treatment* (pp 183–213). New York: Wiley.

Goldstein, A. J., & Chambless, D. L. (1978). A reanalysis of agoraphobia. *Behavior Therapy, 9,* 47–59.

Guidano, V. F., & Liotti, G. (1983). *Cognitive processes and emotional disorders.* New York: Guilford.

Hallam, R. S. (1978). Agoraphobia: A critical review of the concept. *British Journal of Psychiatry, 133,* 314–319.

Jansson, L., & Ost, L. G. (1982). Behavioral treatment for agoraphobia: An evaluative review. *Clinical Psychology Review, 2,* 311–336.

Kendall, P. C., & Korgeski, G. P. (1979). Assessment and cognitive-behavioral interventions. *Cognitive Therapy and Research, 3,* 1–21.

Klein, D. F. (1981). Anxiety reconceptualized. In D. F. Klein & J. Rabkin (Eds.), *Anxiety: New research and changing concepts* (pp. 235–265). New York: Raven.

Last, C. G. (1984). Cognitive treatment of phobia. In M. Hersen, R. M. Eisler, & P. M. Miller (Eds.), *Progress in behavior modification: Volume 16* (pp. 65–82). New York: Academic Press.

Locke, H. J., & Wallace, K. M. (1959). Short marital adjustment and prediction tests: Their reliability and validity. *Marriage and Family Living, 21,* 251–255.

Mahoney, M. (1979). Psychotherapy and human change processes. *APA Master Lecture Series: Psychotherapy research and behavior change.* Washington, DC: American Psychological Association.

Marks, I. (1983). Behavioral concepts and treatment of neuroses. In M. Rosenbaum, C. M. Franks, & Y. Jaffe, (Eds.), *Perspectives on behavior therapy in the eighties* (pp. 54–73). New York: Springer Publishing Co.

Marks, I. M., & Gelder, M. G. (1965). A controlled retrospective study of behaviour therapy in phobic patients. *British Journal of Psychiatry, 111,* 571–573.

Marks, I. M., Mathews, A. M. (1979). Brief standard self-rating for phobic patients. *Behaviour Research and Therapy, 17,* 263–267.

Mavissakalian, M., Michelson, L., Greenwald, D., Kronblith, A., & Greenwald, M. (1983). Cognitive-behavioral treatment of agoraphobia: Paradoxical intention vs. self-statement training. *Behavior Research and Therapy, 21,* 75–86.

Meichenbaum, D. H. (1977). *Cognitive behavior modification: An integrative approach.* New York: Plenum Press.

Mullaney, J. A., & Trippett, C. J. (1979). Alcohol dependence and phobias: Clinical description and relevance. *British Journal of Psychiatry, 135,* 565–573.

Rachman, S. (1983). The modification of agoraphobic avoidance behavior: Some fresh possibilities. *Behavior Research and Therapy, 21,* 567–574.

Rathus, S. A. (1973). A 30-item schedule for assessing assertive behavior. *Behavior Therapy, 4,* 498–506.

Rosenbaum, M. (1980). A schedule for assessing self control behaviors: Preliminary findings. *Behavior Therapy, 11,* 109–121.

Rosenbaum, M. (1983). Learned resourcefulness as a behavioral repertoire for the self-regulation of internal events: Issues and speculations. In M. Rosenbaum, C. M. Franks, & Y. Jaffe (Eds.), *Perspectives on behavior therapy in the eighties* (pp. 54–73). New York: Springer Publishing Co.

Roth, M. (1959). The phobic-anxiety-depersonalization syndrome. *Proceedings of the Royal Society of Medicine, 52,* 587–595.

Shafar, S. (1976). Aspects of phobic illness—a study of 90 personal cases. *British Journal of Medical Psychology, 49,* 221–236.

Simons, A. D., Lustman, P. J., Wetzel, R. D., & Murphy, G. E. (1985). Predicting response to cognitive therapy of depression: The role of learned resourcefulness. *Cognitive Therapy and Research, 9,* 79–89

Snaith, R. P. (1968). A clinical investigation of phobias. *British Journal of Psychiatry, 114,* 673–698.

Watson, D., & Friend, R. (1969). Measurement of social-evaluative anxiety. *Journal of Consulting and Clinical Psychology, 33,* 448–457.

Williams, S. L., & Rappoport, A. (1983). Cognitive treatment in the natural environment for agoraphobics. *Behavior Therapy, 14,* 299–313.

Wilson, G. T. (1982). Adult disorders. In G. T. Wilson & C. M. Franks (Eds.), *Contemporary behavior therapy* (pp. 505–562). New York: Guilford.

Wolpe, J., & Lang, O. J. (1964). A fear survey schedule for use in behavior therapy. *Behaviour Research and Therapy, 2,* 27–30.

8

Learned Resourcefulness and Depression

Peter M. Lewinsohn
Carolyn Alexander

There are several reasons for postulating a relationship between depression and learned resourcefulness. Depression is a common emotional disorder (e.g., Amenson & Lewinsohn, 1981), and one would, therefore, expect the variables that are related to the occurrence of depression to be widely distributed in the general population. Although there is considerable controversy about relative importance of specific etiological variables (cf., Lewinsohn & Hoberman, 1982, for a review), the central importance of the occurrence of stressful life events in the chain of events leading to depression has been recognized by most theorists (Aneshensel & Frerichs, 1982; Billings & Moos, 1982; Brown & Harris, 1978; Lewinsohn, Hoberman, Teri, & Hautzinger, 1985). Initially, stress was found to be associated with depression on the basis of retrospective data (Paykel et al., 1969), but recent prospective studies (e.g., Lewinsohn, Hoberman, & Rosenbaum, 1988) clearly show that the occurrence of stressful life events increases the probability for the future occurrence of depression. In particular, the literature suggests that stressors that disrupt important aspects of the individual's performance such as marital conflict, social exits, and unemployment bear an especially important relationship to the development of depression. The correlation between stress and depression, however, has typically been found to be quite low ($r = 0.20$), indicating that there are large individual differences in the depressive response following the occurrence of stressful life events. We thus hypothesized that learned resourcefulness moderates the relationship between stress and depression. Specifically, we predicted that people who are low on learned resourcefulness would be more likely to become depressed under conditions of elevated stress.

Several other findings from the literature on depression served as the basis for additional hypotheses about the relationship between depression and learned resourcefulness. It is well known that there are large individual differences in duration of episodes of depression, and that most people have relatively short episodes. In a recent study of episode duration (Lewinsohn, Fenn, Franklin, & Stanton, 1986) it was found that about 25% of the episodes last less than 1 month; 50% last less than 3 months, and only 25% last 1 year or longer. Furthermore, most people who experience a depressive episode do not seek treatment (Vernon & Roberts, 1982). It appears, therefore, that most people are able to terminate their depression relatively quickly without professional assistance. To date, there have been few attempts to study the psychological processes that enable people to terminate their depression without professional help (Hautzinger & Hoffman, 1979; Parker & Brown, 1982; Rippere, 1977). Although somewhat limited conclusions can be drawn from these studies, it does appear that people are able to effectively use a wide range of behaviors and cognitions to terminate their depression. Hence we hypothesized an inverse relationship between learned resourcefulness and episode duration.

Another important finding from the depression literature is that a history of previous episodes substantially increases the risk for future depression. Thus, Amenson and Lewinsohn (1981) found the incidence of depression in persons with a previous history to be twice as high as that of persons without such a history. Related findings have been reported by Keller, Shapiro, Lavori, and Wolfe (1982), and by Gonzales, Lewinsohn, and Clarke (1984), who found that about 30% of depressed patients who were recovered at the end of treatment experienced another episode of depression within one year. As a corollary of our first hypothesis, we predicted that persons with a previous history of depression, but who are not depressed at the time of observation, would be characterized by low learned resourcefulness.

In this chapter, we report results relevant to the above–mentioned hypotheses from a longitudinal, prospective study aimed at the identification of antecedents for depression. Data were collected on 806 elderly persons from the general community, the majority of whom were not depressed at the beginning of the study (T1). These subjects were subsequently followed and additional data were collected. On the basis of the initial and follow-up data, it was possible to categorize the subjects into the following groups: (a) cases, i.e., subjects who were not depressed at point of entry but who became depressed during the course of the study; (b) normal controls, i.e., subjects who were not depressed at any time during the study (an additional subdivision of the controls was determined by whether or not the subject had a previous history of depression); and (c) depressives; i.e., participants who were depressed at point of entry into the study.

In addition to measures of depression and of stress, the data set also included a host of other psychological variables. This made it possible to examine the construct validity of the Self-Control Schedule (SCS) (Rosenbaum, 1980; Chapter 1, this volume). Our general expectation was that persons who score high on the SCS have better coping skills and hence would report themselves more satisfied with the important aspects of their lives (including their social supports) would perceive themselves as more socially competent, and would report themselves as experiencing fewer psychological symptoms and complaints.

Method

Participants

Potential participants were identified through a list of licensed drivers obtained from the Oregon Department of Motor Vehicles. A complete listing was obtained of persons over age 50 residing in three zip code areas of Eugene-Springfield, Oregon. A randomly selected subset ($N =$ 4,133) were mailed letters and invited to participate in psychological research aimed at "the understanding of psychological health and its relationship to what people do, think, and feel." The results to be reported are based on the first 806 individuals who indicated interest in participating, filled out an initial questionnaire, and participated in a diagnostic interview. At point of entry into the study (T1), all subjects filled out a 286-item questionnaire. Shortly after completing the questionnaire subjects came in for a diagnostic interview at which time the Center for Epidemiologic Studies Depression Scale (CES-D) (Radloff, 1977) was administered. Thereafter subjects completed the CES-D periodically. Subjects with high scores on the CES-D were asked to come in for an additional interview; a total of 573 follow-up interviews were completed.

Assessment of Depression

Depression was assessed by means of the CES-D given to subjects at intake and by means of a clinical interview based on the Schedule for Affective Disorders (SADS) and Research Diagnostic Criteria (RDC) procedures (Spitzer and Endicott, 1978).

The CES-D is a self-report measure of the frequency of occurrence of 20 symptoms of depression. Subjects report on how they felt during the past week. The CES-D was specifically developed for use in studies of depression symptomatology in the general population, and has demonstrated utility as a screening instrument (Roberts & Vernon, 1983; Weissman, Sholomkas, Pottenger, Prusoff, & Locke, 1977; Lewinsohn & Teri, 1982; Amenson & Lewinsohn, 1981). The CES-D has been shown to be correlated substantially with self-report depression measures, such as the Beck Depression Inventory (Beck, 1967) and to adequately differentiate depressed from nondepressed group (Husaini, Neff, Harrington, Hughes, & Stone, 1980; Radloff, 1977).

Diagnoses of depression and other psychopathological syndromes were based on information gathered from participants in a two-hour semi-structured interview, the SADS (Endicott & Spitzer, 1989). Decision rules specified by the RDC (Spitzer, Endicott, & Robins, 1978) were used to classify the information obtained during the interview into specific RDC diagnostic categories.

Diagnostic interviewers probed for the presence of symptoms at time of the interview and for all times prior to the interview. Thus, past as well as current episodes of depression were diagnosed. For each diagnosis, onset age durations were recorded. To be diagnosed as depressed, a subject had to have met RDC criteria for major, minor, or intermittent depressive disorder. Subjects were excluded from the study if, in addition to being depressed, they met criteria for one of the following diagnoses: (a) schizophrenia, alcoholism, panic or anxiety disorder as the dominant symptom, (b) an RDC life-time diagnosis of bipolar disorder with either mania or hypomania, or (c) organic brain syndrome or mental retardation. Thus, in the context of this study, depression has been defined as pure unipolar depression.

On the basis of diagnostic information gathered during the initial interview, 70 of the subjects were judged to meet criteria for a diagnosis of depression.

Case Finding

Following the initial interview all subjects were administered the CES-D periodically. A total of eight CES-D's were given at intervals of 2-3 months. On the basis of the follow-up interview, 63 subjects were determined to have become depressed (i.e., Cases). To be defined as a case, a subject had to have had a low score on the CES-D at T1 (<9), to not have met criteria for a diagnosis of depression at T1, and to have developed an episode of depression during the interim. There were 189 subjects who had a history of depression prior to the study but who did not become depressed during the course of the study ("Not During") and there were 324 normal controls, i.e., subjects who had never been and who did not become depressed during the course of the study.

The diagnostic interviewers were a carefully selected group of graduate and advanced undergraduate students who were enrolled in a year-long didactic and experiential diagnostic interviewing course in which they learned to conduct a semi-structured clinical interview (SADS) and to diagnose subjects according to decision rules specified by the RDC. Interviewers were blind to questionnaire data, subject selection procedure, and the specific hypotheses under investigation.

To evaluate the reliability of the diagnostic assignments, a randomly selected number of interviews were observed by a second interviewer. The Kappa statistic (Cohen, 1960), which measures how well two rates agree beyond the level predicted by chance, was used to measure the reliability of diagnostic classification between interviewer pairs. For diagnoses at the initial interview weighted Kappa were as follows: not mentally ill: 0.98; major, minor, or intermittent depressive disorder: 0.92. For diagnosis at the follow-up interview, weighted Kappas were as follows: not mentally ill: 1.00; major, minor, or intermittent depressive disorder: 0.91.

Assessment of Dependent Variables

Demographic Variables

Subjects reported their sex, age, marital status, educational level, and employment status. The demographic characteristics of he sample are shown in Table 8.1.

Psychological Variables

1. *Self-Control Schedule*: SCS (Rosenbaum, 1980) was included as the measure of learned resourcefulness. This test consists of 36 items dealing with the use of coping skills used by people for the solution of stressful situations (Chapter 1; Appendix A).

2. *Self-Rated Health*: Health ratings were elicited with 10 items dealing with subjects' overall self-perceived health status as well as specific items addressing vision, hearing, physical disabilities, the occurrence of a serious illness during the past six months, and the use of medications.

3. *Stressful life Events*: Two separate scales probing for the occurrence of micro-and macrostressors were included. Macrostressors ($N = 25$) were measured with a subset of items from the Social Readjustment Rating Scale (Holmes & Rahe, 1967). Each event was rated as to

TABLE 8.1. Demographic characteristics of the sample $(N = 806)$

Parameter	Percentage of sample
Gender	
Female	55.8
Male	44.2
Age[a]	
50–59 yrs.	33.1
60–69	44.0
70+	22.9
Employment status	
Employed	30.8
Unemployed	10.7
Retired	58.3
Educational level	
Grade school	1.8
8th grade	3.8
High school	20.3
Some college or vocational school	41.6
College degree	19.2
Professional degree	13.2
Marital status	
Married	77.5
Divorced/separated	8.7
Widow/er	12.6
Never married	1.2

[a]Mean age = 63.7; SD = 7.9; range = 50–96 years.

whether it had occurred during the past six months to the subject, to a close relative, to a friend, or to the spouse. Based on the life change unit score for each event, a total stress sum was computed for each subject. These scores were then converted to standard scores.

Microstressors were assessed with 44 items from the mood-related events scale of the Unpleasant Events Schedule (Lewinsohn, Mermelstein, Alexander, & MacPhillamy, 1985). These items describe aversive experiences that are part of everyday life, such as having arguments with one's spouse and having to do things one does not like to do. The subjects rated these events on a 3-point scale in terms of their occurrence during the past 30 days. A sum was computed for each subject and these scores were also converted to standard scores. A total stress score was then computed for each subject by summing his or her macro- and microstressor scores.

4. *Social Support Network*: The subjects' social support network was assessed with nine items dealing with the frequency of contacts made by the subjects with members of their network.

5. *Perceived Social Support: Family and Friends*: Abbreviated versions of the two scales of the Perceived Social Support Questionnaire (Procidano & Heller, 1979) were included. These scales are intended to assess the degree to which the subject feels that he or she is supported by family members (10 items) and by friends (10 items).

6. *Satisfaction with Relationships*: Seven items designed to ascertain the subjects' satisfaction with the quality and quantity of their interaction with relatives and friends were included. A total sum was computed for these items.

7. *Life Satisfaction*: Ten items assessed the subjects' degree of satisfaction with the quality and frequency of their activities, accomplishments, family life, marital interaction, and recreational activities were included.

8. *Availability of Help*: Six items were included to assess the potential availability of help from members of the subjects' social network.

9. *Activities*: Five items were included to assess the subject's involvement with pets, plants, television, hobbies, and physical activity (e.g.,"Do you exercise on a regular basis" and "Do you have any hobbies").

10. *Interpersonal Dependency*: The Emotional Reliance ($N = 18$) and Social Self-Confidence ($N = 16$) Scales of the Interpersonal Dependency Questionnaire (Hirschfeld et al., 1976) were included. The items on the Emotional Reliance Scale focus on the subjects' need for attachment and dependency; i.e., the items express a wish for contact with and emotional support from other persons. The items on the Social Self-Confidence Scale reflect wishes for help in decision-making situations and in situations that require taking an initiative.

11. *Cognitive Dysfunction*: Six items selected from the Inventory of Psychic and Somatic Complaints-Elderly Scale developed by Raskin (1979) to measure the degree to which the subjects felt themselves to be experiencing confusion and difficulties with memory, concentration, and thinking.

12. *Pleasantness of Activities*: Seven pleasant activities from the mood-related scale of the Pleasant Events Schedule (MacPhillamy and Lewinsohn, 1971) were included (e.g., "Being with friends"). The subjects were asked to rate the enjoyability of each item on a three-point scale.

13. *Self-Perceived Social Skill*: Subjects were asked to rate themselves, using a 7-point scale, on 16 adjectives (e.g., "Friendly," "Popular," "Assertive") designed to elicit the subjects' self-rated social competence. These items were selected from a previous study (Lewinsohn, Mischel, Chaplin, & Barton, 1980).

14. *Self-Perceived Dysphoria-Anxiety*: The subjects also rated them-

selves on the degree to which being anxious, sad, optimistic and pessimistic was characteristic of them. These were also derived from a previous study (Lewinsohn, Mischel, Chaplin, & Barton, 1980). Each item was rated on a 7-point scale (1 = not at all characteristic, 7 = extremely characteristic).

15. *Anti-depressant Behaviors*: A set of items were derived from recent studies (Rippere, 1977; Parker & Brown, 1982) on the types of responses people make when they feel depressed. From these studies two scales were constructed: (a) effective behaviors ($N = 12$), e.g., thinking through the problem; (b) Ineffective behaviors ($N = 11$), e.g., avoiding other people.

16. *Use of Caffeine, Tobacco, and Alcohol*: Three items were included to assess the degree to which the subject consumes coffee and tea, smokes cigarettes, and drinks alcoholic beverages.

17. *Social Desirability*: Ten items from the Crowne-Marlow Social Desirability Scale (Crowne & Marlow, 1960) were included.

Results

Relation Between Learned Resourcefulness, Stress, Gender, Age, and Depression

From the available data, the potential effects of the following variables (singly and in interaction) upon diagnostic category could be assessed: learned resourcefulness, stress, age, gender, and diagnostic category. Multiway frequency table analysis (BMDP3F, 1979) was selected as the most appropriate statistical technique. This analysis allows for the simultaneous inclusion of the effects of all the variables of interest and is not sensitive to the skewness of any of the variables. The analysis provides chi-square estimates based on the log linear model. This model specifies probabilities as the linear sum of the logarithms of the frequencies, and allows all probabilities to be expressed as the sum of marginal probabilities. As such the design corresponds to the model used in the analysis of variance. Thus, the independence of association for two variables is referred to as first order interaction; independence for the combined effects of three variables is referred to as a second order interaction; and so on. Interactions and main effects in this analysis are interpretable exactly as in the analysis of variance (Everitt, 1977). As the use of this statistical procedure requires categorical variables, age and the SCS scores were categorized to generate approximately equal number of subjects in each of the intervals. Age was trichotomized into high, intermediate, and low subgroups (<60; 60-69; 70+ years). Diagnostic groups were constituted by Cases ($N = 63$), Not

During ($N = 189$), Depressed at TL ($N = 70$), and Normal Controls ($N = 324$).

The multi-way analysis revealed a significant relationship between the SCS and diagnostic group [$\chi^2(6, N = 646) = 20.8, p < 0.002$]. The mean SCS scores of the four groups are shown in Table 8.2. Post hoc contrasts showed Cases to be lower on the SCS than those who were not depressed at TL [$\chi^2 (2, N = 576) = 10.1, p < 0.01$]; the Depressed at TL to be lower than those who were not depressed at T_1 [$\chi^2 (2, N = 646) = 11.8, p < 0.003$]; and for the Not During not to differ from the Normal Controls [$\chi^2 (2, N = 513) = <1$, NS].

The analysis also revealed a significant effect due to stress [$\chi^2 (6, N = 646) = 29.7, p < 0.001$] with a greater proportion of the Cases [$\chi^2 (2, N = 576) = 11.8, p < 0.003$] and the Depressed at T_1 [$\chi^2 (2, N = 646) = 6.5, p < 0.04$] being in highest stress, and the Not During [$\chi^2 (2, N = 513) = 11.8, p < 0.003$] having higher stress scores than the normal controls. The critical interaction between diagnostic group by SCS group by stress group, however, did not attain statistical significance [$\chi^2 (12, N = 646) = 9.2$. NS] (see Table 8.3).

While age was not found to be related to SCS [$\chi^2 (4, N = 646) = 3.0$, NS], gender was [$\chi^2 (2, N = 646) = 6.45, p < 0.04$], with women having slightly higher SCS scores than men, as shown in Table 8.4. Replicating earlier findings women were overrepresented among the Cases and Depressed [$\chi^2(2, N = 646) = 16.7; p < 0.001$; however, women did not show more stress [$\chi^2(2, N = 646) = 2.3$, NS].

Relation Between SCS and Duration of Episodes

For this analysis, we identified all subjects with a previous history of major or minor depressive disorder. Subjects with intermittent de-

TABLE 8.2. Mean age and mean SCS scores of the diagnostic groups

	Cases ($N = 63$)	Not During ($N = 189$)	Depressed ($N = 70$)	Normal Controls ($N = 324$)
Age				
M	61.6	61.9	61.6	65.3
SD	7.4	7.4	7.4	7.9
SCS				
M	24.43	25.13	23.80	25.0
SD	16.0	15.8	13.8	14.9

TABLE 8.3. Distribution of diagnostic groups on the stress measure

Diagnostic group	Stress			
	Low	Intermediate	High	*N*
Cases	19.0%	30.2%	50.8%	63
Not During	25.9%	40.7%	33.3%	189
Depressed	20.0%	34.7%	45.7%	70
Normal Control	41.0%	35.2%	23.8%	324
Total	32.2%	36.2%	31.6%	646

pressive disorder were omitted because, by definition, the duration of such episodes is indeterminate. There were 185 subjects with a previous episode of major or minor depressive disorder. The mean interval between the occurrence of the episode and the time the subjects were interviewed was 15 years; standard deviation was 12.5 years; range was 0–59 years.

Because the frequency distribution of duration values is known to be very skewed (Lewinsohn, Fenn, Franklin, & Stanton, 1986), the values were categorized into four categories (<7 weeks, 7-19 weeks, 19-51 weeks, 1 year+) as shown in Table 8.5. The SCS scores of the four groups were then compared by means of an ANOVA. Differences were small and did not attain statistical significance [$F(3,177) = 1.3$, NS].

Construct Validity of the SCS

In order to clarify the psychological characteristics associated with the SCS, we computed its correlation with all other variables, performed a multiple linear regression with the SCS as dependent variable, and a discriminant function analysis. For the latter, the subjects were trichotomized on the SCS into three groups with approximately equal *N*.

TABLE 8.4. Percentage of women and men in each of the three SCS groups

SCS	Women	Men
Low	24.7%	34.5%
Intermediate	24.2%	21.4%
High	51.1%	44.1%
N	356	290

TABLE 8.5. Mean SCS scores for
groups who had a previous episode of
depression ($N = 189$) and who differed
in duration

SCS	Duration (in weeks)			
	1–6	7–19	19–51	52
M	25.1	25.2	25.6	24.8
SD	17.0	15.3	14.0	16.2
N	46	31	38	70

As can be seen in Table 8.6, the following variables were significantly correlated with the SCS: Self-Perceived Social Skill, Self-Perceived Dysphoria/Anxiety, Life Satisfaction, Antidepressant Behaviors: Interpersonal Problem-Solving, Pleasant Activities, Antidepressant Behaviors: Maladjusted Behaviors, Cognitive Dysfunction, Antidepressant Behaviors: Activities, CESD, Antidepressant Behaviors: Effective Behaviors, Perceived Social Support: Friends and Family, Social Support Network, and Self-Rated Health.

Correlation of the following variables with SCS did not attain significance at the 0.05 level: Satisfaction with Relationships: Friends and Others, Availability of Help, Help from Friends/Children/Grandchildren, Helping Others, Addictive Behaviors, Social Desirability, Emotional Reliance, and all of the stress measures (see Table 8.6).

The multiple correlation for the above-mentioned variables with the SCS scores was $R = 0.57$. The use of the discriminant function allowed for the correct classification of 54.2% of the sample (chance $> 33.3\%$).

Discussion

The major finding of the present study is constituted by the fact that persons who were low on learned resourcefulness were more likely to *become* depressed during the course of the study. Being low on learned resourcefulness and therefore presumably being deficient in the kinds of coping skills implied by the learned resourcefulness construct, substantially increased the probability for an episode of depression, independent of status on the stress measure, and is consistent with other findings in the literature (Brown & Harris, 1978; Dohrenwend & Dohrenwend, 1978). However, the predicted interaction between stress and learned resourcefulness was not found. In other words, the appear-

TABLE 8.6. Correlation of the SCS With Each of the Other Measures

Variable	r	F	p
Self-Perceived Social Skill	0.40	56.0	0.001
Self-Perceived Dysphoria/Anxiety	−0.36	44.9	0.001
Self-Confidence	0.30	33.5	0.001
Life Satisfaction	0.28	29.0	0.001
Pleasant Activities	0.26	25.9	0.001
Antidepressant Behaviors			
Interpersonal Problem-Solving	0.27	23.5	0.001
Maladjusted Behavior	0.25	20.4	0.001
Cognitive Dysfunction	0.24	17.4	0.001
CES-D	−0.21	19.4	0.001
Activities	0.22	18.0	0.001
Antidepressant Behaviors: Effective Behaviors	0.20	17.8	0.001
Perceived Social Support-Friends	0.20	12.7	0.001
Cognitive Dysfunction	0.24	17.4	0.001
Satisfaction with Relationships	0.12	3.8	0.02
Perceived Social Support-Family	0.19	12.7	0.001
Social Support Network	0.18	11.0	0.001
Antidepressant Behaviors: Ineffective Behaviors	0.18	12.9	0.001
Self-Rated Heart	0.15	7.4	0.001
Antidepressant Behaviors: Activities	0.15	10.5	0.001
Satisfaction with Relationships: Children	0.13	3.8	0.02
Addictive Behaviors	−0.11	2.2	0.11
Helping Others	0.10	1.7	0.18
Emotional Reliance	−0.10	2.3	0.09
Social desirability	−0.08	<1	NS
Help From Friends/Children/Grandchildren	0.07	<1	NS
Satisfaction with Relationships			
Others	−0.06	1.8	0.17
Friends	0.04	<1	NS
Availability of Help	0.03	1.1	NS
Stress			
Spouse	−0.03	<1	NS
Microstressors	−0.02	<1	NS
Self	0.02	<1	NS
Family	−0.02	<1	NS
Antidepressant Behaviors: Interpersonal Help-Seeking	−0.02	<1	NS

NS, not significant.

ance of stressful life events increased probability for becoming depressed, and being low on learned resourcefulness increased the probability for becoming depressed; but, learned resourcefulness did not moderate the relationship between stress and the onset of depression. These two risk factors acted in an additive but not in a multiplicative or interactive way.

The fact that the duration of episodes of depression that our subjects had experienced prior to the onset of the study was not associated with learned resourcefulness was unexpected. In other words, being high on learned resourcefulness reduced the probability of *becoming* depressed, but once somebody had become depressed, their learned resourcefulness level was irrelevant. It may tentatively be suggested that while having the kinds of coping skills measured by SCS helps one to avoid becoming depressed, but once depressed, the depression process overrides these skills.

While both the Cases and the Depressives scored low on the SCS, the Not Durings did not differ from the Normal Controls. This constitutes another unexpected and challenging finding. Because we assumed that learned resourcefulness is a trait, we expected the Not During to score lower on the SCS than the Normal Controls. Our findings tentatively suggest that learned resourcefulness also has state characteristics; i.e., that it is diminished by the depression state, but once depression has terminated it reverts to its previous level. It needs to be emphasized, of course, that the above mentioned inferences about temporal fluctuations in learned resourcefulness are speculative and that they need to be studied longitudinally in the same subjects after they have recovered from their depressive episode.

Consistent with other studies (e.g., Amenson & Lewinsohn, 1981; Weissman & Paykel, 1974) women were more likely to become Cases and to be depressed. Our women participants, however, did not differ from the men participants in regard to stress level, and were slightly but significantly higher than men on the SCS. Thus, as we found in our earlier study (Amenson & Lewinsohn, 1981), psychological variables that are related to depression are relatively unsuccessful in accounting for the substantial difference in the prevalence and incidence of depression among men and women.

The fact that learned resourcefulness did not moderate the relationship between stress and depression also deserves discussion, as the concept that learned resourcefulness allows people to function effectively in stressful conditions has been central to previous theorizing (Rosenbaum, 1983; Chapter 1, this volume). Are our results inconsistent with previously reported findings of disrupted performance by those who are low on learned resourcefulness but not on the part of those who are high on learned resourcefulness? We think not. In these previous studies, the performance of groups differentiated on learned resourcefulness has been compared only under stressful conditions. On the basis of our results, we would predict that performance differences would be found between groups differentiated on the basis of learned resourcefulness even under *low* stress conditions.

Our results provide good support for the construct validity of the SCS. Consistent with theoretical expectations, the SCS was found to be correlated with other scales designed to identify behaviors shown to be both effective and ineffective in coping with depression. The SCS was also correlated with measures reflecting one's confidence and self-perceived skill in social interaction, with being satisfied with one's relationships and with major life roles, with being more active and enjoying one's activities, and with feeling oneself to be cognitively competent and healthy. The variables that were not correlated with the SCS also add to its discriminant validity. Most importantly, the SCS was not found to be associated with the Social Desirability Scale, suggesting that the SCS is relatively stable in terms of responses biases. Also, the SCS was not correlated with whether or not people felt themselves to be emotionally dependent on others, with the rate of occurrence of stressful life events, with the frequency of contacts with others, or with the perceived availability of help.

In sum, the picture that emerges of the person who has skills measured by the SCS is that of an individual who feels self-confident about the ability to cope with the problems posed by daily life and who is less likely to become depressed.

Whether being low on learned resourcefulness constitutes a specific vulnerability for depression or whether, as one would expect on theoretical grounds, it is also a risk factor for the occurrence of other problematic behaviors such as anxiety and psychosomatic disorders is an important question which needs to be addressed in future studies.

References

Amenson, C. S., & Lewinsohn, P. M. (1981). An investigation into the observed sex difference in prevalence of unipola depression. *Journal of Abnormal Psychology, 90,* 1–13.

Aneshensel, C. S., & Frerichs, R. R. (1982). Stress, support, and depression: A longitudinal causal model. *Journal of Community Psychology, 10,* 1392–1396.

Beck, A. T.(1967). *Depression: Clinical experimental and theoretical aspects.* New York: Harper and Raw.

Billings, A. C., & Moos, R. H. (1982). Stressful life events and symptoms: A longitudinal model. *Health Psychology, 1,* 99–117.

Brown, G. W., & Harris, T. (1978). *Social origins of depression.* New York: The Free Press.

Cohen, J. (1960). A coefficient of agreement for nominal scales. *Educational and Psychological Measurement, 1,* 37–46.

Crowne, D. P., & Marlowe, D. A. (1960). A new scale of social desirability independent of psychopathology. *Journal of Consulting Psychology, 66,* 547–555.

Dohrenwend, B. S., & Dohrenwend, B. P. (1978). Some issues in research on stressful life events. *Journal of Nervous and Mental Diseases, 166,* 7–15.

Endicott, J., & Spitzer, R. L. (1978). A diagnostic interview: The schedule for affective disorders and schizophrenia. *Archives of General Psychiatry, 35,* 837–844.

Everitt, B. S. (1977). *The analysis of contingency tables.* New York: Halstead.

Gonzales, L., Lewinsohn, P. M., & Clarke, G. (1985). Long term follow-up of Coping With Depression course participants. *Journal of Consulting and Clinical Psychology, 53,* 461–469.

Hautzinger, M., & Hoffman, N. (Eds.) (1979). *Depression und Umwelt.* Salzburg, Austria: Otto Muller Verlag.

Hirschfeld, R., Klerman, G. L., Chodoff, P., Korchin, S., & Barret, J. (1976). Dependency of self-esteem clinical depression. *Journal of the American Academy of Psychoanalysis, 4,* 373–388.

Holmes, T. H., & Rahe, R. H. (1967). The social readjustment rating scale. *Journal of psychosomatic Research, 11,* 213–218.

Husaini, B. A. & Neff, J. A. Harrington, J. B., Hughes, M. D., & Stone, R. H. (1980). Depression in rural communities: Validating the CES-D scale. *Journal of Community Psychology, 8,* 20–27.

Keller, M. B., Shapiro, R. W., Lavori, P. W., & Wolfe, N. (1982). Recovery in major depressive disorder. *Archives of General Psychiatry, 39,* 905–910.

Lewinsohn, P. M., Fenn, D., Franklin, J., & Stanton, A. K. (1986). Relation of age at onset to duration of episode in unipolar depression. *Journal of Psychology and Aging, 1,* 63–68.

Lewinsohn, P. M., & Hoberman, H. M. (1982). Depression. In A.S. Bellack, M. Hersen, & A.E. Kazdin (Eds.), *International handbook of behavior modification and therapy.* (pp. 173–208). New York: Plenum Press.

Lewinsohn, P. M., Hoberman, H., & Rosenbaum, M. (1988). A prospective study of risk factors for unipolar depression. *Journal of Abnormal Psychology, 97,* 251–264.

Lewinsohn, P., Hoberman, H., Teri, L., & Hautzinger, M. (1984). *An integrative theory of depression. In S. Reiss & R. Bootzin (Eds.), Theoretical issues in behavior therapy* (pp. 331–359). New York: Academic Press.

Lewinsohn, P. M., Mermelstein, R. M., Alexander, C., & MacPhillamy, D. J. (1985). The Unpleasant Events Schedule: A scale for the measurement of aversive events. *Journal of Clinical Psychology, 41,* 483–498.

Lewinsohn, P. M., Mischel, W., Chaplin, W., & Barton, R. (1980). Social competence & depression: The role of illusory self-perceptions. *Journal of Abnormal Psychology, 89,* 203–212.

Lewinsohn, P. M., & Teri, L. (1982). Selection of depressed and non-depressed subjects on the basis of self-report data. *Journal of Consulting and Clinical Psychology, 50,* 590–591.

MacPhillamy, D. J., & Lewinsohn, P. M. (1971). *A scale for the measurement of positive reinforcement.* Unpublished communication, University of Oregon.

Parker, G. B., & Brown, L. B. (1982). Coping behaviors that mediate between life events and depression. *Archives of General Psychiatry, 39,* 1386–1391.

Paykel, E. S., Prusoff, B. A., & Uhlenhuth, E. H. (1969). Scaling of life events. *Archives of General Psychiatry, 21,* 753–760.

Procidano, M. E., & Heller, K. (1983). Measures of perceived social support from friends and from family: Three validation studies. *American Journal of Community Psychology, 11,* 1–24.

Radloff, L. S. (1977). The CES-D scale: A self-report depression scale for research in the general population. *Applied Psychological Measurement, 1,* 385–401.

Raskin, A., & Jarvik, L. (Eds.) (1979). *Psychiatric symptoms and cognitive loss in the elderly.* Washington DC: Hemisphere Publications.

Rippere, V. (1977). What's the thing to do when you're feeling depressed a pilot study. *Behavioral Research & Therapy, 15,* 185–191.

Roberts, R. E., & Vernon, S. W. (1983). The center for epidemiological studies depression scale: Its use in a community sample. *American Journal of Psychiatry, 140,* 41–46.

Rosenbaum, M. (1980). A schedule for assessing self-control behaviors: Preliminary findings. *Behavior Therapy, 11,* 109–121.

Rosenbaum, M. (1983). Learned resourcefulness as a behavioral repertoire for the self-regulation of internal events: Issues and speculations. In M. Rosenbaum, C. M. Franks, & Y. Jaffe (Eds.), *Perspectives on behavior therapy in the eighties* (pp. 54–73). New York: Springer Publishing Co.

Spitzer, R. L., Endicott, J., & Robins, E. (1978). Research diagnostic criteria (RDC). *Psychopharmacology Bulletin, 11,* 22–24.

Spitzer, R. L., Endicott, J., & Robbins (1978). Research diagnostic criteria: Rationale and reliability. *Archives of General Psychiatry, 35,* 773–782.

Vernon, S. W., & Roberts, R. E. (1982). Prevalence of treated and untreated psychiatric disorders in three ethnic groups. *Social Science Medicine, 16,* 1575–1582.

Weissman, M. M., & Paykel, E. S. (1974). *The depressed woman: A study of social relationships.* Chicago: University of Chicago Press.

Weissman, M. M., Sholomkas, D., Pottenger, M., Prusoff, B. A., & Locke, B. Z. (1977). Assessing depressive symptoms in five psychiatric populations: A validation study. *American Journal of Epidemiology, 106,* 203–214.

9

Resourcefulness in Coping with Severe Trauma: The Case of the Hostages

Calvin Jeff Frederick

Initially, the notion that severe trauma can have positive sequelae appears highly improbable. An old aphorism states, however, that out of conflict and crisis comes creativity and growth. While differential responses appear among traumatic events, illustratively, sufficient similarities exist across stressors to permit focusing on a single stressor for our purposes in this treatise. Let us take hostage-taking as an avenue through which to pursue the issues under discussion. Given the view that some victims of severe stress evince positive outcomes to it, what motivates them toward constructive action? Need for survival? Political idealism? A cause celebre? Media publicity? Anger and revenge? Emotional or mental disturbance? All of the above seem to be evident in selected circumstances. Can stress, per se, elicit immunization to further stress? Will treatment for psychic trauma produce immunization? Is resiliency innate or is it developed and enhanced after psychological trauma? Are characteristics of persons who display resistance to stress identifiable and reproducible? What are the differences between persons who react positively and those who respond negatively? Some answers may lie in the eye of the beholder. Since traumas are not unidimensional, they must be placed in the proper context.

In 1981, the author was privileged to participate in a conference at the Hague cosponsored by the World Health Organization and the Dutch government to address the *Psychosocial Consequences of Violence*. During the conference, Professor Leo Eitinger, the distinguished medical researcher and survivor of Auschwitz and Buchenwald, spoke upon the debilitating physical and psychological outcomes of the holocaust. Whereupon, a young psychiatrist insisted that it was important to consider the rewarding components of the holocaust, including its positive effects upon the survivors. Professor Eitinger's reaction was intense when he said, "I could not disagree more with Dr. X! If there was any positive effect from the holocaust experienced by the survivors, it was in spite of it and not because of it!" Clearly then, one must acknowledge the fact that some qualitatively different stressors require evaluation in their own right.

Growth Through the Experience of Stress

Stress and coping issues have continued to generate an expanding body of literature, particularly over the past fifteen years. The literature is extremely diverse due to approaches of a number of investigators from various disciplines (Cameron & Meichenbaum, 1982). Early authors addressed the topic primarily from three points of view; namely, anthropological (Cannon, 1942), biological (Selye, 1952) and psychological (Janis, 1951, 1958, 1971). Burrowes, Hales, and Arrington (1988) cite the influence of biochemical, electrical, genetic, environmental and interpersonal stress variables contributing to violent behavior. Perhaps the most challenging current biologic variable is the inverse relationship between cerebrospinal fluid 5-hydroxyindolacetic acid (5-HIAA) and violent acts. This finding has been duplicated in numerous populations throughout the world to date. Thus, in some instances coping with stress may be enhanced via biochemical routes. The differences between victims developing post traumatic stress syndrome (PTSD) and those who do not remain to be more fully understood (Frederick 1987; Sonnenberg (1988). However, we do know that coping styles vary with basic personality structure, type of stress, and supportive resources. Utilization of these factors may be molded into either of the two models: (a) cognitive-behavioral (Meichenbaum, 1977) and (b) transactional (Lazarus, 1966; Lazarus & Launier, 1978). In the former, the coping process is emphasized as opposed to classification, per se. In the latter model, coping appraisals plus coping responses are underscored.

Various tension reduction procedures have been employed by some victims, on occasion, without being taught. There is little doubt, however, that prior knowledge of such techniques can be most useful during periods of prolonged stress. Niehous (1985), an American business executive who was held hostage in South America, offers these suggestions for potential victims: (a) engage in active forms of communication with captors on nonthreatening topics, (b) attempt to get captors to recognize the victim as a human being rather than an object, (c) set personal goals for oneself, (d) attend to personal health—eat and exercise, and (e) maintain faith in something outside oneself. Weisaeth (1989) reports that among 13 Norwegian sailors who were tortured after being taken hostage near the coast of Libya in 1984, "not a single seaman gave in to the torture." However, seven of the 13 developed PTSD, whereas six seaman did not. Although not marked enough to warrant a diagnosis, some psychological symptoms appeared in virtually all subjects. Differences between subjects with clear psychological distress symptoms versus those without such symptoms seemed to be due to (a) premorbid vulnerability, (b) productive routine work during captivity, and (c) severity of treatment. Variations on these themes have been employed by persons from all walks of life in many other situations. Curiously, Freud (1949) and former president of Egypt, Sadat (1978), have written in a strikingly similar vein with regard to the importance of love, narcissism and responses to group stress. In Freud's original work (1922), republished in 1949, he wrote "So long as a group formation persists . . . individuals behave as though they were uniform, tolerate other people's peculiarities . . . and have no feeling of aversion toward them. Such a limitation of narcissism can . . . only be produced by one factor, a libidinal tie with other people. Love for oneself knows only one barrier—love for others . . . And in the development of mankind as a whole, just as in individuals, love alone acts as the civilizing factor in the sense that it brings a change from egoism to altruism" (pp. 56 and 57). Freud then alluded to war neuroses as being due primarily to what was clearly a coping problem. He stated that since the Army officer loves all his men equally, they are comrades among themselves. A disruption in libidinal attachment however, as an aspect of narcissism, leads to trouble. War neurosis arises from the conflict the soldier feels between the part he is expected to play in the army and his maltreatment by his superiors. Freud felt the latter was the foremost motive in the development of his neurosis, which was tantamount to what is now known as PTSD.

President Sadat described his own psychic trauma in graphic detail following prolonged imprisonment. Although victims draw on different inner resources to sustain themselves, Sadat emphasized that, initially, an individual must recognize the source of trouble within oneself and second, the presence of some kind of belief system or faith. He placed great importance on the value of love; specifically, love of God, love of oneself, and love of another human being. This perspective, of course, helps to foster hope. He stated "no problem should ever be regarded as insuperable. There are always solutions to everything. To love means to give, and to give means to build, while hate is to destroy . . . The hate that prevailed in Egypt for eighteen years before I assumed the presidency was a destructive force, which razed everything to the ground—and we are still suffering from its consequences" (1978, pp. 76–87).

Sadat felt that suffering could, indeed, become a positive force for personal growth when he wrote, "one of the most important factors that facilitated . . . peace of mind was suffering. Great suffering builds up a human being and puts him within reach of self-knowledge. And great suffering really follows from lofty human ideals . . . I hold friendship to be sacred . . . Now that I had discovered this . . . I had actually begun to live . . . my narrow self ceased to exist" (1978, p. 85).

Thus, it is apparent that great stressors can be bearable in some circumstances; growth is, indeed, possible. Let us hope that humankind's inhumanity to humans will abate so that growth can occur in more pleasant circumstances.

Significant Case Examples

Pursuing our use of hostage-taking to develop a paradigm for coping strategies, the author conducted personal interviews again with a number of former hostages on December 13, 14, 26, and 29, 1988. These recent interviews disclosed the following information and illustrative reactions.

David Jacobsen, former hospital administrator and hostage in Beirut, Lebanon, speaking with regard to any positive outcomes of hostage-taking, revealed that he had developed the following reactions: (a) feeling of increased self worth, (b) solidification of ego strength, (c) enhanced sense of humor, (d) realization of value of an individual's basic body strength and good health, and (e) renewed faith in higher power. Not unlike many executives in the United States, Jacobsen had a tendency toward mild hypertension prior to his capture. Contrary to what might be expected, however, the hostage experience brought about an actual decrease in blood pressure. This was likely due to the practice of stress-reduction techniques and self-awareness while in captivity. The captors deprived their hostages of everything possible. Nevertheless, Jacobsen affirms with deep conviction that they were unable to exert mind control over the hostages. He asserts "there were two things they could not take away from us: (a) the freedom to think and (b) the freedom to pray."

Although responding individually, by and large, the hostages exercised in order to (a) counter the effect of ill treatment and deprivation and (b) remain prepared physically to undertake and execute a successful escape in the event the occasion presented itself. Jacobsen employed humor to ventilate veiled anger and hostility when speaking to his guards. He made frequent remarks but always made a point to grin or smile while doing so. He noted that some of the other hostages were amazed that he was able to get away with speaking to a guard in a contentious manner. Several of the hostages, in particular, Tom Sutherland, Terry Anderson, Father Martin Jenco, and David Jacobsen, often argued with each other about politics, books, and games they played, which served to keep them from sinking into depth of depression and despair. They kept hope alive regardless of time or circumstances. Jacobsen firmly asserts that in his view, none of the hostages with whom he was associated during captivity became victims of the Stockholm Syndrome or were "brainwashed" by the captors. In fact, he proudly affirms that the hostages "brainwashed" their captors in large measure. Assuming that one is of sound mind and body, any individual possessing such assertiveness must be viewed as strong willed to say the least. Another individual acting in a similar fashion without an awareness of specific cultural differences might appear foolhardy, lacking in judgment and ordinary prudence.

His familiarity with the culture and his experienced interplay with such persons told Jacobsen that any risk of harm was small, based on his youthful captors, since they were mere followers of the avowed wishes of their leaders.

Moorhead Kennedy (1986), Director, Council for International Understanding, former member of the U.S. diplomatic service, and ex-hostage held in Iran for 444 days, emphasizes emotional difficulties arising after release followed by an enhanced appreciation for life. He noted that his wife observed one man who left but still another who came back. In many ways, the man who returned was to be preferred over the one who left. Kennedy underscored how the Iranian hostages were demeaned. "For example, we were treated like children and were not allowed to go to the bathroom alone."

Such treatment tends to reawaken early life conflict while evoking childlike aggression or passive rebellion, which may not be in the subject's best interest. The nature and depth of the trauma must be sensitively grasped by close friends, family, and therapists. It is impossible for anyone to fully understand the issues of captivity who has not "seen the other side of the mountain," as Kennedy puts it. As full awareness of the captivity sets in and self-worth is reevaluated, the victim often comes to believe that he or she can endure anything.

Out of adversity comes strength, so to speak. Basic strength must be present in the first place, however. While deepening their appreciation for good health and the conveniences of modern democratic life, some former hostages find themselves experiencing a corresponding impatience with the immature behavior shown by many adults in our society.

James Dozier, United States Brigadier General Retired, held hostage in Italy, speaks of his faith and personal strength, despite 6 weeks of marked physical restriction by being placed in a box during his captivity. Even though his captors guarded him like an animal, and were never more than 4 or 5 feet away, he maintained his sense of basic self-worth through personal discipline. Like, David Jacobsen, Dozier voiced his annoyance and frustrations to his captors because they refused to contact Italian government authorities, despite his insistence that they do so. Moreover, he complained to them openly about his displeasure at being subjected to such severe restrictions of movement. By deliberately adhering to his own disciplined personal routine, he believes that such predictable behavior on his part caused the captors to be less rigorous in their oversight of him than they would have been otherwise. His disciplined routine convinced his captors that they knew what he would be doing at any given point in time; hence, they felt less need to watch him so closely and let him alone. Thus, for the enterprising person, captivity can help one realize his or her own resourcefulness and innovative capabilities. General Dozier continues to share his experiences in teaching and lecturing to armed services personnel, in an effort to prepare them for various problems encountered in the hostage-taking experience, in the event such a fate should befall them.

Father Martin Jenco, former Beirut hostage and Servite priest, used the positive aspects of his religious beliefs to cope with stress by conducting daily services each morning during captivity, irrespective of the cramped quarters where he was held. Undoubtedly, Father Jenco's deep faith and religious beliefs served him well during the ordeal of his capture. Moreover, he gained strength and satisfaction by sharing knowledge and performing church rituals. He could, thereby, function as a positive catalyst for the needs of other hostages with whom he came in contact.

Father Jenco, Tom Sutherland, David Jacobsen, and Terry Anderson were able to co-mingle for periods of time during their incarceration.

Despite marked differences in their political views and life styles, a common bond of mutual confinement provided an interstitial linkage which could transcend strong disagreements and even heated arguments. Father Jenco confirms that the very process of argument was, in itself, helpful since, adventitiously, it served as a useful coping mechanism. It helped to focus psychic energy and gave direction to a barren and otherwise degrading, and potentially hopeless existence. One of the best antidotes for depression is the mobilization of energy into activity, preferably motor activity. Illustratively, if an individual rises to his feet and/or executes firm movements with the hands, arms and face, such behavior undercuts the insidious malignant quality which is inherent in psychological depression.

David Collett, son of Alec Collett who was a United Nations journalist and is still missing and presumed to be a victim of hanging by Abu Nidal and his group, was interviewed. This heinous act against his father was directed against the British in retaliation for sentencing terrorists to Parkhurst prison for a murder attempt on the life of the Israeli Ambassador to England who was shot and paralyzed for life. After the initial shock and disbelief of his father's apparent death at the hands of terrorists, Collett's resolve to assist hostage victims and their families helped direct the recovery process. It became a courageous and psychologically solidifying means of focusing thoughts and energy upon a constructive cause. This was not mere repression of the negative because Collett sustained his ready access to vitriol when called for. Being able to express feeling openly and even publicly provided an acceptable therapeutic outlet to assist in the reinforcement of self-worth.

Covictims

A number of former hostages have informed the author that their relatives and family members have suffered greater long-term psychological difficulties from the ordeal more than the hostages themselves. Family members, close relatives, and friends are, indeed, covictims with special problems that are frequently overlooked and slighted. Most of the focus remains on the former hostages as primary victims by professionals, the media and work associates. Family members feel ignored or neglected. Then, the stress inoculation training they were offered was resented because it espoused the medical model and the assumption of a sick role.

Apart from the gratitude that fate has brought in returning an imprisoned family member, feelings need expression, whereas doubts and conflicts require resolution. Family members invariably welcome an opportunity to be heard and express their feelings concerning their roles, conflicts, and views about the hostage-taking experience. Some continue to feel anxiety about how their lives will fit into the scheme of things, how their lives will resume in the future, and how they can restructure relationships that may require mending. Some feel annoyance, anger, and resentment in varying degrees. The wife of a former hostage told me that she had become so frustrated with her exhostage husband that she hurled a glass ashtray at him. Marital discord and divorce may follow in the aftermath of terrorist experiences. Family members are, by no means, always drawn closer together following the release. Many persons endeavor to busy themselves with constructive activities, which may or may not be directly related to the hostage crisis. Although many family members receive consolation from intermingling with other hostage families, some do not and prefer to relate on an individual basis to a professional or a trusted, close friend. Whatever the personal preference, it must be respected.

Attempting to cajole or coax an individual into a group or activity about which they have marked negative feelings can frequently be quite damaging. Particularly sensitive areas can be unwittingly addressed and poorly managed creating further trauma and needless ill will on the part of the victim or covictim. It is of vital importance to assist the individual in experiencing resolution and growth in a manner that permits the feeling of personal responsibility for one's own mastery of the trauma. This can be enormously ego building in the wake of an ego-shattering ordeal.

An assessment of coping responses by the author (1987) among family members of hostages discloses the fact that specific behaviors were evident before, during, and after the event. Before and during the event the following were present: (a) efforts to employ problem solving, (b) use of social support within and outside the immediate family, (c) engagement in activities related to hostage taking, (d) need to be regarded as normal, without psychopathology. They resented any allusions to the possibility of mental or emotional illness. After the event, unexpected tensions arose within the family, even though they had been told such phenomena might develop.

In distilling the gist of what has been put forward by former hostages and family members as coping mechanisms, one finds the following: (a) belief in the innate strength of oneself, (b) reflections and thoughts of loved ones and friends, (c) faith in some superordinate power, (d) hope that captivity will end favorably, (e) use of calculating powers to interact and plan for possible escape, (f) physical exercise, (g) expression of anger via appropriate self assertion, and (h) ability to focus attention and become task oriented.

Stress cannot be measured or even defined without considering both stressor and "stressee," so to speak. Stress cannot exist without a host. Coping may be manifested as a passive or indifferent response. Stress must be personal. The energy that goes into managing or controlling it is an implicit part of stress itself. Just as in the field of public health, a bacteria, pest, or virus must find an acceptable host for disease (stress) to manifest itself. If one resists or becomes immune to the pest (stressor) then neither stress nor a viable host (stressee) will become a reality. The state of immunity will produce a negative host. Hence, both prevention and treatment must be aimed at the heart of the issue.

Psychological immunization, similarly termed "psychological inoculation," by Cameron and Meichenbaum (1982), and incident-specific treatment (Frederick, 1987) are both directed toward amelioration of stress problems in a vulnerable host. The latter, in particular, underscores the value of healthy ego strength and deemphasizes the sick role. Although the Stress Reduction Model set forth in Figure 9.1 is clearly analogous to an epidemiologic/public health paradigm, it is important to note that victims of traumatic stress strongly object to being viewed as sick. Hence, without careful structuring, a medical model, per se, may be distasteful and even evoke marked resentment among family members as covictims of traumatic incidents. In a similar vein, victims and their families often become disenchanted with the stress inoculation training offered to them. The model set forth below, however, can provide a useful instructional tool for the clinician to share in open discussion. It can assist affected persons with an understanding of those conditions which accompany continuing stress. It can help structure areas of accountability and responsibility in the

Independent Variable	Intervening Variable	Dependent Variable	
		Person\Host	Condition
Stressor	Stress[——————— →	+ Stressee ——→	PTSD
	[——————— →	-Stressee ——→	NoPTSD
TB Bacilli	Tuberculosis[————→	+ Host ———→	Disease
	[—→(Immunity) ——→	-Host———→	NoDisease

FIGURE 9.1. Stress reduction model.

treatment process and provide encouragement with respect to symptom amelioration and improvement.

The pertinent stress factors delineated here have been distilled from more than two thousand cases reported by the author (Frederick, 1987) from a variety of stressors. Although the weight of each of these may vary in a given situation, their contributions to the impact of trauma are consistently reliable.

Pertinent stress factors are: (a) duration of stress, (b) severity of stress, (c) physical environment, (d) restrictions of movement, (e) being alone during periods of stress, (f) presence of premorbid vulnerability, (g) age, and (h) support systems during and after stress periods. Considering each in turn, moderate positive correlations exist with the duration of stress, physical environment, and premorbid vulnerability. Stronger positive correlations occur with severity of stress, restriction of movement, being alone, and the presence of support systems. A moderate negative correlation occurs with age, that is, persons over 40 often endure stress better than those below the age of 40.

Physiological and biochemical factors are related to general health as mediators of stress. Although it appears that central and autonomic nervous system changes coexist along with psychological reactions, the use of medication to alleviate PTSD symptoms has brought mixed results at best. Modlin (1986) reported poor outcomes from drug therapy usage, and he noted that in the total treatment context drug therapy can actually do more harm than good. Hogben and Cornfield (1981) and Davidson, Swartz, Storck, Krishnan, and Hammett (1985) have reported more positive results but subjects in the former study were severely disturbed hospitalized patients in contrast to the other populations studied. Psychophysiological measures such as pulse rate, blood pressure, electromyelogram (EMG), and incident-specific focusing during relaxation have been most successfully employed by the author for both diagnostic and treatment purposes. The author is convinced that the latter, in particular, is a sine quae non trauma mastery and effective problem resolution.

References

Burrowes, K. L., Hales, R. E., & Arrington, E. (1988). Research on the biologic aspects of violence. In Tardiff, K. (Ed.) *The psychiatric clinics of North America* (pp. 499–509). Philadelphia: W.B.Saunders & Co.

Cameron, R. & Meichenbaum, D. (1982). The nature of effective coping and the treatment of stress related problems: A cognitive-behavioral perspective. In Goldberger, L. & Breznitz, S. (Eds.) *Handbook of Stress* (pp. 695–71). New York: The Free Press.

Cannon, W. B. (1942). "Voodoo death." *American Anthropologist, 44,* 169–181.

Davidson, J., Swartz, M., Storck, M., Krishnan, R., & Hammett, E. (1985). A diagnostic and family study of post traumatic stress disorder. *American Journal of Psychiatry, 142,* 90–93.

Frederick, C. J. (1987). Psychic trauma in victims of crime and terrorism. In G. R. VandenBos & B. K. Bryant, B. K. (Eds.) *Cataclysms, crises and catastrophes* (pp. 55–108). Washington, DC: American Psychological Association.

Freud, S. (1949). *Group psychology and the analysis of the ego.* New York: Liveright Publishing Co.

Hogben, G. I. & Cornfield, R. B. (1981). Treatment of traumatic war neuroses with phenelzine. *Archives of General Psychiatry, 38,* 440–445.

Janis, I. L. (1951). *Air, war and emotional stress.* New York: McGraw-Hill.

Janis, I. L. (1958). *Psychological stress.* New York: John Wiley.

Janis, I. L. (1971). *Stress and frustration.* New York: Harcourt.

Kennedy, M. (1986). The Ayatollah in the Cathedral: Reflections of a hostage. New York: Hill and Wang.

Lazarus, R. S. (1966). Psychological stress and coping process. New York: McGraw-Hill.

Lazarus, R. S., & Launier, R. (1978). Stress related transactions between person and environment. In L. A. Pervin & M. Kewis (Eds.), *Perspectives in interactional psychology* (pp. 287–327). New York: Plenum.

Meichenbaum, D. (1977). *Cognitive-behavior modification: An integrative approach.* New York: Plenum.

Modlin, H. C. (1986). Post traumatic stress disorder: No longer just for war veterans. *Post Graduate Medicine, 70,* 26–44.

Niehous, W. F. (1985). Surviving captivity II. The hostage's point of view. In B. M. Jenkins (Ed.), *Terrorism and personal protection* (pp. 423–433). Stoneham, MA: Butterworth. Publishers.

Sadat, A. L. (1978). *In search of identity.* London: Collins.

Selye, H. (1952). *The story of the adaptation syndrome.* Montreal: Acta.

Sonnenberg, S. M. (1988). Victims of violence and post-traumatic stress disorder. In K. Tardiff (Ed.), *The psychiatric clinics of North America* (pp. 581–589). Philadelphia: W.B. Saunders & Co.

Weisaeth, L. (in press). Torture of Norwegian ship's crew. *Acta Psychiatrica Scandinavia.*

Appendix A:
Self-Control Schedule

Scoring instructions

1. Reverse the scoring of the following eleven items: 4,6,8,9,14,16, 18,19,21,29,35. For example: if a subject circled item 4 , −3 the reverse score would be +3. Similarly −1 would be +1, −2 will be +2.
2. Sum up all the scores of the individual items. The total score of the scale could range from −108 (36 × −3) to +108 (36 × +3). For normal populations the score is usually +25 with a standard deviation of 20.

Rosenbaum, M. (1980). A schedule for assessing self-control behaviors: Preliminary findings. *Behavior Therapy, 11,* 109–121. Copyright 1980 by the Association for Advancement of Behavior Therapy. Reprinted by permission of the publisher and author.

The Self-Control Schedule

This questionnaire is designed to find out how different people view their thinking and their behavior. A statement may range from very characteristic of you to very uncharacteristic of you.

There are no right or wrong answers. We simply want to know how you feel each statement applies to you.

Please answer every item, and circle only one answer for each item. Use the following code to indicate whether a statement describes your thinking or behavior:

-3 very uncharacteristic of me, extremely undescriptive

-2 rather uncharacteristic of me, quite undescriptive

-1 somewhat uncharacteristic of me, slightly undescriptive

+1 somewhat characteristic of me, slightly descriptive

+2 rather characteristic of me, quite descriptive

+3 very characteristic of me, extremely descriptive

1.	When I do a boring job, I think about the less-boring parts of the job and about the reward I will receive when I finish.	-3	-2	-1	+1	+2	+3
2.	When I have to do something that makes me anxious, I try to visualize how I will overcome my anxiety while doing it.	-3	-2	-1	+1	+2	+3
3.	By changing my way of thinking, I am often able to change my feelings about almost anything.	-3	-2	-1	+1	+2	+3
4.	I often find it difficult to overcome my feelings of nervousness and tension without outside help.	-3	-2	-1	+1	+2	+3
5.	When I am feeling depressed, I try to think about pleasant events.	-3	-2	-1	+1	+2	+3
6.	I cannot help thinking about mistakes I made.	-3	-2	-1	+1	+2	+3
7.	When I am faced with a difficult problem, I try to approach it in a systematic way.	-3	-2	-1	+1	+2	+3
8.	I usually do what I'm supposed to do more quickly when someone is pressuring me.	-3	-2	-1	+1	+2	+3
9.	When I am faced with a difficult decision, I prefer to postpone it even if I have all the facts.	-3	-2	-1	+1	+2	+3
10.	When I have difficulty concentrating on my reading, I look for ways to increase my concentration.	-3	-2	-1	+1	+2	+3
11.	When I plan to work, I remove everything that is not relevant to my work.	-3	-2	-1	+1	+2	+3
12.	When I try to get rid of a bad habit, I first try to find out all the reasons why I have the habit.	-3	-2	-1	+1	+2	+3
13.	When an unpleasant thought is bothering me, I try to think about something pleasant.	-3	-2	-1	+1	+2	+3
14.	If I smoked two packs of cigarettes a day, I would need outside help to stop smoking.	-3	-2	-1	+1	+2	+3

15. When I feel down, I try to act cheerful so that my mood will change.   -3 -2 -1 +1 +2 +3
16. If I carried the pills with me, I would take a tranquilizer whenever I felt tense and nervous.   -3 -2 -1 +1 +2 +3
17. When I am depressed, I try to keep myself busy with things I like.   -3 -2 -1 +1 +2 +3
18. I tend to postpone unpleasant tasks even if I could perform them immediately.   -3 -2 -1 +1 +2 +3
19. I need outside help to get rid of some of my bad habits.   -3 -2 -1 +1 +2 +3
20. When I find it difficult to settle down and do a task, I look for ways to help me settle down.   -3 -2 -1 +1 +2 +3
21. Although it makes me feel bad, I cannot help thinking about all sorts of possible catastrophes.   -3 -2 -1 +1 +2 +3
22. I prefer to finish a job that I have to do before I start doing things I really like.   -3 -2 -1 +1 +2 +3
23. When I feel physical pain, I try not to think about it.   -3 -2 -1 +1 +2 +3
24. My self-esteem increases when I am able to overcome a bad habit.   -3 -2 -1 +1 +2 +3
25. To overcome bad feelings that accompany failure, I often tell myself that it is not catastrophic and I can do something about it.   -3 -2 -1 +1 +2 +3
26. When I feel that I am too impulsive, I tell myself to stop and think before I do anything.   -3 -2 -1 +1 +2 +3
27. Even when I am terribly angry at someone, I consider my actions very carefully.   -3 -2 -1 +1 +2 +3
28. Facing the need to make a decision, I usually find out all the alternatives instead of deciding quickly and spontaneously.   -3 -2 -1 +1 +2 +3
29. Usually, I first do the things I really like to do even if there are more urgent things to do.   -3 -2 -1 +1 +2 +3
30. When I realize that I am going to be unavoidably late for an important meeting, I tell myself to keep calm.   -3 -2 -1 +1 +2 +3
31. When I feel pain in my body, I try to divert my thoughts from it.   -3 -2 -1 +1 +2 +3
32. When I am faced with a number of things to do, I usually plan my work.   -3 -2 -1 +1 +2 +3
33. When I am short of money, I decide to record all my expenses in order to budget more carefully in the future.   -3 -2 -1 +1 +2 +3
34. If I find it difficult to concentrate on a task, I divide it into smaller segments.   -3 -2 -1 +1 +2 +3
35. Quite often, I cannot overcome unpleasant thoughts that bother me.   -3 -2 -1 +1 +2 +3
36. When I am hungry and have no opportunity to eat, I try to divert my thoughts from my stomach or try to imagine that I am satisfied.   -3 -2 -1 +1 +2 +3

Indices

Author Index

Subject Index